Revealing and Concealing Gender

Revealing and Concealing Gender

Issues of Visibility in Organizations

Edited By

Patricia Lewis
Senior Lecturer in Management, Kent Business School, University of Kent

Ruth Simpson
Professor of Management, Brunel Business School, Brunel University

palgrave
macmillan

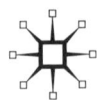

Selection and editorial content © Patricia Lewis and Ruth Simpson 2010
Individual chapters © the contributors 2010

All rights reserved. No reproduction, copy or transmission of this publication may be made without written permission.

No portion of this publication may be reproduced, copied or transmitted save with written permission or in accordance with the provisions of the Copyright, Designs and Patents Act 1988, or under the terms of any licence permitting limited copying issued by the Copyright Licensing Agency, Saffron House, 6–10 Kirby Street, London EC1N 8TS.

Any person who does any unauthorized act in relation to this publication may be liable to criminal prosecution and civil claims for damages.

The authors have asserted their rights to be identified as the authors of this work in accordance with the Copyright, Designs and Patents Act 1988.

First published 2010 by
PALGRAVE MACMILLAN

Palgrave Macmillan in the UK is an imprint of Macmillan Publishers Limited, registered in England, company number 785998, of Houndmills, Basingstoke, Hampshire RG21 6XS.

Palgrave Macmillan in the US is a division of St Martin's Press LLC, 175 Fifth Avenue, New York, NY 10010.

Palgrave Macmillan is the global academic imprint of the above companies and has companies and representatives throughout the world.

Palgrave® and Macmillan® are registered trademarks in the United States, the United Kingdom, Europe and other countries

ISBN-13: 978-0-230-21211-4   hardback

This book is printed on paper suitable for recycling and made from fully managed and sustained forest sources. Logging, pulping and manufacturing processes are expected to conform to the environmental regulations of the country of origin.

A catalogue record for this book is available from the British Library.

A catalogue record for this book is available from the Library of Congress.

10 9 8 7 6 5 4 3 2 1
19 18 17 16 15 14 13 12 11 10

Printed and bound in Great Britain by
CPI Antony Rowe, Chippenham and Eastbourne

In memory of Edwin Carr, 1965–2009

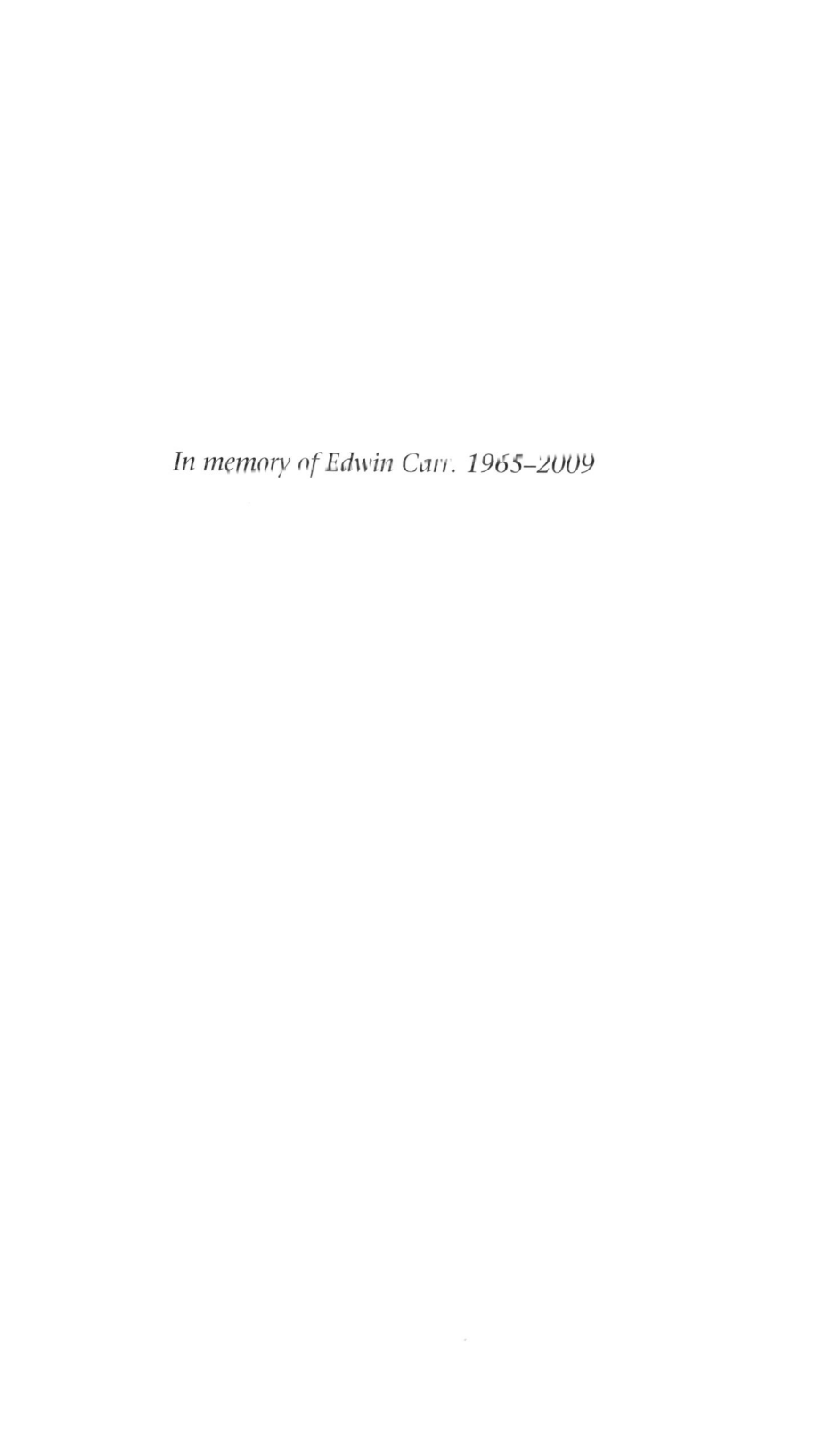

Contents

Biographies of Contributors		ix
	Introduction: Theoretical Insights into the Practices of Revealing and Concealing Gender within Organizations *Patricia Lewis and Ruth Simpson*	1
1	Living and Working in Grey Areas: Gender (In)visibility and Organizational Space *Melissa Tyler and Laurie Cohen*	23
2	A Question of Membership *Heather Höpfl*	39
3	Pregnancy Centre Stage, Please: Contesting the Erasure of Pregnant Bodies from Workplace Space *Caroline Gatrell*	54
4	'Mothered' and Othered: (In)visibility of Care Responsibility and Gender in Processes of Excluding Women from Norwegian Law Firms *Selma Therese Lyng*	76
5	Organizing Entrepreneurship? Women's Invisibility in Self-employment *Deborah Kerfoot and Caroline Miller*	100
6	'Mumpreneurs': Revealing the Post-feminist Entrepreneur *Patricia Lewis*	124
7	Masculinities in Practice: The Invisible Dynamics in Sports Leadership *Irene Ryan*	139
8	Leadership and the (In)visibility of Gender *Jennifer Binns*	158
9	'Now you see me, now you don't': The Visibility Paradox for Women in a Male-Dominated Profession *Jacqueline H. Watts*	175

viii *Contents*

10	The Critical (and Subversive) Act of (In)visibility: A Strategic Reframing of 'Disappeared and Devalued' Women in a Densely Masculinist Workplace *Susan Harwood*	194
11	A Reversal of the Gaze: Men's Experiences of Visibility in Non-traditional Occupations *Ruth Simpson*	219
12	Gender, Mask and the Face: Towards a Corporeal Ethics *Alison Pullen and Carl Rhodes*	233

Index 249

Biographies of Contributors

Jennifer Binns is a Labour Relations Adviser in the Department of Commerce, Western Australia. She has drawn on extensive experience at senior management levels in the public sector to develop her understanding of leadership as a gendered concept and practice. Other research interests include government employment policy, gender mainstreaming and work-life balance.

Laurie Cohen is Professor of Organization Studies and Associate Dean for Research in the Faculty of Social Science and Humanities at Loughborough University. One strand of her research concerns aspects of careers including careers of professional workers, career sense making and enactment in offshoring contexts, and most recently examining the interplay of career and Diaspora. Another strand focuses on gender, organization and home/work dynamics. She has published in diverse journals and edited collections, and is on the editorial board of Human Relations and Management Learning.

Caroline Gatrell is a Lecturer in the Lancaster University Management School. Her intellectual project focuses on the maternal body, examining changes and changing relationships in the context of family practices, motherhood, fatherhood and paid/unpaid work. Her work has been published in a range of journals including *Journal of Gender Studies, The Sociological Review, The International Journal of Human Resource Management, European Journal of International Management, Feminist Review and Gender, Work and Organization*. In addition she has recently published two books: *Embodying Women's Work* and *Gender and Diversity in Management: A Concise Introduction* (with Elaine Swan).

Susan Harwood is an experienced equal opportunity and gender diversity researcher, practitioner and consultant. Her PhD thesis – *Gendering Change: An Immodest Manifesto for Intervening in Masculinist Organisations* (2006) describes a major collaborative, participatory action research project between the University of Western Australia and an Australian policing jurisdiction. This project was awarded the Griffith University Prize for Excellence in Research in 2005 and in 2008 Susan's thesis was awarded an industrial relations prize by the University of Western

Australia's School of Business for 'most outstanding thesis'. Susan is currently working on bringing a community engagement programme to women in the Pacific. *Women Leading Change* is a gender equity initiative that brings together women in policing with women in the community on a leadership development programme.

Heather Höpfl is Professor of Management at the University of Essex and Visiting Professor at UvH, Utrecht and the University of South Australia. She has worked in a number of different jobs and fields including working on the design of the Thrissell letter-sorter with a large engineering company in Bristol, as an Economics teacher at a Liverpool HS, as tour manager for a touring theatre company and a researcher with ICL, Logica, and the *(then)* DHSS. In the 1990s she worked with British Airways on developing a safety culture. She is co-editor of *Tamara, Journal for Critical Organization Inquiry* and European editor of the *Journal of Management Spirituality and Religion* and publishes widely. Recent publications have been on theorization and reflection, the Bhopal disaster with Sumohon Matilal, on the loss of heroines and on visual ethnography. She is married to Harro Höpfl and has two sons, George and Max.

Deborah Kerfoot lectures in Organizational Analysis at Keele University. Her research interests and publications are in the sociology and critical study of management, empirical research on employment, poststructuralism and gender, sexuality and diversity in organizations. Deborah is currently writing on entrepreneurship and masculinity in organization. She is joint Editor in Chief of the Wiley Blackwell journal *Gender, Work and Organization* and is organizer and Chair of the biennial international interdisciplinary conference of the same name. She is an editorial board member of the *Journal of Management Studies,* also published by Wiley Blackwell.

Patricia Lewis is a Senior Lecturer in Management in the Kent Business School, University of Kent. Her work on gender and emotion, gender and enterprise, the development of enterprise culture and entrepreneurial identity has been published in a range of journals including *Gender, Work and Organization, British Journal of Management, Work, Employment and Society, Human Relations and Journal of Business Ethics*. She is currently writing on the identity work of female entrepreneurs, exploring how the gendered nature of entrepreneurial identity impacts on this and how the masculinity of entrepreneurship is denied, desired and challenged by women business owners.

Biographies of Contributors xi

Selma Therese Lyng is a sociologist working at the Work Research Institute of Oslo. Current research projects include studies of gender and work-family conflict and balance in 'high commitment' professions, particularly lawyers and management consultants. Additional publications and research are related to educational exclusion and inclusion in secondary school.

Caroline Miller worked as a researcher at Manchester Metropolitan University before joining Keele University where she currently lectures in Marketing. Caroline has also spent 14 years working in the steel industry. She has experience of running family owned small/medium sized business. Caroline gained a PhD studying women and entrepreneurship at Keele University and a Masters in Research. Her research interests have a wide focus and include business start-up, gender, social exclusion (difference), sustainable practices in marketing and critical marketing. Publications are international and interdisciplinary including *International Journal of Business and Economics, International Journal for Management Theory and Practice and Journal of Marketing Management.*

Alison Pullen is amongst other identity labels Associate Professor of Organization Studies at The Centre for Management and Organization Studies (CMOS), UTS, Australia. Alison is author of *Managing Identity* (2006), *Identity and Organization* (2005) and *Thinking Organization* (2005). She has published widely and is currently writing on gender, ethics and affect using feminist philosophy and practice.

Carl Rhodes works at the University of Technology as Professor of Organization Studies. His current research focuses on ethics and organizations, and organizations in popular culture. Recent books include *Bits of Organization* (2009 with Alison Pullen) and *Critical Representations of Work and Organization in Popular Culture* (2008 with Robert Westwood).

Irene Ryan is a Senior Lecturer, Department of Management, Faculty of Business and Law at AUT University, Auckland, New Zealand. She holds a PhD in Management and Employment Relations from the University of Auckland. Her research interests build on her interdisciplinary background and work experiences in both the voluntary and paid work sectors. Broadly, areas of current interest include the intersectionality of gender and age in paid employment and sport, leadership in sport, dimensions of diversity, careers and men and masculinities. She is a keen participant, volunteer and avid spectator of a variety of sports.

Ruth Simpson is a Professor of Management at Brunel Business School and Director of the Centre for Research in Emotion Work and Employment Studies (CREWES). She is author and co-author of several books in the area of Gender and Organizations and has published in *Human Relations, Work, Employment and Society, Gender, Work and Organization, Management Learning* and the *Academy of Management (Learning and Education)* journal. Her research interests include gender and management education, gender and emotions and the careers of men in non-traditional occupations.

Melissa Tyler is a Senior Lecturer in Organization Studies at Loughborough University Business School. Her work on the organizational aspects of emotion, aesthetics, gender, sexuality and the body has been published in a range of journals and edited collections. Her current research is on emotional and aesthetic labour in Soho's sex shops. She is an Associate Editor of *Gender, Work and Organization*, and a co-editor of the *International Journal of Work, Organization and Emotion*. Her most recent book, co-edited with Philip Hancock, is *The Management of Everyday Life*.

Jacqueline H. Watts is Senior Lecturer and Staff Tutor in the Faculty of Health and Social Care at the Open University, UK. This role follows a long first career as a training and technology transfer consultant in the civil engineering industry. Her research interests include feminist theory, gendered labour markets, professions and the social context of death and dying. Her work has been published in a number of journals including *Qualitative Research, Gender, Work and Organization, Work, Employment and Society, Feminism & Psychology, International Journal of Work, Organisation and Emotion* and *Illness Crisis & Loss*. Her most recent work is a sole-authored book entitled *Death, Dying & Bereavement*.

Introduction: Theoretical Insights into the Practices of Revealing and Concealing Gender within Organizations

Patricia Lewis and Ruth Simpson

Introduction

Issues of visibility and invisibility are becoming increasingly apparent in gender research in organizations. Such work is based on a recognition of the significance of (in)visibility in understanding experiences of advantage and disadvantage in work contexts – and how these experiences can impact on identity, attitudes, culture and careers. From a variety of perspectives, such work has highlighted how visibility and invisibility 'play out' in organizations – revealing the often hidden and gendered processes of organizing and how these processes can be concealed within norms, practices and values. Thus, early research in organization studies critiqued the gender blind orientation to theorizing about work and organization (e.g. Linstead, 2000; Wilson, 1996) which universalized male subjectivity and sought to make visible women's experiences in organizations. More recent work has helped to make visible those 'suppressed' aspects of organizational life, hidden by dominant management and masculine discourses, such as violence and sexuality (e.g. Hearn and Parkin, 2001). Other work has explored the problems women face as highly visible 'tokens' in different male dominated contexts (Cross and Bagilhole, 2002; Kanter, 1977; Simpson, 2000); how traditionally feminine skills are 'disappeared' into the embodied dispositions of women (Fletcher, 1999; Tyler and Abbott, 1998; Taylor and Tyler, 1998); how equal opportunity policies, through a rhetoric of meritocracy and gender justice, can serve to conceal continuing gender disadvantage. Within masculinity studies, authors have highlighted how men are often blind to issues of gender in their own behaviours and practices as well as how the advantages and privileges of masculinity are obscured within the norm (Hearn, 1996; Kerfoot and

Knights, 1993, 1998; Lewis, 2006; Simpson and Lewis, 2005, 2007; Whitehead, 2001).

The implications of these practices and processes around (in)visibility are highly complex – often dependent on gender and organizational context. Visibility in organizations can be encountered differentially, often as constraining and detrimental for women but potentially advantageous for men (Heikes, 1991; Simpson, 2004, 2005, 2009; Williams, 1993). Heightened visibility can afford men in non-traditional roles developmental opportunities and exposure to challenging situations – so that they are often 'fast-tracked' in their careers (Simpson, 2004, 2005). Women by contrast often face a 'dense' masculinity (Harwood, this volume) in male dominated occupations and a chilly working environment which excludes and marginalizes them. Invisibility can also be experienced in different ways and have implications for the negotiation of identity as men and women 'manage gender' in organizations. In the context of management, men are invisible as gendered and privileged subjects (Whitehead, 2001). They evade scrutiny and interrogation and so have less difficulty performing a (masculine) management identity. Women however are 'marked' as gendered Other and have to work hard to manage both gender and occupational identity (Lewis, 2006). While invisibility (and occupancy of the normative position) is a source of power for men, paradoxically, it can be a symptom of powerlessness for other groups that are marginalized, neglected and hidden from view – and who have to work hard to gain recognition and to be seen. On an equally paradoxical level, the disciplinary gaze that is often bestowed on women and which captures the power relations between the viewer and the viewed can be both resisted and embraced. This relates to the display of female bodies (Hancock and Tyler, 2007) as well as to how men may draw on the masculine 'gaze' to position themselves hierarchically in relation to women (Alvesson, 1998) – and how women may both defy and instrumentally or strategically manipulate the visibility and eroticism implicated in being 'under view'.

In order to make sense of these often contradictory processes, we have previously mapped out the concepts of visibility and invisibility as theoretical constructs (discussed below) and highlighted how they can tell 'rich stories' about organizational life (Lewis, 2006; Simpson and Lewis, 2005, 2007). However, to fully understand the complex relationship between visibility and invisibility and the contradictions within the experiences of each, we need further empirical and conceptual analysis of how they manifest themselves in contemporary organizations – a task which this book sets out to do. The studies presented here provide us with the opportunity to revisit the concepts and encourage us as researchers to critically reflect on and perhaps rethink their aspects. In putting together a series of empirical and conceptual studies around the concepts of revealing, concealing and (in)visibility, we hope to challenge the value of these concepts as well as highlight their innovative explanatory potential for understanding gender issues within organizations.

Surface and deep conceptualizations of (in)visibility

Our previous discussions of visibility and invisibility sought to make sense of these complexities and contradictions at a theoretical level by drawing a distinction between 'surface' and 'deep' conceptualizations (Simpson and Lewis, 2005, 2007). At a 'surface' level, which we aligned largely with liberal feminist orientations, we examined literature which focused on states of exclusion and difference arising from numerical imbalance while from a 'deep' (and largely post-structuralist) perspective, we considered processes of maintaining power through invisibility and the struggles around the norm. In terms of the former, a key focus was on the dynamics of asymmetric groups and the implications of visibility and difference for the subjective state of members of the minority and for relations between those groups. Thus, for token women, high visibility can create performance pressures and a fear of making mistakes (Kanter, 1977; Maddock, 1999, Marshall, 1994); can lead to marginalization and exclusion as, through 'homosociability', men choose other men for friendships, teams and networks; and can limit behavioural repertoires available as token women are assigned to a variety of stereotypical and highly constraining roles. Visibility can have negative consequences for women through performance pressures, heightened career barriers and the creation of a hostile working environment as well as through strong social constraints on behaviours in social interactions (Kanter, 1977; Simpson, 1997, 2000). While the experience of token men may well differ, as assumptions that men are careerist, seek authority and hold special expertise feed into career success, visibility at this 'surface' level is largely associated with a negative state of exclusion and difference – disadvantages that can, according to liberal feminist principles, be overcome by an increase in numbers of women in organizations and hence a more gender balanced group.

At a deeper level, we went beyond surface states of exclusion and difference to explore power dynamics. In particular, drawing on Robinson's (2000) work, we highlighted the processes of maintaining power through the invisibility of the normative position, the power struggles around the norm and the effects of visibility as individuals and groups are subsequently de-centred and no longer hidden from view. Thus, men can be shown to benefit from invisible privileges of masculinity through their location within the 'dominant centre' (Hearn, 1996) where their experiences and privileges are taken as the norm and where they evade scrutiny and problematization (Kusz, 2001; Robinson, 2000). However, as Robinson points out, this privileged and powerful position has been threatened by women and other marginalized groups as they seek recognition and mobilize social and cultural identities – in so doing throwing the spotlight on the (hitherto concealed) advantages and resources of men. Men accordingly have become marked (and visible) as a gendered and privileged group. As Robinson argues, men have responded to this part de-centring from the normative position and new experience of visibility by claiming victim status. This is evidenced by recent concerns (e.g. Beynon, 2002) that men are in crisis – failing in education, in employment and within the family structure. By taking up a victim identity, men can not only benefit by being distanced from (and hence dis-identify with) an oppressor group, but can in so doing continue to conceal their ongoing material and cultural advantages over women – a theme we discuss in more detail below.

While our conceptualization of surface and deep (in)visibility sought to map existing literature, to consolidate a fragmented field and help make sense of its different orientations, this book is more exploratory in intent. In other words, while partly informed by the above conceptual distinction (i.e. between surface and deep orientations), it sets out to position recent empirical and conceptual work on the processes of revealing and concealing as well as on the related experiences of visibility and invisibility in organizations. How do men and women experience visibility? What aspects of the gendered organization are concealed within taken for granted thinking and normative routines? How does (in)visibility link to power and how are these dynamics played out in day-to-day organizational life? These are some of the questions this edited book sets out to address – and in so doing, the chapters themselves 'reveal' in that they seek to uncover some of the hidden, gendered processes and practices in organizations. We start with further consideration of the significance of the distinction between surface and deep conceptualizations referred to above and, in particular, the importance of the norm – something we foreground in this book as we 'scope' issues of revealing and concealing, of visibility and invisibility in the context of employment and work. We go on to develop a frame in the form of a 'vortex' for the analysis of the way revealing, concealing and (in)visibility play out in organizations and how they are experienced and managed.

The invisible norm

From our discussion so far, we can identify the following features of the norm, or what Hearn (1996) refers to as the 'dominant centre'. First and foremost, the norm is largely invisible, 'opaque to analysis (Collinson and Hearn, 1994), unproblematized and evading scrutiny. Individuals who occupy the normative position (such as white, middle class men) tend to go unnoticed. They do not represent a particular (e.g. gendered, raced) category and in this sense they are 'unmarked'. While women are marked by and embody gender (and non-whites marked by and embody race), white men represent universal personhood and carry what Robinson (2000) refers to as a 'disembodied normativity'. Thus, in Whitehead's (2001) study of male further education managers, when asked how gender had influenced their behaviour as managers, men were nonplussed. 'I don't know, I'm not a woman' was a typical response. In other words, men routinely fail to see themselves as gendered and position gender (as well as race) as an issue that attaches to another. Their bodies are thus unmarked by these identity categories and they are accordingly invisible as a gendered (and racial) group.

Secondly and relatedly, the material and cultural privileges that attend the normative position also go unnoticed. They are concealed as privileges and are often seen as inevitable rewards that accompany the dominant centre. We tend not to question the advantages of masculinity or position them as such, but instead focus on disadvantages that attach to femininity. As we have pointed out elsewhere (Simpson and Lewis, 2005, 2007), gender only gets noticed when it is a source of harm. Gender as advantage therefore escapes from view and remains concealed within what are seen as the 'natural' rewards of masculinity. The centre is accordingly a site of power in that material and cultural advantages that come from privilege and from positioning as One are hidden, protected and hence perpetuated. In Foucauldian terms, invisibility thus underpins power.

Thirdly, the centre or norm can be seen to be insecure and subject to challenges as individuals from the margins seek to enter and as others dispute and reveal its privileged status. In terms of the former, through defensive strategies entry from the margins is contested by the norm so that the core normative category remains overwhelmingly white, middle class and male and its domain supportive of hegemonic understandings that are the basis of definitional power. For example, while women have made in-roads into key areas of organizational and public life, occupying positions of power and influence and gaining arguably some of the material benefits of the dominant centre, they are still in terms, symbolically 'cast as Other'. They are never fully accepted as leaders, as managers or as members of the board. As Höpfl argues in Chapter 2, they cannot be full members of organizations because they lack members – the condition for entry. They remain strangers – visibly marked as women, embodying gender and often pushed to the margins or infantilized in a discursive regime and symbolic order of hegemonic masculinity and instrumental rationality. They may seek the cultural and symbolic privileges of invisibility but the quest is likely to fail.

In this respect, as our other work has shown (Lewis, 2004, 2006; Simpson, 2004, 2005, 2009; Simpson and Lewis, 2005, 2007) both women and men can make strategic moves to enter the dominant centre from the margins but their positioning is incomplete. Thus, from Lewis (2004, 2006), some female entrepreneurs often deny the salience of gender in their organizational lives and seek to align themselves with the world of men – to be symbolically associated with the 'serious business' of (male) enterprise rather than the 'non-serious' business that appears to epitomize the world of entrepreneurial women. As Lewis has argued, this may be seen as a 'quest for invisibility' and, from her study, considerable anger is expressed towards those women who do take up a 'feminine' entrepreneurial identity and who accordingly subvert other women's attempts to integrate into the norm. In fact, women business owners in general are rarely seen as entrepreneurs per se and are not accepted as the norm. Instead, they are marked, gendered, Othered and labeled as 'female entrepreneurs' so they carry all the meanings (e.g. of non-serious business, of slow growth and risk aversion) that the label implies. Simpson (2004, 2005, 2009, also this volume) has shown how male nurses draw on ties of fraternity to align themselves with the world of higher status male medical practitioners such as doctors and consultants – the dominant centre of the hospital organization. Drawing on occupational ideologies around 'equal partnership' and presenting arguments relating to how doctors value their specialist expertise, male nurses position themselves as equals despite the differences in professional status. However, visibly marked as Other in a feminine and lower status occupation, that entry into the centre is incomplete and male nurses have often had to confront alterity through a variety of interactions and work practices where male doctors exclude and marginalize them.

For the Other, on the periphery, to enter the norm or the domain of the One, is therefore fraught with difficulty and can never be fully complete. Other challenges to the norm are more radical in nature. As Robinson (2000) has pointed out, and as referred to above, the rise of feminism and of black power and, more recently, the organization of social difference around sexuality, age, faith, disablement as well as gender and race, has helped to throw the spotlight on the hitherto hidden privileges of white (and of course heterosexual) masculinity and to mark white men as a racial and gendered group. At an organizational level, as we shall see in the following chapters, individuals and groups position themselves against the dominant order and so create space for non hegemonic meanings. In so doing they challenge the invisibility of male privilege, the definitional power of masculine discourses and the disembodied normativity of men. They have helped reveal men for what they are as a categorical group and reveal their privileges as just that – namely the benefits and rights that attend upon white men. The privileges of the centre and the meanings that attach to that centre therefore are not fully secure and, through challenges to men's normative status, may not remain hidden from view. On this basis, men's hold on power can be seen as fragile so there may be considerable instability as men respond to challenges to their privileged position – drawing for example on traditionally gendered and essentialist rhetoric to support the *status quo* or, *in extremis*, on violent behaviours and displays.

The norm therefore can be seen to be the largely invisible site of power and advantage and insecure as individuals and groups from the margins seek to enter the centre and as others challenge and reveal its privileges. These dynamics of (in)visibility and power and of revealing and concealing are evident in many of the chapters that make up this book. As we have seen, Heather Höpfl draws attention in her chapter to male notions of order based on membership and how women, lacking members, are 'strangers' in their world. Melissa Tyler and Laurie Cohen's chapter on (in)visibility and organizational space is founded on the significance for women of the 'norm' of the masculine academic career that demands traditionally feminine support and availability from women but which fails to recognize them as such; similarly Selma Theresa Lyng refers to the normative high commitment 'up and go' career in the legal profession and how discourses of meritocracy and individual choice help conceal the gendered nature of its dynamics – as well as how women are constrained in any attempts to reveal the career structure as inequitable; Jennifer Binns focuses on the masculine norm of leadership and calls for an 'outing' of masculinity as a dominant practice; Irene Ryan looks at the hidden dominant centre of sports leadership, highlighting how, in a similar vein to Lyng, the gendered nature of sport and its management are concealed within a rhetoric of equal opportunity and Susan Harwood shows how, in an organization based research project looking at gendered culture in the police, female officers use the margins to help reveal some of the hidden attributes and practices within the dominant centre of the force. All these papers highlight the durability and invisibility of the norm, how it conceals gendered practices and processes through normalizing discursive regimes, as well as the challenges that are being made to its dominant status. In different ways, the margins seek to reveal, in Pullen and Rhodes's terms, the 'mask' of gender while the norm draws defensively on taken for granted discourses and rhetoric to conceal a privileged status that is, in different ways, under challenge.

Visibility and invisibility within the margins

What of those outside the norm – on the margins, the periphery, designated as Other? How does (in)visibility play out in these contexts? We argue here that while the norm is strongly associated with invisibility and with dynamics (practices, processes behaviours, rhetoric) that seek to conceal, both visibility and invisibility are implicated in different ways within the margins. Thus, as tokens in male dominated occupations and roles, women stand out and are highly visible. They symbolize their category and experience material consequences of over-exposure and the marking of their bodies as gendered. Jacqueline Watts, looking at women's experiences in the male dominated engineering profession demonstrates how as tokens women are both conspicuous, as 'physical spectacle' and invisible in terms of authority required for the job. Tyler and Cohen's chapter shows how women from a range of occupations in a university setting are expected to be available for support and emotion work. They are visible within the organization's emotional as well as aesthetic regimes. From Gatrell, pregnant women are highly visible, their bodies marked as disturbing and potentially disruptive to organizational routines while from Lyng, female lawyers with children are visible as mothers – different from the norm of the fast track, high commitment career. As both Gatrell and Lyng suggest, women may therefore seek invisibility as a coping mechanism – creating spaces where they can remain unnoticed, erasing markers of motherhood. However, as we have seen, while invisibility within the norm is associated with power and privilege, outside the norm it can signify lack of power as individuals are hidden, marginalized and neglected. Outside this volume, Rollins (1985), looking at the largely powerless world of domestic cleaning, refers to the invisibility of women – how, enshrouded in oblivion, conversations by employers and their families take place around them as if they are not there. In the present volume, we can see how being invisible in the context of the professional career can be a symbol of worthlessness and lack of value – in Tyler and Cohen's terms, to represent 'cultural marginalization and symbolic negation'. Keeping a low profile or undertaking invisible emotion work is to 'invisibilize' one's merit and potential so that individuals can be erased.

Nevertheless, as Harwood has also shown in the context of an interventionist culture change project in the police, invisibility can also be used strategically to challenge the norm; equally visibility as Other can be a site of resistance and change. In Harwood's study, female officers exploited their invisible, marginal and subservient roles to gain knowledge of gender dynamics which formed the basis of new understandings and which they used, in highly visible contexts, in subsequent debriefings to senior personnel. Other work outside this volume (e.g. Davies and Thomas, 2004) has demonstrated how individuals can use visibility and difference to challenge the *status quo* – rejecting subjectivizing effects of competitive masculine discourse to present 'trailblazing' identities that actively challenge current practices and champion different ways of doing. To be visible is not therefore always to be exploited, the subject of gaze or to be marked detrimentally as gendered – but as Davies and Thomas point out, also to be epistemologically advantaged in that in some contexts 'difference' can allow individuals to do and say things that are denied within the mainstream.

The '(In)visibility Vortex'

These dynamics paint a complicated picture of the implications of visibility and invisibility both inside and outside the norm and of how different forms of (in)visibility are lived, experienced and managed. In order to make sense of these complexities, we present a 'map' of the terrain. This we present through the concept of a vortex. A vortex is a flow, usually in spiral motion, around a centre. The speed of rotation and the level of turbulence are greatest at the centre and decrease progressively with distance towards the margins. This dynamic, we suggest, is resonant with the processes of concealment that occur within the norm as well as the challenges that take place from outside it. In other words, the norm can be seen to be a site of agitation and defensive action as individuals and groups seek to maintain the invisibility of their privileged state and to hang onto its material and cultural advantages – and as dominant meanings that preserve the *status quo* struggle to suppress alternative interpretations. As we have argued elsewhere (Simpson and Lewis, 2007) the closer individuals or groups lie in relation to the norm, the more likely they are to secure access to its privileges. Effective challenges are therefore likely to emanate from those closest to that centre such as, from Watt's chapter, female engineers who already have made claim to a specialist expertise and the material and cultural advantages of a (masculine) professional status or, from Binns, senior women managers who draw on the culture (and masculine) resources of leadership. The concept of a vortex therefore captures the turbulence and insecurity that occurs both within and immediately outside the centre – the latter in the form of challenges to the norm and the processes of revealing its privileged status.

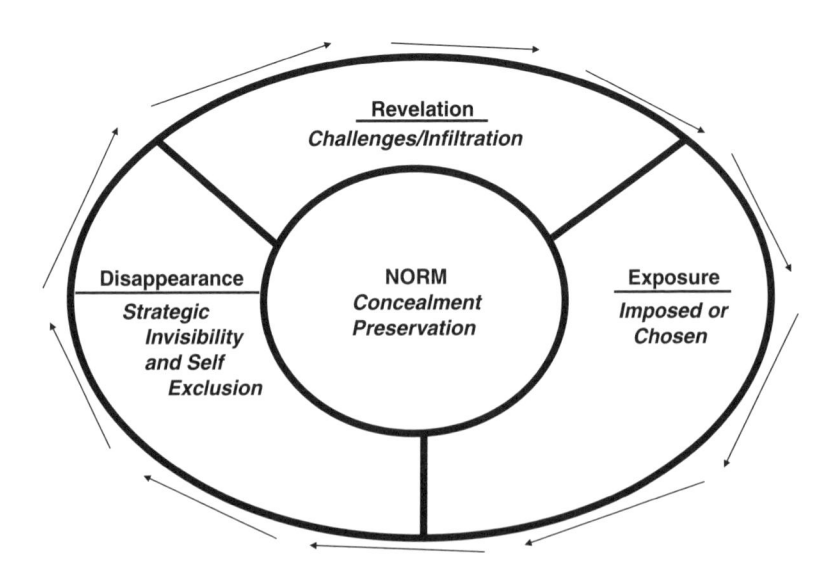

Figure I.1 The (In)visibility Vortex

Concealment and preservation within the norm

As Figure I.1 illustrates, and based on our earlier discussion, the norm is characterized by specific processes that relate to its invisible status of power – namely processes of *concealment* (of privilege and advantage) and *preservation* (of that order). Thus, from Watt's chapter, we see how attempts are made to reject female engineers from the masculine norm of privileged and expert professionalism through practices of erasure, put-down humour and a hyper-sexualization that demeans their status. Similarly Höpfl refers to how a university restructuring and subsequent organizational manoeuvrings led to the 'disappearance' of women Heads of School so that masculine order was regained and Ryan discusses how restructuring of the governance of field hockey meant that men positioned themselves to take control of key aspects of leadership while drawing on discourses of equal opportunity to conceal their quest for power. Concealment and preservation of a dominant status thus require the power to control work practices as well as the power to define and to suppress alternative meanings – a power that, from Robinson (2000), is both fragile and insecure. Preserving order and concealing political intent require strategic manoeuvring, surveillance, speed, contrivances, tactics, machinations – in short they involve a turbulent 'ebb and flow'.

Revelation, exposure and disappearance in the margins

The vortex as presented above additionally captures the dynamics of movement outside the centre and how (in)visibility plays out in the margins. Here, we conceptualize key processes as *revelation, exposure and disappearance*.

Revelation

In terms of revelation, those in the margins, through radical acts, subversive stories and interpersonal relations, can reveal and so challenge normative practices and discourses that privilege masculinity. Thus, in Harwood's study of the police, women on an in-house culture change project engaged in critical acts while centre stage in their debriefings about inequitable attitudes and practices to senior managers – while other women pooled experiences to highlight gendered power; Watts' study shows how female engineers 'stood up' to male foremen who resisted their authority and used their positions of influence to challenge the *status quo*. Revelation can also come through simple presence as women infiltrate leadership and management positions, bringing in new ways of thinking and doing. Revealing however is not easy. Some chapters accordingly explore the difficulties of challenging the norm – how, from Gatrell, men mobilize the notion of 'unreasonable demands' to support the norm of the male body and to undermine pregnant women's demands for change while, from Lyng, revealing the dominance of masculinity is risky: women are, in Fournier's (2001) terms 'framed as Other' and hence outside the normative career.

Exposure

These 'politics of revealing' and the dialectics between revealing and concealing highlight the links between revelation and exposure. To reveal dominant practices for what they are or even to simply enter from the margins and hence challenge the masculine domain is to draw attention to alterity and to be framed by dominant discourses as Other – as *mothers*, as *female* leaders, lawyers, academics, engineers. To challenge and reveal is to render oneself visible and exposed. Pregnant women are highly visible in a negative sense and some resist being framed by struggling to conform to the demands of disembodied work practices; mothers become visibly gendered in the legal career, symbolizing reduced work dedication and unavailability. As Binns points out, in performing leadership women stand out as aberrations – as strangers to be diminished and dismissed; in academia, from Tyler and Cohen, they are exploited and overexposed. At the same time, however, visibility can be *chosen* rather than imposed and exposure can be valued for its alternative positioning. Simpson finds men who choose a non-traditional career can experience a 'special status' as visible Other and gain ontological satisfaction from the exposure their token status brings. From Lewis's study 'Mumpreneurs' embrace alterity in their specific choice of motherhood *and* entrepreneurship signalling oppositional identity to the male norm of enterprise.

Disappearance

Despite this, in many contexts visibility as Other is a problematic state of alterity. From the empirical sites that make up this book, one response is to seek invisibility – to overcome abjection and to disappear. For Tyler and Cohen, invisibility is a coping mechanism to counter the demands of availability referred to above and to manage the competing demands of work and home. Women working in a university setting found physical spaces where they could effectively vanish from view – even though invisibility is also symbolic of lack of worth and negation and even though the emotion work of 'availability' and service to others is similarly disappeared. Equally, in Harwood's study, women made strategic use of invisibility and their Other status to gather information for a change project and to 'eavesdrop' on conversations they would not normally hear. They strategically 'disappeared'. Keeping a low profile is thus a response to visible alterity. A further response, as we have seen, is to seek to enter and remain invisible within (disappear into) the norm. Thus, in Simpson's account male nurses attempt to distance themselves as visible Other in a non-traditional occupation by seeking to enter the 'dominant centre' of male doctors and male medical practice. Finally, from Kerfoot and Miller, individuals may 'self exclude' and make a choice to disappear. Here, as Other to male entrepreneurship, women are shown to internalize their exclusion through the weight of a gendered rhetoric of enterprise which evidently disadvantages them. Disappearance can thus be a strategic choice (to overcome Otherhood; to exploit invisibility and alterity; to enter the invisible norm) or an act of self exclusion in response to perceived disadvantage.

Complexities within the vortex

The vortex paints a complicated picture of agitation and turmoil both within and around the norm. The processes of concealing and preservation within the norm and of Revelation, Exposure and Disappearance in the margins imply a constant motion that relates to the maintenance of power and to the countervailing dynamics of alterity From our conceptualization there is a flow which could move from revelation to exposure as other and then to disappearance as a strategic response or an act of self exclusion. However despite this circularity these processes are by no means always sequential or discrete. As Tyler and Cohen have aptly demonstrated, women can be simultaneously over-exposed and disappeared in that their contributions in the form of 'support work' are marginalized and undervalued; Harwood demonstrates how women move strategically between visibility and invisibility to initiate change. They disappear into alterity and then make themselves visible to challenge the *status quo*. Binns points out that women experience visibility and invisibility – if they perform femininity and their gender is exposed, their worth as leaders disappears.

To make visible the so-called 'female advantage' is to also expose what women lack as 'real leaders' and to further conceal the masculinity of the norm. These processes therefore interact in complicated ways in the manoeuvrings that underpin privilege and disadvantage, in the preservation of power and in the strategies of resistance to being framed.

We started this chapter with a discussion of the diverse ways in which visibility and invisibility have been implicated in organizational experience and some of the contradictory processes involved. Our aim was therefore to try to make sense of this complicated terrain. But just as we feel we may have captured some of these experiences within a conceptual framework and so helped reveal underlying processes and practices of gender, our final chapter throws all this into disarray! As Pullen and Rhodes provocatively and persuasively suggest, the notion that gender *can* be revealed is in itself subject to question. There is no 'true meaning' to uncover as with a hidden face beneath a mask. In fact the mask itself reflects our normative understandings of masculinity and femininity and is inscribed with masculine knowledge. In revealing the so-called 'truth' about men, masculinity and the norm, we must be aware that gender itself is an understanding and practice that performs its own act of concealment as a mask. How can we reveal when the revelation conceals; when the exposure also disappears?

These questions disrupt our carefully ordered positioning of processes within and outside the norm and our understandings of revealing and concealing. We may think we have captured some elements of the dynamics of (in)visibility, but they then evade our grasp and new issues are raised. This further supports the complexity of the dynamics involved and of the contestable nature of our understandings of gender. The concepts of visibility and invisibility as played out in the gender dynamics of organizations are at best slippery and insecure. However, it is through these disjunctures and these gaps in understanding; through these contradictions and tensions that new research areas can be framed. The (in)visibility vortex – as well as the concepts and dynamics of Concealment, Revelation, Exposure and Disappearance – is accordingly a modest step in the direction of an appreciation of the implications of the dynamics of visibility and invisibility as well as of the spaces in between that can form the foundations of future work.

The structure of the book

In Chapter 1 'Living and Working in Grey Areas: Gender (In)visibility and Organization Space', Melissa Tyler and Laurie Cohen explore the relationship between gender in/visibility and organizational space, demonstrating how visibility and invisibility helps us to understand the ways in which space is involved in the practicing of gender. Through an exploration of Sofia Hulten's video installation 'Grey Area', as well as through the interpretations and experiences of women working within a university setting, they reveal how women are positioned as Other in and through space. They show how women are both overexposed and erased and how different forms of visibility and invisibility are lived out, experienced and managed through space. For example, women often feel they must be available to others (and hence visible) – but the identity and emotion work of 'availability' is often invisible and under-valued. Similarly, while women may seek out invisibility as a coping mechanism to counter over-exposure, to counter expectations of availability and to manage the competing demands of work and home, invisibility can at the same time be a symbol of worthlessness and negation. Tyler and Cohen aptly demonstrate the complexities of the connections between structural and numerical disadvantage and the cultural marginalization and symbolic negation of women as they seek to manage their position as Other within specific organizational and spatial regimes.

In Chapter 2 'A Question of Membership', Heather Höpfl highlights the power of the norm and women's position as strangers in that space. She does this by looking at the masculine symbolism which is deeply embedded in organizations. She argues that organizations are conventionally understood in terms of abstract relationships and rational actions manifest in rankings and league tables. Through these metrics individuals can achieve membership of an organization. However, what is concealed is the masculine nature of these access points making it easier for men to achieve a sense of belonging while also constructing women as strangers. Within this context the only membership available to women is as a plaything or else a quasi-man. In this sense women can adopt a visible role as 'woman' and Other or alternatively seek invisibility by acquiring a metaphorical 'member'. However, for those women who set out on a quest for invisibility within the masculine norm, the cost of this strategy is impotence. Drawing on a range of her own experiences, Höpfl illustrates beautifully the constant battle women face in seeking recognition of their membership of the masculine world of organizing.

In Chapter 3, 'Pregnancy Centre Stage, Please: Contesting the Erasure of Pregnant Bodies from Workplace Space', Caroline Gatrell draws on internet site discussions among pregnant women to explore experiences of pregnancy and to highlight the disappearance and erasure of the maternal pregnant body in the workplace space. She links this absence to the neglect of the pregnant body from management and organizational scholarship. Against a background of the universalizing of the healthy male body as the norm, she argues persuasively that women's contribution and their place in the public world are often discounted in a context where pregnant bodies are either metaphorically invisible (and therefore ignored) or deemed out of place and 'other' and therefore highly visible in a negative sense. Through her data, she demonstrates how pregnant bodies are unreliable, unwelcome and treated as a threat to social order and control and how they elicit feelings of disgust. In response, women attempt to manage their pregnant bodies to conform to organizational routines and often seek to disappear by rendering their bodies and the physical aspects of their pregnancy, 'off-stage'. Through her rich and evocative data, Gatrell argues for the inclusion of the pregnant body within management scholarship as a legitimate topic for study and for pregnant bodies to 'take their position in a positive spotlight'.

In Chapter 4, '"Mothered" and Othered: (In)visibility of Care Responsibility and Gender in Processes of Excluding Women from Norwegian Law Firms', Selma Therese Lyng explores care responsibility as a symbolic principle of Othering in the context of the legal profession in Norway. Here, she describes how women (and some men) are marginalized from the normative high commitment 'up and go' career on the 'A' team within Norwegian law firms – a career type that symbolizes loyalty, commitment and high dedication. While childless women experience few barriers in this career, as mothers they become exposed as gendered and come to symbolize reduced work dedication and unavailability – with material consequences in the form of exclusion from advantageous positioning such as high profile client networks. Through her data, Lyng shows how women engage in counter 'de-mothering' strategies, such as excessive work patterns, to 'disappear' or render invisible the signifiers of contract deviation and to signal commitment to the job. Challenges to the norm of unencumbered commitment are constrained by the consequent exposure of motherhood should women demand fairer treatment. By revealing the inequalities in the legal career, any professional merit or potential that women may possess also disappears. Lyng demonstrates how the process of Othering of workers with care responsibilities as well as the unequal patterns of exclusion within the normative career are rendered invisible and unchallenged through dominant discourses that draw on a rhetoric of individual choice and on essentialized notions of gendered care.

In Chapter 5, 'Organizing Entrepreneurship? Women's Invisibility in Self-employment', Deborah Kerfoot and Caroline Miller explore the underlying masculine norm of entrepreneurship and how traditional female gender roles are oppositionally constructed. Drawing on data derived from a micro-ethnography of a self-employment access and learning programme and interviews with 42 respondents from a variety of self-employment programmes, the chapter explores the self-employment workshop as a specific organizational site where entrepreneurship and the entrepreneur are constituted and sustained as self-evidently male. Kerfoot and Miller argue that the consequence of this is to position women as outside of what it means to be a successful entrepreneur. The self-employment programmes reveal the masculinity of entrepreneurship while at the same time disappear other ways to be entrepreneurial. One reading of the consequences of this is to suggest that women make themselves invisible by choosing not to set up a business. However Kerfoot and Miller argue that women's invisibility in the ranks of entrepreneurs must be understood as something more than choice – rather they highlight the processes through which this invisibility is constructed. Thus women didn't simply 'choose' not to set up a business, they clearly recognized how being a woman would significantly disadvantage them.

In Chapter 6, '"Mumpreneurs": Revealing the Post-feminist Entrepreneur', Patricia Lewis explores the emergence of a new feminized entrepreneurial identity labelled 'mumpreneur'. What is notable about the adoption of this identity by some women business owners is their willingness to embrace entrepreneurship while also choosing to retain and make visible their traditional mothering role. While motherhood and entrepreneurship are conventionally understood as being in opposition to each other, the post-feminist mumpreneur chooses to put her caring responsibilities at the centre of her entrepreneurial activities. However one significant consequence of such a choice is that mumpreneurs who seek independence and self-reliance through entrepreneurship do so by setting limits on their participation in entrepreneurial activity. While this compromise allows women to take part in the public world of work, this participation is dependent on a retraditionalization of gender particularly within the home. Thus for these women, entrepreneurship is certainly not about transgressing the traditional categories of gender, rather it may, as Adkins (1999: 136) suggests create '…new lines of demarcation and domination'.

In Chapter 7, 'Masculinities in Practice: The Invisible Dynamics in Sports Leadership', Irene Ryan explores sport leadership and how, with a specific focus on field hockey, organizational discourses of equality, based on parity in terms of numbers of men and women at 'ground level', serve to conceal how gender is implicated in leadership and coaching practice. Here, Ryan shows how the liberal quest for equal opportunities and restructuring of the organization and government of hockey along managerialist lines, have left men's sport largely intact and further legitimized discourses of hegemonic masculinity that have historically permeated the sports landscape. In this way, government initiated changes in sports administration, based on positivistic logic and hierarchies of authority have solidified gender suppressive practices and institutionalized invisible forms of normativity. Through her data, she shows how women are exposed and highly visible within the sport, experiencing barriers to full advancement while the 'ordinary and inevitable' privileges of masculinity are hidden within the norm. Gender is accordingly rendered invisible through the overpowering presence of a form of hegemonic masculinity and resistance effectively silenced through a dominant rhetoric of equality of opportunity and choice.

In Chapter 8, 'Leadership and the (In)visibility of Gender', Jennifer Binns in an Australian based study on leadership, demonstrates how (in)visibility, rather than being aligned to gender categories (e.g. visible man/invisible woman), can operate in ambivalent and contradictory ways. She uses her data to establish the significance of three different forms of visibility and invisibility. Discursive (in)visibility refers to the absence of feminine values and characteristics from dominant understandings of leadership and here she highlights how normative values of heroism, individualism, toughness and decisiveness permeate accounts of leadership behaviours. The concept of corporeal (in)visibility captures the material and physical absence of women's bodies from leadership as well as their visibility, as embodied femininity, in these roles. Binns shows how women, if they take up a masculine model of leadership, often invoke hostility from men and encounter moves to render them 'disappeared'; if they practice unassuming femininity, they are not seen as real leaders – though they can gain power through displays of embodied femininity in ways which are not similarly required of men. Finally, (in)visibility as identity work is concerned with how gender and leadership are enacted as a dual process where gender is sometimes exposed and at other times disappeared. Through these powerful conceptualizations, Binns foregrounds and reveals the gendered construction of leadership in ways that go beyond the highlighting of a feminine alternative to the main/male gaze.

In Chapter 9, '"Now you see me, now you don't": The Visibility Paradox for Women in a Male Dominated Profession', Jacqueline Watts explores the way in which female engineers cope with their minority position within the masculine work environment of civil engineering. Focusing on the way in which this minority position renders them highly visible, she considers how this visibility can have negative as well as positive effects. Female engineers experience their visibility negatively in terms of being highly conspicuous while at the same time 'unseeable' i.e. their authority is ignored. On the other hand when they are requested to make visible their 'femaleness' in a way that can be of advantage to the organization, benefits may accrue and prevent a woman from being completely disregarded. However, the differing impact of the positive and negative aspects of being a visible minority can lead to role overload where a female engineer has to work extra hard to be accepted on the same terms as her male colleagues, while role confusion can result from the request to privilege her 'femaleness' over her technical skills when dealing with business clients.

In Chapter 10, 'The Critical and (Subversive) Act of (In)visibility: A Strategic Reframing of "Disappeared and Devalued" Women in a Densely Masculinist Workplace', Susan Harwood examines in the context of policing and through data collected during an interventionist research project aimed at uncovering problems of a gendered workplace culture, some of the ways in which women used their (in)visibility within a densely masculinist workplace to mask their collective activity and to subvert male authority. By highlighting how women on the culture change project, often working at low levels of the organization, managed their visibility as project members (and hence were able to potentially 'report' on higher status male colleagues) and their invisibility in some of the support and 'menial' work required of them in their work roles, Harwood demonstrates how strategic moves between visibility and invisibility can be a force for change. Thus, women were able to draw on their largely invisible support roles (one woman activated the slide show in a high-powered meeting) to report 'findings' to the group – thereby making strategic use of deferential behaviour to mask 'fact finding' activities associated with their role within the research project. In fact, as she clearly demonstrates through her data, the capacity to move between the visible and the invisible was crucial to women's continuing project participation and that strategic 'disappearing' into subservience and deference could be the foundations of radical change.

In Chapter 11, 'A Reversal of the Gaze: Men's Experiences of Visibility in Non-traditional Occupations', Ruth Simpson explores the implications of visibility and of the reversal of the gaze for men's experiences in four gender a-typical roles: nursing, primary school teaching, cabin crew and librarianship. She shows how some men claim to enjoy the visibility their token status brings, activating a 'special' identity and benefiting from assumptions, on the part of colleagues and managers, that they possess special expertise as well as enjoying in some contexts the opportunity to display a corporate aesthetic ideal. At the same time, visibility and marking can be an uncomfortable experience when that is associated with Other (different, devalued) identities and identity work can also be seen in the struggles that take place around the dominant centre as men resist Otherhood and seek the invisibility and privileges of the norm. The gaze can thus be experienced as pleasure and as a source of discomfort and pain and the chapter shows how it both highlights and conceals – supporting partial truths and obscuring what remains outside of its view.

In our final chapter, 'Gender, Mask and the Face: Towards a Corporeal Ethics' Alison Pullen and Carl Rhodes problematize the very notion that gender can be revealed. Here they consider meanings behind revealing and concealing to examine gender itself as a mask. The mask does not hide or conceal the true identity of the wearer but is part of that identity and is made up of the matrix of ways in which we mark divisions between ourselves in relation to others. We therefore have different layers of masks which mutate and develop through the mobilization, adoption and reflection of sameness and difference to and from others. The mask can be seen as a 'culturally dominant means through which we become who we are by locating ourselves in relation to what we understand by masculinity and femininity'. Their central question: 'What lies beneath when the mask is removed?' is explored by turning to the work of Levinas and his view of ethics as the site of the ontological relationship with other – a relationship which can be considered ethical in the care, responsibility and love shown to that other and where the mask removed reveals a face that is, in its individuality and uniqueness, unknowable and which therefore precedes gendered description. As Pullen and Rhodes argue, gender as a mask and the categorization of men and women in terms of gender identity is a violation of ethics in that the 'masking' forecloses individuality, inscribing (masculine) 'knowledge' of gender onto the mask and reducing the totality of humanity to just two tropes. The gendering of human bodies is thus ethically questionable in that such practices overwrite people with masks that violate their status as unique and particular. On this basis, as they persuasively argue, any politics of gender must work towards the unmasking or undoing of gender itself, seeking to disrupt gendered distinctions while recognizing that gender is a form of knowledge and practice that performs an act of concealment as a mask.

Through these chapters, this book attempts to make sense of the complexities and contradictions inherent in the way visibility and invisibility is experienced and managed in organizations. We have captured some of these complexities within the notion of the vortex which we hope can form the basis of future research.

References

Adkins, L. (1999) 'Community and economy: A retraditionalization of gender?', *Theory, Culture and Society*, 16(1):119–139.
Alvesson, M. (1998) 'Gender relations and identity at work: A case study of masculinities and femininities in an advertising agency', *Human Relations*, 51(8): 969–1006.
Beynon, J. (2002) *Masculinities and Culture*. Buckingham: Open University Press.
Collinson, D. and Hearn, J. (1994) 'Naming men as men: Implications for work, organization and management', *Gender, Work and Organization*, 1(1): 2–22.
Cross, S. and BagiChole, B. (2002) 'Girls' jobs for the boys? Masculinity and non-traditional occupations', *Gender, Work and Organization*, 9(2): 204–226.
Davies, A. and Thomas, R. (2004) 'Gendering resistance in the public services', in Thomas, R., Mills, A. and Helms Mills, J. (eds) *Identity Politics at Work: Resisting Gender, Gendering Resistance*, pp. 105–122. London: Routledge.
Fletcher, J. (1999) *Disappearing Acts: Gender Power and Relational Practices at Work*. Boston: MIT Press.
Hancock, P. and Tyler, M. (2007) 'Un/doing gender and the aesthetics of organizational performance', *Gender, Work and Organization*, 14(16): 512–533.
Hearn, J. (1996) 'Deconstructing the dominant: Making the One(s) the Other(s)', *Organization*, 3(4): 611–626.
Hearn, J. and Parkin, W. (2001) *Gender, Sexuality and Violence in Organizations*. London: Sage.
Heikes, J. (1991) 'When men are in the minority: The case of men in nursing', *The Sociological Quarterly*, 32(3): 389–401.
Kanter, R. (1977) *Men and Women of the Corporation*. New York: Basic Books.
Kerfoot, D. and Knights, D. (1993) 'Management, masculinity and manipulation: From paternalism to corporate strategy in financial services in Britain', *Journal of Management Studies*, 30(4): 659–677.
Kerfoot, D. and Knights, D. (1998) 'Managing masculinity in contemporary organizational life: A man(agerial) project', *Organization*, 5(1): 7–26.
Kusz, K. (2001) 'I want to be the minority: The politics of youthful white masculinities in sport and popular culture in 1990s America', *Journal of Sport and Social Issues*, 25(4): 390–416.
Lewis, P. (2004) 'Using conflict to highlight the gendered nature of entrepreneurship: The case of the "career woman" entrepreneur', *British Academy of Management Conference*, St. Andrews, Scotland, 30 August–1 September.

Lewis, P. (2006) 'The quest for invisibility: Female entrepreneurs and the masculine norm of entrepreneurship', *Gender, Work and Organization*, 13(5): 453–469.

Linstead, S. (2000) 'Gender blindness or gender suppression? A comment on Fiona Wilson's research note', *Organization Studies*, 21(1): 297–303.

Maddock, S. (1999) *Challenging Women: Gender, Culture and Organization*. London: Sage.

Marshall, J. (1994) 'Why women leave senior management jobs: My research approach and some initial findings', in Tantum, M. (ed.) *Women in Management: The Second Wave*. London: Routledge.

Robinson, S. (2000) *Marked men: White Masculinity in Crisis*. New York: Columbia University Press.

Rollins, J. (1985) *Between Women: Domestics and the Employers*. Philadelphia: Temple University Press.

Simpson, R. (1997) 'Have times changed? Career barriers and the token woman manager', *British Journal of Management*, 8, 121–129.

Simpson, R. (2000) 'Gender mix and organizational fit: How gender imbalance at different levels of the organization impacts on women managers', *Women in Management Review*, 15(1): 5–20.

Simpson, R. (2004) 'Masculinity at work: The experiences of men in female dominated occupations', *Work, Employment and Society*, 18(2): 349–368.

Simpson, R. (2005) 'Men in non-traditional occupations: Career entry, career orientation and experience of role strain', *Gender, Work and Organization*, 12(4): 363–380.

Simpson, R. (2009) *Men in Caring Occupations: Doing Gender Differently*. London: Palgrave.

Simpson, R. and Lewis, P. (2005) 'An investigation of silence and a scrutiny of transparency: Reexamining gender in organization literature through the concepts of voice and visibility', *Human Relations*, 58(10): 1253–1275.

Simpson, R. and Lewis, P. (2007) *Voice, Visibility and the Gendering of Organizations*. Basingstoke: Palgrave Macmillan.

Taylor, S. and Tyler, M. J. (1998) 'The exchange of aesthetics: women's work and the gift', *Gender, Work and Organization*, 5(3): 165–171.

Tyler, M. J. and Abbott, P. (1998) 'Chocs away: Weight watching in the contemporary airline industry', *Sociology*, 32(3): 433–450.

Whitehead, S. (2001) 'The invisible gendered subject: Men in education management', *Journal of Gender Studies*, 10(1): 67–82.

Williams, C. (1993) (ed.) *Doing Women's Work: Men in Non-Traditional Occupations*. London: Sage.

Wilson, F. (1996) 'Research note: Organizational theory: Blind and deaf to gender', *Organization Studies*, 17(5): 825–842.

1
Living and Working in Grey Areas: Gender (In)visibility and Organizational Space

Melissa Tyler and Laurie Cohen

Introduction

Our focus in this chapter is on the relationship between gender (in)visibility and organizational space. Initially, our interest in this area was sparked by two seemingly unrelated experiences. The first occurred when an academic colleague who was visiting our department commented on the unprofessional appearance of our respective offices, a state she attributed primarily to the fact that we had chosen to display photographs of our families and friends, and particularly children's drawings, on our walls and notice boards. In her view, this reduced us both to the status of 'mother' and undermined our efforts to be perceived as competent academics; the two, from her point of view, being mutually exclusive. This set us thinking about how we display ourselves in our offices; that is, about how we perform our gender identities in and through our workspace.

In our minds, at least initially, an unrelated experience that occurred at roughly the same time was our visit to an art exhibition on office life held at The Photographers' Gallery in London (Cohen and Tyler, 2004). Here we encountered a video installation by contemporary artist Sofia Hulten called *Grey Area*. In *Grey Area* the artist herself performs in a grey suit which she seemingly uses as camouflage as she hides in various places – behind a plant, in a rolled up carpet, beneath a desk – until she eventually gets into a bin liner and throws herself away. The effect is comical, but also deeply disturbing because of what it seemingly says about how women feel about themselves, and about each other, in their workplace (as one of the women who took part in our subsequent research put it, 'it's funny but also very depressing'). We found the video extremely unsettling yet also strangely compelling,

24 *Living and Working in Grey Areas*

evoking as it did feelings we hadn't previously been conscious of or articulated in relation to our own experiences of work. Having been 'moved' in this way ourselves, and having made connections between our feelings about this video and the comments made by our academic colleague about our own workspaces, we were interested to find out if our interpretations and the thoughts and feelings they provoked in us, resonated with those of other women. To this end we used still images (reproduced here in greyscale) from *Grey Area* (Figure 1.1) as the basis for a series of focus groups and interviews with women in which we discussed their gendered experiences of the workplace. During these interviews, we asked women to reflect not only on their responses to the images in the stills, but also on the thoughts and feelings these images provoked in relation to their own, and each others', lived experiences of work.

There is now a relatively well established body of literature focusing on the ways in which women continue to be positioned as Other – *in* the organization but not *of* it (Bruni *et al*, 2004; Knights and Kerfoot, 2004; Tyler, 2005). Some of this literature makes sense of women's relatively precarious position with reference to the concepts of visibility and invisibility and draws attention not only to the structural disadvantages women face (Alvesson and Due Billing, 1997) – to what

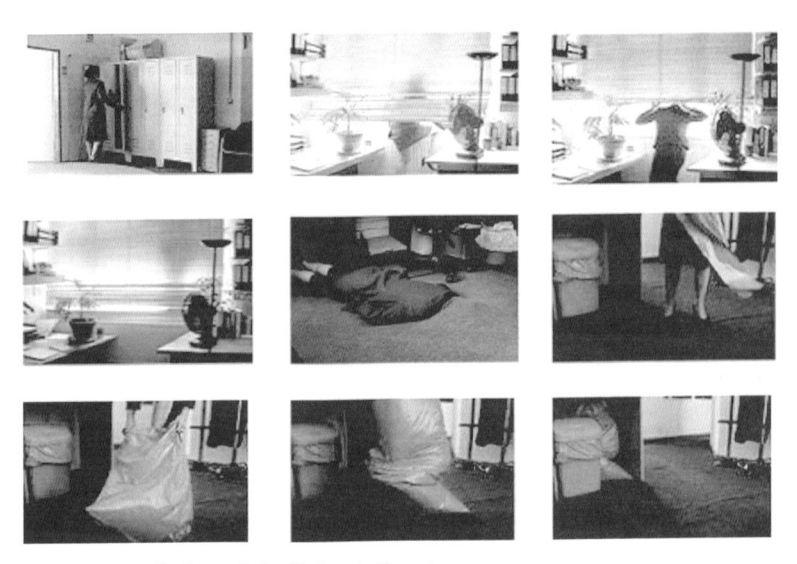

Figure 1.1 Stills from Sofia Hulten's *Grey Area*

Simpson and Lewis (2007) describe as 'surface' meanings of invisibility, but also to their relative cultural marginalization and symbolic negation (Gherardi, 1995; Czarniawska, 2006), to 'depth' meanings of invisibility in Simpson and Lewis's terms, as well as to the connections between the two in the gendering of organizations (Simpson and Lewis, 2007). It has also highlighted the ways in which women tend to be equated with the embodied and emotional aspects of organizational life, so that female employees especially are required to manage their presentation of self in such a way as to engender a particular emotional or aesthetic experience in others. In practice, this suggests that many women have to induce or suppress particular aspects of their embodied selves in accordance with the aesthetic and emotional regimes defined largely by their employing organization (Witz et al, 2003; Pettinger, 2004), or by their occupation (Entwistle and Wissinger, 2006), while at the same time being required to perform often highly visible aesthetic or emotional roles (Wolkowitz, 2006). This means that, coupled with these different forms of invisibility, women often also experience a high level of visibility, one that is either imposed on them, as their gendered presentations of self are co-opted and commodified by their employing organizations, or which they consciously seek out as a coping strategy. Consequently women, particularly those women who find themselves over-exposed in male dominated or normatively masculine environments, where their gender identity becomes an unrelenting marker of difference, may pursue a chameleon-like 'quest for invisibility' (Lewis, 2006), through which they simply seek to blend in.

However, in our thinking about how these different forms of invisibility and visibility are lived, experienced and managed, the gendering of organizational space and the role of space in constructing women as both invisible and over-exposed remains relatively neglected. Indeed, in their study of gendered spaces of organization and consumption, Gregson and Rose (2000) call for more research which teases out the performative qualities of space and the gendered practices that bring particular organizational spaces into being. In their view, more work needs to be done exploring the diverse ways in which organizational spaces compel the practising of gender in particular ways. Through exploring the extent to which other women's readings of *Grey Area* resonated with their thoughts and feelings about their workplaces and spaces, we sought to shed light on some of these issues.

Researching *Grey Areas*

We began our research by circulating a 'call for participation' on the university campus on which we both work. We decided to base the research here for two main reasons. The first was pragmatic: we were concerned to make the methodology as open and accessible as possible and to encourage participation, and so thought that by arranging the focus groups in our own institution we would be able to provide a relatively convivial setting for the research. Our feeling was that undertaking the research in an organizational setting in which we were ourselves immersed would strengthen the methodology, although we were of course also conscious that it would impose certain limits. Second, we felt that a university campus would be a particularly interesting site on which to base the research. Echoing the insights in the literature on women's organizational Otherness cited above, there is a growing body of research focusing specifically on women's lived experiences of academic life, much of which highlights continuing structural disadvantage and cultural marginalization, manifest for instance in the persistence of the gender pay gap and in sedimented patterns of horizontal and vertical segmentation (Knights and Richards, 2003). Ramsay and Letherby (2006: 26, emphasis added) sum this up when they argue that the gendered organization of academia is characterized by a wealth of practices 'which render women academics' participation undervalued, unrecognized and marginalized, leading to *an overwhelming feeling of 'otherness'*.

While in the main this literature focuses on the experience of women academics, universities are clearly host to a whole range of very different occupations; they are complex organizations incorporating a variety of often competing or conflicting workplace cultures, identities, roles and workspaces. Furthermore, the boundaries between work and non-work, especially as these are materialized in spatial terms, are relatively blurred for many but not all of us working in a university setting. Through our study we sought to capture something of this complexity, and to link it to our interest in women's (in)visibility, and to the apparent struggle for recognition that we had encountered in Hulten's work, as well as to the discomfort we had both experienced following the comments made about our own workspaces.

The response we had to our call for participation was overwhelming. Many women were extremely keen to be involved, partly (they suggested) because they were intrigued by the methodology, but also because many of them felt that they had no other forum in which to talk about their own, or listen to others' experiences of the workplace.

We undertook three focus groups, each held a week apart. Nine women took part in the first one, which lasted for an hour and 20 minutes (amounting to 22 pages of transcript); 11 women in the second, which lasted for one hour and ten minutes (amounting to 20 pages of transcript), and ten women in the third group, which lasted for an hour and 30 minutes (producing a 24-page transcript). Of those 30 women who took part in the focus groups, 23 agreed to take part in a follow up interview; an additional ten women who had volunteered for the focus groups after they were full but asked to be interviewed instead also took part in individual interviews, plus a further 14 who volunteered subsequently. So, in total, 30 women took part in the focus groups and 47 women were interviewed individually (23 of whom had already taken part in one of the three focus groups).

Participants (referred to here using pseudonyms) worked in a broad range of departments: some in mainly female work groups, others in gender-mixed groups, and some worked in largely male groups. Most were in departments in which the senior members of staff were disproportionately male, and a few in groups in which they were the only women. Participants represented a broad range of age groups and work roles, from very senior to entry level, manual and non-manual occupations, and included women who described themselves as single, cohabiting with partners, as married, divorced or widowed, and identifying with various sexual identities. However, the nature of the sampling technique we used and our choice of research site meant that the sample was relatively ethnically homogenous and did not represent a full range of socio-economic groups. We fully recognize that this is a limitation of the research, but also see the university as a rich research site, given the features noted above.

We used printed colour sheets of stills from *Grey Area* as a starting point for the focus groups (see Figure 1.1, above), laying the room out so that participants sat around a large table facing each other, with an A3 sheet of the stills in front of them. We were (loosely) guided by an interview schedule, in which we asked the women taking part to reflect on the images and on how they might relate (if at all) to their own experiences of the workplace, and of their own workspace. We asked participants about their first impressions, if there were any images in the sequence that struck them as particularly interesting or important, and why. We then talked about how the images made them feel, and about how they thought the woman in the video might be feeling. At various points we focused on the theme of hiding, and particularly on the woman throwing herself away at the end of the sequence. We also had lengthy discussions in each group about why the video is called *Grey Area*, and about what greyness connotes in relation to gender, identity and work. In each of the sessions, participants asked questions of themselves, of us, and of each other. With participants' consent, we recorded these discussions in their entirety and had these transcribed, subjecting the transcripts to in depth analysis using manual coding informed by the conceptual and theoretical insights gleaned from the literature discussed above.

When we arranged and undertook these focus groups we worked with two other researchers, one of whom was a part-time researcher within our work group, the other was an experienced research student. One took charge of the recording equipment, leaving us free to concentrate on the discussion itself, the other took notes on the discussion, observing for instance, the participants' body language and interaction, as well as the apparent power relations that emerged within each group. We also annotated our own hard copies of the stills during the discussions. The four of us met straight after each group to reflect on the discussion, incorporating the notes we all made. We had the recording of each focus group transcribed immediately so that we could talk about it before the next group met. Once all three transcripts were available, we spent time working through them, immersing ourselves in the data over the course of several readings, discerning themes that seemed to be particularly important to participants, or which recurred throughout the course of each group session, and/or across all three.

Following the focus groups and our iterative analysis, we developed an interview schedule based on the themes that had emerged from this first phase of the research. We used this as the basis for a second phase of research consisting of a series of individual interviews in which we asked women to reflect on their lived experiences of their workspace. Here as in the focus groups we asked participants to talk not only about their current employment, but also previous jobs. Interviews, like the group discussions, were recorded and fully transcribed and we made notes on our own observations of the interview and of the setting. The interviews were all conducted in participants' workspaces, some of which were private, others shared. While we were conscious that an interview might not always be the most appropriate method for collecting data on the actual practices of everyday working life (De Certeau, 2002), we aimed to mitigate against some of these limitations by conducting the interviews *in situ*.

Interviews lasted between 50 minutes and two hours, the average being one hour and ten minutes, and the average length of a transcript being about 20 pages. This meant that in total, we derived some 940 pages of transcribed material, in addition to the 66 pages collected from the three focus groups. We subjected these transcripts to in-depth thematic analysis, reflecting on the findings of the focus groups and again, taking part in regular discussions with each other, before undertaking the next few interviews. This meant that data collection and analysis became part of an ongoing, integrated and largely interactive process throughout both phases of the research.

Inspired by O'Neill's (2002) work on 'ethno-mimesis', our intention was to use the images from *Grey Area* to 'move' respondents, and so to encourage them to reflect on aspects of their own and other women's lived, embodied experiences that they might not otherwise think about or find easy to articulate. In this sense, our research sought to create a 'space' within which those who took part in it could interact and reflect on their own and each others' working organizational lives. Thus the research was never intended to be disinterested, disembodied or detached. On the contrary, as we outlined at the outset of our discussion here, it was prompted by what might be regarded as two 'moments' of auto-ethnography. Our aim, though, was to encourage other women to reflect on their own and each others' lived experiences of their work environments, incorporating the stills from *Grey Area* that we had found so compelling in order to draw them into the research and encourage a greater sense of involvement.

Gender, space and work in *Grey Areas*

Spatial matters recurred both in the group discussions and the interviews, coalescing around participants' simultaneous sense of erasure and over-exposure, and their reflections on how this related to their positioning, as women, within organizations. Sometimes respondents actively sought to render themselves invisible or draw excessive attention to themselves, whilst at other times these were states that participants felt had been imposed on them by colleagues, managers or by 'the organization' more generally. Often the data we generated revealed the complex interplay between these processes. As mentioned above, consistent with O'Neill's (2002) concept of 'ethno-mimesis', in both phases of the project participants were encouraged to use their thoughts and feelings about the video stills to reflect on their own, and each others', lived experiences of the workplace. It is through this reflective slippage that the theme of simultaneous negation and over-exposure was articulated.

Working in a goldfish bowl: being shiny, happy and accessible

In the focus groups, the image of simultaneous over-exposure and erasure conveyed by the *Grey Area* stills provided the starting point for a discussion of women's spatial and social availability within their own departments and organizations, and in workplaces more generally. As one participant put it:

> *I think there's a demand that women are accessible. When you're talking about women being in offices where ... where you can't hide away, I don't know, somehow I think as a woman you're expected to be always happy, happy, shiny, accessible to people to come and talk to* (Focus Group Two, November 2005, emphasis added).

This sense that within their organizations women are expected to be constantly available to others recurred in all three focus groups and was likewise a theme that women wanted to develop further in their interviews. Notable above is the speaker's (failed) attempts to take control of this situation by becoming invisible. Likewise in the course of her interview Anna reflects on her feelings of hyper-accessibility, colleagues' frequent invasions of her workspace and of her futile efforts to hide:

> *I'm very exposed in this space. If they [her male colleagues] see my door ajar they'll knock on it and come in and speak to me. Even if I keep it shut I constantly get interrupted ... It's very stressful* (interview with Anna, March 2006, emphasis added).

Similarly, Debbie commented 'there are occasions when I've felt that my job's like living in a goldfish bowl because I'm watched so closely by others' (interview with Debbie, April 2006). What is interesting here is that while both Anna and Debbie had a formal entitlement to their own workspace, this was frequently disregarded, as male colleagues appeared to transgress this spatial boundary at will. Like the speakers above, in an attempt to gain an element of control over persistent feelings of invasion and vulnerability, Lisa talked about the changes she had recently made:

> *I changed my desk layout a few months back ... I'm tucked round a corner so my space is very limited ... and I'd been sat with my back to anybody*

who was approaching my area and I realised I was very uncomfortable with this because whereas some people would speak as they approached so I knew they were coming, there were a couple of ... men who would come and stand and that was creepy ... So I rotated my desk 'round (interview with Lisa, February 2006).

This continual feeling of over-exposure led some participants to feel bombarded by work, and by the demands of their working environments, a theme we return to below. In her interview, Julia reflected back on the woman in *Grey Area*, linking the images of her apparent attempts to escape with her own feelings of being trapped and physically overwhelmed by her workspace. Julia had a worked in an open plan office and she explained how male colleagues' mess often spilled into her space. Not only did she find this irritating and insensitive, but more importantly it made her feel anxious because she was unable to stop it happening, unable to create boundaries between herself and others which people recognized and respected: 'It's out of control because it's just full of paper and rubbish ... Yes, it gives me the feeling that I just want to escape from it all, but just like the woman in the pictures [laughter]' (interview with Julia, April 2006).

Such feelings were also expressed in the focus group discussions. In the following quote a participant explained:

Generally all of them [the stills] I would perceive as myself ... it's that kind of 'just make the world go away for a minute', you know? You know how you have that feeling sometimes, like 'if the world could just stop and I could catch up, or just be invisible for a bit and get on top of things ... and then it could all start up again', but you that's never going to happen.

The slippage between *Grey Area* and this participant's own experience is notable in this extract. However, for our purposes in this section, what we want to highlight in all of the data we have thus far presented is, first, the dynamic, on-going interplay between women's sense of over-exposure and invisibility and second, that this was experienced in spatial terms. While over-exposure was expressed as others' invasion of respondents' workspace and transgression of spatial boundaries, invisibility was seen as a way of taking control – of redrawing the boundaries, and reclaiming the space.

Fracture and fragmentation: being/becoming (in)visible

In all three focus groups, talk about physical engulfing and of simultaneous erasure and over-exposure was used as a springboard for exploring participants' more general feelings about how their work often fractures and fragments their lives such that different dimensions, like home and work, continually seep into each other. For example:

> Work fragments our lives a lot of the time. It fragments mine totally... I have an impossible relationship between my home and work life. You know, it's a hell, and it's irreconcilable and I suspect a lot of women have that ... <u>both sides are clashing in the middle and you're stretched across</u> really (Focus Group One, November 2005, emphasis added)

Many participants saw this as a struggle experienced, or at least made sense of, in spatial terms. Implicit in many of the quotes provided thus far is a sense that women feel they don't quite belong in their workspaces. Notwithstanding issues of formal entitlement, participants (especially those with children or other caring responsibilities) commented that they often didn't feel entirely comfortable at work or at home. This discomfort was often described in terms of both excessive availability and of invisibility. Echoing the previous section, on the one hand participants explained that at home, as at work, they were expected to be there, always and for everybody, accommodating others' needs, be they material or emotional. At the same time, though, they felt that much of the work this involved (not just the actual physical labour, but also the emotion and identity work) was actually invisible to others – that is, so embedded were others' (colleagues, family members etc) expectations, and the idea that others had a right to these expectations, that they were not recognized as demands and expectations at all. In fact, they weren't recognized as anything. Living in the boundary between the two spaces, in the 'grey areas' between home and work, many of the women who took part in our research continually negotiated for a rightful place in each. As one particular participant in the second focus group suggested (again, slipping between her own experiences and her interpretation of those of the woman in the video stills):

> Maybe it's because at the point I am in my life of having two young children it makes me think ... Is this the way she's treated at home, you know, she's a bit faceless, she's a nobody, she's somebody's mum, she's somebody's wife, she's a homemaker and she goes to work, she's just like, I don't know, maybe she's a secretary and she's the person who makes the coffee... Maybe it's blurred, what she's expected to be at home and

what's expected of her at work, and she just feels not valued in either setting.

While the above speaker describes the similarity between home and work spaces, in the following extract, Claire refers more specifically to work, explaining how her responsibilities at home contribute to a somewhat precarious position in her department:

Because I sort of whiz in, do what I have to do and whiz out again ... I don't really belong. <u>I'm a bit of an outsider and also because it's a very male dominated environment I work in it's difficult to sort of fit in it that way as well</u> (interview with Claire, April 2006, emphasis added).

It is significant though, that while some women experienced not quite belonging as dislocating, for others their perceived status as relative outsiders seemed to be somewhat enabling, providing a degree of temporal and spatial flexibility that was necessary to reconcile the often competing demands made on them. Hence, they relied on a sense of simultaneous (in)visibility, of being a kind of absent presence in their work environments, to manage their different roles and responsibilities. As Abbie describes it:

I have an office over here rather than in the main block so that I can manage my time and space. I have three children so it's very important to be able to manage your time and to, you know, accommodate everybody's needs and I can do that much more effectively if I haven't got people constantly knowing where I am ... I'm sure that ... work actually benefits usually because I can work anywhere which is great for me, but that's what makes this job do-able with children and so, you know, <u>I quite like to be able to be invisible when I need to be</u> (interview with Abbie, April 2006, emphasis added).

Here Abbie consciously strives for invisibility as a coping mechanism; that is, as a technique she can deploy in managing her limited time and availability as she moves between the two spaces of home and work. Here an interesting contrast to the earlier quotes in which office (and indeed home) spaces were seen as fixed, intransigent places in which women were positioned and constructed in particular ways by themselves or others. In contrast in this quote, the spaces themselves and the boundaries between them are depicted as elastic, malleable and subject to re-creation by the individuals and groups working and living in and around them.

There but not there: identifying with the trash

Whilst in the first section hiding was described as a coping mechanism and expressed as an assertive, positive response to an unacceptable level of accessibility, at many other points in the research respondents talked about it in much bleaker terms, as a symbol of worthlessness and negation. Referring to *Grey Area*, this was again expressed in spatial terms – not as people invading the woman's space, but more symbolically, as the space itself engulfing her. These data are interesting and very different from those we have discussed up to now. Whereas previously the quotes we have provided depict space as a place where things happen, when used symbolically, space is constructed as an actor in its own right – having agency, impacting and defining people in different ways.

In the first focus group, for example, discussing the woman in *Grey Area*, a respondent commented how: 'it looks as though the environment is actually closing in on her'. This claustrophobia and sense of being engulfed was linked to the theme of negation. Far from invisibility being used in an agentic way, to reclaim a sense of control, the image here is one of isolation, worthlessness and imprisonment. Like an animal caught in the headlights of an on-coming car, she is trapped in this space, a victim with no apparent value or status but likewise with no apparent means of escape. Here there is little sense of individual agency or control, and an associated stripping of identity. This was articulated in a short exchange between three women, also from the first focus group: 'I think there's definitely a loss of control ... Of rational behaviour ... And possibility a lack of identity'.

Here, a respondent from Group One summed up the views of many of the focus group participants: 'It's like she's hiding in and from the space at the same time ... *It's almost like she's sort of identifying herself with the trash. There but not there* ... She feels unworthy'. Like the rubbish, the woman in *Grey Area* was an unwanted by-product of that space. With limited capacity for individual action (other than getting into the bag), we can only presume that at some point someone will come and remove her, as they do with the rest of the waste. In this sense, participants seemed to interpret the woman's (unsuccessful) attempt to escape as something she was consciously seeking out, a strategy they could clearly relate to themselves. They also reflected on what she might be trying to escape from, articulating both a sense of marginalization and exclusion – of worthlessness, on the one hand, and on the other a constant sense of being watched.

Concluding thoughts: Gender (in)visibility and organizational space

As we have discussed, in our data space was depicted in a variety of ways. Sometimes it was seen as a fixed place in which colleagues, 'organizations' and others imposed particular meanings, definitions and expectations that women negotiated with, accommodated, resisted or sought to reclaim. At other times, though, it was expressed as a much more elastic construct, created, deployed and transformed by people in light of their needs, interests, and aspirations. Space was also used symbolically as an entity that engulfed and trapped women, resulting in their feelings of being constantly on show, but likewise isolated and negated – stripped of identity and value but without means of escape.

In this respect, the women who took part in our study, reflecting on their own and others' lived experiences of the work place in light of the video stills, articulated a clear sense of (in)visibility in their working lives. On the one hand, many reported feeling a sense of negation, erasure, and exclusion, a feeling that several linked to 'identifying with the trash'. In these instances it was not the case that women were not noticed – indeed much of our data suggests there was a powerful sense of being excessively visible and unable to escape from this – but rather of being without value. In the words of one of the participants in the third focus group: 'It's not that people don't notice you. It's just that they notice you, but they don't care'.

Echoing Kanter's (1977) earlier work (cited in Simpson and Lewis, 2007), many participants in our research, especially those women who worked in (numerically or culturally) male dominated environments, reported feeling hyper-visible, over-exposed and relatively vulnerable as a result. Kathy for instance, who worked in senior management, commented, 'When do I feel most like the woman in the images? In a room full of men, then you're a human being being disregarded' (interview with Kathy, March 2006). Consequently, women in these circumstances consciously sought out invisibility as a coping mechanism. Similarly, women who felt they were constantly expected to be accessible, or who felt their workspaces were not respected by (primarily male) colleagues also cultivated invisibility as a way of dealing with the sense of imposition they experienced. In such a way they 'took' the space, and thereby regained a sense of control. In other circumstances women found that seeking out invisibility allowed them to deal with the often competing demands and roles that characterized their lives, particularly in terms of living and working between the two spaces (and responsibilities) of work and home. For them, invisibility became a mechanism through which they pursued and practiced what Bruni *et al* have described as 'gender switching' (Bruni and Gherardi, 2002; Bruni *et al*, 2004), enabling them to move, as seamlessly as they could, between different and often competing gender hegemonies.

Our findings thus echo Simpson and Lewis's (2007: 4) observation that 'visibility and invisibility can be both a privilege and a burden', something which women consciously seek out, or strive to shake off. Recognizing this, what we found in our study is that living and working in the 'grey areas' between what we might call spaces of gender recognition, that is, places with which women identify themselves and each other – is where many women would position themselves. What this means is that women's working lives, at least for those women who took part in our study, are characterized by a perpetual sense of (in)visibility. Recognition of themselves as viable subjects therefore continually alludes them, hence the feeling that many women reported of being 'there but not there'. For many of the women whose thoughts, feelings and experiences we have referred to above, their working lives are characterized by the pressures of living a negotiated yet negated existence, condemned as De Beauvoir (1988 [1949]) put it, to perpetual immanence, something they experienced and attempted to make sense of in largely spatial terms. Thus, returning to Gregson and Rose's (2000) observation that more thought needs to be given to the gendering of space within organizational life, we would suggest that the concept of (in)visibility therefore helps up to begin to understand something of the lived experience of the ways in which organizational space is invoked through the practising of gender. Conversely, it also sheds light on some of the ways in which workspace impacts upon the practising of gender at work, particularly on practices of gender identification, and on the often simultaneous sense of exposure and negation the women in our research experienced. Living and working as they did in the 'grey areas' between spaces of recognition, they experienced themselves as (in)visible: in the words of one participant, 'there but not there'.

Acknowledgements

We are very grateful to the artist Sofia Hultén for kindly granting permission for still images from her video installation Grey Area to be included in the research on which the chapter is based. We wish to clarify that the ideas expressed in the chapter are our own, and do not necessarily reflect the views of the artist herself.

References

Alvesson, M. and Due Billing, Y. (1997) *Understanding Gender and Organizations*. London: Sage.

Bruni, A. and Gherardi, S. (2002) 'Omega's story: The heterogeneous engineering of a gendered professional self'. In Dent, M. and Whitehead, S. (eds) *Managing Professional Identities: Knowledge, Performativity and the 'New' Professional*, pp. 174–198. London: Routledge.

Bruni, A., Gherardi, S. and Poggio, B. (2004) 'Doing gender, doing entrepreneurship: An ethnographic account of intertwined practices', *Gender, Work and Organization*, 11(4): 406–429.

Cohen, L. and Tyler, M. (2004) '*The Office* (27th November 2003–18th January 2004), The Photographers' Gallery, London: A Review', *Work, Employment and Society*, 18(3): 621–629.

Czarniawska, B. (2006) 'Doing gender unto the other: Fiction as a mode of studying gender discrimination in organizations', *Gender, Work and Organization*, 13(3): 234–253.

De Beauvoir, S. (1988 [1949]) *The Second Sex*. London: Jonathan Cape.

De Certeau, M. (2002) *The Practice of Everyday Life*. Berkeley, CA: University of California Press.

Entwistle, J. and Wissinger, E. (2006) 'Keeping up appearances: Aesthetic labour in the fashion modelling industries of London and New York', *The Sociological Review*, 54(4): 774–794.

Gherardi, S. (1995) *Gender and Organizational Symbolism*. London: Sage.

Gregson, N. and Rose, G. (2000) 'Taking Butler elsewhere: Performativities, spatialities, subjectivities', *Environment and Planning D: Society and Space*, 18: 433–452.

Kanter, R. (1977) *Men and Women of the Corporation*. New York: Basic Books.

Knights, D. and Kerfoot, D. (2004) 'Between representations and subjectivity: Gender binaries and the politics of organizational transformation', *Gender, Work and Organization*, 11(4): 430–454.

Knights, D. and Richards, W. (2003) 'Sex discrimination in UK academia', *Gender, Work and Organization*, 10(2): 213–238.

Lewis, P. (2006) 'The quest for invisibility: Female entrepreneurs and the masculine norm of entrepreneurship', *Gender, Work and Organization*, 13(5): 453–469.

O'Neill, M. in association with Giddens, S., Breatnach, P., Bagley, C., Bourne, D. and Judgel, T. (2002) 'Renewed methodologies for social research: Ethno-mimesis as performative praxis', *The Sociological Review*, 50(1): 69–88.

Pettinger, L. (2004) 'Brand culture and branded workers: Service work and aesthetic labour in fashion retail', *Consumption, Markets and Culture*, 7(2): 165–184.

Ramsay, K. and Letherby, G. (2006) 'The experience of academic non-mothers in the gendered university', *Gender, Work and Organization*, 13(1): 25–44.

Simpson, R. and Lewis, P. (2007) *Voice, Visibility and the Gendering of Organizations*. Basingstoke: Palgrave Macmillan.

Tyler, M. (2005) 'Women in Change Management: Simone De Beauvoir and the Co-optation of Women's Otherness', *Journal of Organizational Change Management*, 18(6): 561–577.

Witz, A., Warhurst, C. and Nickson, D. (2003) 'The labour of aesthetics and the aesthetics of organization', *Organization*, 10(1): 33–54.

Wolkowitz, C. (2006) *Bodies at Work*. London: Sage.

2
A Question of Membership
Heather Höpfl

Not part of the game

Recently I was invited to be the external examiner for a PhD where the candidate was a member of staff and so had two external examiners. The other external was a man, like me a professor, and the supervisor was also a man, also a professor. We assembled in a small room to discuss the thesis and the supervisor began by asking the other external, 'Well, how many PhDs have you examined?' Prof X pondered for a moment and then said, 'How many have you?' to which the supervisor replied, 'Four'. 'I have examined seven' was the response. To this the supervisor said, 'But, if you count internal examinations, I have examined eight'. 'I have examined seven *external* PhDs' was the confident riposte. A pecking order was established and the male external examiner had announced himself as the chief cock. They didn't ask me. They weren't at all interested in how many PhDs I had examined. This was purely a male game and I wasn't invited to play. Later, after the viva had taken place and when we were summing up the report I did say, 'Actually, having examined over *fifty* PhDs, I would like to comment...' but it didn't mean anything to either of them. I was irrelevant to their game. I could have examined five or 500 for all it mattered to them. This was a male competition. They were totally oblivious to excluding me from their power play. After all it was about who was the biggest cock in the yard and I didn't come into the pecking order because I wasn't a cock. This is the point that is made by Jenny Firth-Cozens in her provocative book, *To Have and to Hold: Men, Sex and Marriage*, in which she cautions that to understand the behaviour of men in organizations the first thing you have to realize is that 'the penis becomes the biggest cigar, the sportiest car, the largest desk, the best reserved parking space, the deadliest weapon, the biggest mausoleum' (Firth-Cozens, 1995: 71) and I well remember her saying to me over a dinner in Newcastle that it is important to remember that 'most men never grow out of comparing the size of their d**ks [sic]'. Clearly, the acquisition of membership requires more than competence. Membership requires a *virile member*: either literal or metaphorical.

Men only (irrespective of gender)

It is abundantly clear from the study of any organization that there is a contemporary obsession with measurement. Organizations are preoccupied with the idea that planning is the means of achieving targets; that metrics are the way of ensuring that progress into the future is being achieved. The league-table, the term itself comes from football, is an established way of understanding the pecking order of any number of institutions: universities, schools, hospitals and, of course, football teams. There is a belief that destinies can be determined by analysis, prediction and monitoring and an emphasis on progress and improvement leads to a concern with measurement.

In this way, conventional representations of the organization reduce *organization* to abstract relationships, rational actions and purposive behaviour. This can be seen in the numerous check-lists which infest institutions at the present time. Organization, it seems, is subject to obsessive 'alpha male' behaviour, frenetic male posturing, and a compulsive desire to see who has the biggest member. In order to make the contest appear rational and abstract, organization becomes synonymous with regulation and control via metrics. In this way, metrics preserve the pecking order and retain an apparent justification for hierarchy and status. This is achieved primarily by the imposition of definition and measurement. Under such circumstances, organization comes to function in a very specific sense to establish a notion of *membership* and it is quite clear that the definition at work here is a male one. Men do not realize the extent to which women live as strangers in their world. What is normal and taken for granted is a world which is defined, constructed and maintained by male notions of order where membership is determined by male notions of what constitutes *the club*, by what determines the pecking order and, by who is able to exercise power.

In this respect, Kristeva's analysis of *foreigners* provides a range of issues which can be applied to the position of women in relation to membership. In her book, *Strangers to Ourselves* (1991 [1988]), Kristeva does not apply theories of difference to race, class or gender yet her analysis of the foreigner appears to offer significant insights into what it is to be a woman and a stranger in a male world: into what it is to lack membership. Of course, some might reject this notion out of hand as creating the world of the organization as enemy territory. Some would argue that the world has changed over the past 30 years and that, in any case, the world is what you make of it. However, these are also the self assurances which the foreigner offers him/herself. 'It is not too bad'; 'You can make of it what you want'. 'If you are prepared to work, you can achieve anything'. This is the simple rhetoric of those who desire to be assimilated. It is the language of resignation and stoicism.

Put simply, in terms of membership, women can either be playthings or else quasi-men. Either way women are dismembered to sustain the notion of membership. To become a member of the organization, a woman must either conform to the male projection offered her or else acquire a metaphorical 'member' as the price of entry into 'membership'. Women who do conform by acquiring a metaphorical member are assumed into the body and made homologues/homomorphs of men. There is also scope for women to become playthings or daughters but this is a different order of membership. The daughter might be cherished and indulged. The price, however, is infantilization. The plaything – however successful, always occupies a service role in relation to male reality definitions. To gain membership, to achieve the status of honorary man, women must accept impotence. They do not possess real members so they cannot be real members. They are rewarded for not re-membering the body. In other words, by accepting the prevailing reality definitions and accepting the validity of the pecking order, women gain entry to a club in which they can never gain full membership because they *de facto* lack the conditions for entry. Ultimately, this is a matter of potency: about the power to define since it is definition itself which determines the extent of women's participation.

The phallus as an emblem of membership

In conventional terms, the strategic direction of the organization involves the construction of the organization as a purposive entity with a trajectory towards a desired future state. Consequently, many of the organizational metrics with which we are all so familiar are concerned with the achievement of this future state, the measurement of progress towards this state and the use of corrective measures to modify and improve deficient performance. There is a privileging of the future over the present. Moreover, the aspirational goals of the trajectory mean that, in the present, all members of an organization are deficient relative to the targets which have to be achieved (Höpfl, 2007). However, for women this is more serious because entry into the organization is already accompanied by the acknowledgement of a lack. Without a phallus, membership is at best only partial and conferred only at the discretion of those who have the power to define the boundaries of the organization and the conditions of entry. Sometimes this is quite explicit. Once I was visiting the Health Centre at the university where I worked and was irritated that when the patient in front of me, a biologist, was called to see the doctor, the receptionist said, 'Prof X. The doctor will see you now' yet when my appointment was called the receptionist leaned over the counter and said simply, 'Heather'. Friends have told me that I am reading too much into this and that perhaps she was simply being friendly one woman to another. My reading of it is rather different. Women are frequently infantilized in this way and when I asked her, after my appointment, why she had called the previous patient Prof X when she could have called me 'professor' or 'doctor' or 'Mrs.' but had called me *Heather*, she swung the computer screen toward me and said, 'It wasn't me. It was the computer'. There on the orange and brown screen of the computer of this vintage I read, 'CONFLICT BETWEEN GENDER AND TITLE – VERIFY?' 'I'm afraid that is not the computer', I said tartly, 'that is the perversity of the programmer'. Well, it explains how my title was rendered suspect but it does not explain why like children and the aged, I was diminished by the use of my first name: not taken entirely seriously.

In the presence of huge erections

Elsewhere (Höpfl, 2007), I have examined what a commitment to metrics and other abstract representations of the organization have excluded. Of course, there is any number of ways in which the organization constructs itself in textual and representational terms: the explicit use of rhetoric in marketing the products and images of organizations is one such construction. It is also present in the construction of statements, strategies and structures, in its use of representation for regulation. The fundamental characteristic of the organization as a purposive entity is its *directedness* and, clearly, there is a relationship between the direction (as orientation) and direction (as command) of the organization and the rhetorical trajectory. De Certeau (1986) has said that a particular characteristic of rhetoric is that its trajectory is completed by *the other*. That is to say that rhetoric requires something from the audience to which it is directed. It is completed by a response. In a specific sense, the organization as a rhetorical entity *wants something* of the employee, of the customer, the competitor, the supplier, the general public. Ironically, the organization as an abstract entity transfers its own lack to its members who are thereby rendered deficient in relation to the abstract desires of the organization. This is the subtle fear of falling below some expectation: of failing to have a big enough member. It is a male fear. In response to the endless rhetoric which outlines the implications of failure and the endless commitment to monitoring, it is not surprising that the consequence is a paralysing state that sets the individual at odds with the world, alienated from it, terrified of it, unable to act, react, or to adopt a moral disposition: unable to sustain the erection. So everything falls, institutions collapse, membership is lost. It is what happens in the face of the fear of the disordered other. It is the fear of disorder brought by women as the already deficient other (see Lacoue-Labarthe, 1989: 129). When '…women's only power was the ability to take away men's power, whether by fostering his dependency or denying him sex or making him feel a failure because he couldn't satisfy her sexually or economically…[it]…makes woman always a threat, always something to fear' (Firth-Cozens, 1995).

Women lack membership

This is the most primitive of fears, the fear of castration. In his discussion of the role of the phallus, Žižek says that symbols which confer power such as the insignia of office, the sceptre or the crown, are external to the wearer and worn only in order to exert power. As a consequence, he argues, they 'castrate', and deprive him of his virility. So that symbolic castration 'introduces a gap between what I immediately am and the function that I exercise (i.e., I am never fully at the level of my function). …. [this is] the castration that occurs by the very fact of me being caught in the symbolic order, assuming a symbolic mandate'. Castration is the very gap between what I immediately am and the symbolic mandate that confers on me this 'authority'. Leaving aside for a moment the gender implications of this statement although, of course, *my* symbolic mandate is more equivocal, authority in such terms is like a mantle that signifies office. Authority then resides in the symbolic order and likes to make its presence felt in the behaviour of a community, displays of potency, the destruction of difference. After all, as Žižek argues, this constructed phallus is an 'organ without a body...an excessive supplement' (Žižek, 2003: 87) and it demands deference. We cower under the power of the erection. To act with authority requires that contradictions, discontinuities, collisions of meaning and so forth must be regulated to preserve the appearance of order. This makes monitoring and measuring important activities which preserve the erection of order.

Of course, the organization requires that its prospective representations – images and texts – are received as convincing by its various audiences. Gesture and strutting are an important part of establishing the pecking order. Not surprisingly then, recent years have seen the elaboration of the rhetoric of organizations directed at employees in terms of the pursuit of greater commitment, improved performance, invocations to quality and the construction of ornate narratives of organizational performances. I think of these elaborate representations as enormous erections which serve to regulate the organization by their staying power. However, in producing these elaborate constructions/ erections, which exist only as emblems and abstract representations, the organization represents itself as synecdochal where the *member* and ownership of the *member*, that is, membership, assume more importance than the body *per se* – whether corporate or physical. The organization comes to be regulated by the phallus and the phallus is the single most important determinant of membership. At the same time, the emphasis on rigidity and tumescence is a symbolic one. As such, ironically, it signifies that the organization has lost contact with the physical bodies of which it is made up. To repeat myself, it is an 'organ without a body...an excessive supplement' (Žižek, 2003: 87). Not surprisingly, women can only enter into membership by the acquisition of a metaphorical phallus: by becoming ciphers of men and *real member*ship has status over symbolic membership on every count. Most women who are professors will have had the experience of arriving at a hotel with a male companion or partner only for the receptionist to smile broadly and welcome the male as 'Prof. X'. This has happened to me too many times to mention over the past 20 years. The assumption is that status always rests with the man. In contrast, I must *wear* my amulet to signify *my* membership. I must wear the *fascinum* as a symbol of my metaphorical phallus, my symbol of membership. In classical times, the *fascinum* was a phallic amulet worn around the neck of children and cattle to protect the wearer from the evil eye. The metaphorical phallus serves the same function. It is an amulet against the other: a reminder of a membership I never had but which is *remembered* only by the fascinum: a token membership.

Women as strangers

In her book, *Strangers to Ourselves* (1991 [1988]), Kristeva examines conditions of exile and looks at the position of the foreigner. Her translator, Leon Roudiez, is quite specific in rendering the strangers of the title *Strangers to Ourselves* (*Etrangers à nous même*), as foreigner because it invites a different range of connotations than 'stranger'. This notion of being alien, being exotic to a place, to be ectopic – to grow in the wrong place – is readily understandable in terms of the experiences of women in organizations. It is not possible to do more than sketch some of the implications of Kristeva's characterization of the foreigner for an understanding of the position of women in organizations but the analogy works well. First perhaps one might consider Kristeva's description of the foreigner as being *defined by work*. The foreigner, she argues, unable to speak freely in a tongue other than the mother tongue is first reduced to silence and then defines him/herself by a commitment to work. Over a working life, I have seen myself and other women meeting deadlines that men might deign to meet eventually, been in work earlier, worked later, not had a network to fall back on for favours (unless as *largesse*), certainly worked. Of course, I am not saying that some men are not equally committed and hard working but I do recall in a previous post a female colleague who missed an afternoon's work because of a sick child and behind her back the male staff moaned and commented on her partial commitment. However, on one occasion when our immediate boss had to take time off to take his son to the dentist, the same male colleagues applauded him as though his actions were extraordinary and heroic. So, women are not only expected to be invisible or at least not intrude too much in the business of organization but they should be physically present as a demonstration of their commitment. Women, it seems, should be 'seen and not heard'.

Women should be seen and not heard

I think of my mother, now well over 80, who has for years told me that I should 'not say anything'. 'Don't say anything' she counsels every time I look as if I might be angry or fed up particularly in matters matrimonial. 'Don't say anything, keep quiet, smile'. My mother is a strong woman: not at all meek, and she offers me this advice more in defiance than in submission. 'Don't say anything or he will know he has got you'. She is saying don't place yourself into a position where you can be manoeuvred. Her words are meant to salve and she is telling me, 'Don't get into competition. Men can't stand that. Don't get involved. Don't submit'. I remember when I was working at a new university in the north east of England and the new Vice Chancellor announced a restructuring. At that time there were 22 Heads of School of which ten were women and 12 were men. After the reconstruction and following amalgamations, there were 11 new schools and they were to be headed by ten men and one woman (a woman who left within 18 months of the new regime). This was an extermination. Rationality and the logic of the change were seen to prevail. Order was restored to the site and the place of the slaughter was ritualistically cleansed. It was as if the possibility of contamination from the mere presence of women in the hierarchy was unbearable. These women had to be removed from sight, to *'disappear'*. Following this period of displacement, and when fates were sealed and it was too late to attempt to bring about changes, the newly displaced women consoled each other. 'Don't let them know how you are feeling. Smile and nod' they said to each other. They were not reduced to a mute compliance but rather united by a sense of outrage and impotence: spectators as their own destinies unfolded and yet completely unable to act. Grief and distress was private. It took place in the homes of mainly female colleagues where a 'tearful face [was] turned towards the lost homeland' (Kristeva, 1991 [1988]: 9, 10). They had disappeared from a place which was merely constituted by the construction of appearance and this is perhaps rightly so. The organization constructed as it was of aspirations, rhetoric, abstractions, desires and metrics was no place for women of flesh and blood whose physical presence might cause damage to the illusion.

Not a world of flesh and blood

So, what of Kristeva's explanation that the foreigner, unable to speak, puts every effort into activity whether it be domestic, leisure or work. Certainly, women work. Studies of women at work seem to suggest that women do more to achieve the same degree of promotion as men. There is a polite collusion which indicates that women are now accepted in organizations on an equal footing as men. However, the reality is rather different. Just as is the case with Kristeva's own experiences and the support she received through influential men, it is still arguably the case that women achieve participation in organizations to the extent that they first, renounce or annihilate themselves in order to conform more fully to the male desire for organization, which Jung has described as the pursuit of 'sterile perfection' (Dourley, 1990: 51). Certainly, in the example above, it is possible to see the enormous erections that organizations create to promise the satisfaction of all desires, to reassure the organization's members that they are wanted and worthy, and male. The second condition is that women learn to speak in the *prosthetic* language of the patriarchal discourse. *Sterile perfectionism* (Dourley, 1990: 51), according to Jung, is one of the defining characteristics of patriarchal consciousness. Order and rationality function to exclude the physical. The organization is not a world for real women of flesh and blood.

Whitmont puts forward the view that the *control* of passions and physical needs traditionally have been valorized because they idealize maleness (Whitmont, 1991: 243) and give emphasis to the '*merely* rational' [italics added] (Whitmont, 1991: 243). Organizations then, as expressions of collective expectations and abstractions, render physicality 'dirty' corrupting and, by implication, to be excluded. Indeed, the corollary of this emphasis on rationality is a distrust of natural affections and the loss of compassion (Whitmont, 1991. 245): rationality and abstraction are qualities which have been both valorized and equated with professionalism. Flesh is exiled. Women can only enter the organization as ciphers: as homologues or as objects of desire. Recently, I had a conversation with a young woman academic in her early 30s. She had recently finished her doctorate and contemplated improving her publications, 'But', she confided, 'I haven't given up the idea of having a family. But it would be so difficult. I don't have family nearby who could help and the university is no place for that sort of thing'. That sort of thing – the physical, pregnancy, with all that goes with it such as a changing body, the smells and realities of maternity – have no place in a world dedicated to abstraction and tidy rationality (Höpfl and Matilal, 2007). Women *must be seen* to dedicate themselves to work as the price of their participation They cannot permit a personal life, the life of the homeland, to enter the ordered world of organization. So, in effect, women can enter the organization as quasi-males but in order to do this they must first be neutered – just as a foreigner might be naturalized in order to be granted citizenship in the country of exile.

Women permitted to enter are not real *members* and do not possess real *members*. Such quasi-men cannot become the 'fathers' of the organization. In any event, since organizations only produce 'sons', reproduction of the organization is entirely phallocentric. Women who become true homologues renounce the friendship of other women, declare themselves to prefer the company of men and make phallic shows to confirm their *member*ship. There is a lot of 'bad faith' (Sartre, 1989 [1943]) amongst women about the extent of their permission to participate. Women have to be *converted* in order to achieve standing in this male world. They must be converted to reason and rule by logic, to the language of order and to the rules of their adopted country. They must demonstrate that they are believers. As converts they must not only conform but do more. They must actively demonstrate their commitment to the values and customs of their new land.

Management tools

The concern for the achievement of future states involves a desire for well-defined means of determining whether or not any progress towards future goals has been made. Management tools are all about measurement and comparison. The concept of benchmarking, for example, typifies this need for performance measures and suggests a fundamental need for reassurance that the organization is, after all, a sustainable erection. Of course, the trajectory of strategic development is not only about an organization establishing parameters of *normal* expectations but also about improvement: about bigger, better and more. Organizational life is replete with the exhortation to increase and extend, to do more, achieve more, to 'be the best', to seek improvement without end. So, all aspects of organizational life are subjected to the 'totalizing discourse' (Knights and McCabe, 1997) of quality management, culture change or whatever is the current vogue in change terminology. Management tools are one means by which this discourse reinforces itself. Its logic is not only phallogocentric, it is self-reinforcing. Consequently, that women should not care about measurement and comparison is sufficient reason for their exclusion. The construction of tools which facilitate measurement and comparison demands admiration and approval and this should preferably be both visible and sustained.

However, the situation is worse than this. In order for the organization to sustain itself it must erect for itself symbols of what is lost to logic and rationality. It must erect the feminine emblematically. If real women cannot be admitted, what is lost to the organization must be elevated to fill the gap. Instead of flesh and blood, the organization creates for itself a representational version of what is no longer there. So, the organization erects itself in diagrams and charts, texts and metrics which seek to uphold the representation of the feminine, the body, but which inevitably achieve a cancellation. It is little wonder, therefore, that notions of quality and care, the ubiquitous valorization of staff, the commitment to service improvement and so forth, have more in them of absence rather than presence. Hence, the patriarchal organization is concerned with logic and order and rationality, with location and hierarchy, with allocation and definition. It is organization which has lost contact with the body.

Women as leaders

Implicit in all this is the curious issue of what is valued. Studies of manager behaviour have frequently shown that subordinate workers often prefer female managers. This appears to be related to the interpersonal skills and caring which women managers seem to bring to the role. However, this does not seem to hold true for studies of leadership. Women it seems are judged on their performance as leaders using different criteria. It is not their interpersonal skills which let them down. Rather, it seems that women are perceived to lack order, logic, direction and rationality. Consequently, unless they can be converted to reason, in other words, to become homologues of men (Lyotard, 1989: 114), they are thought to lack the necessary leadership skills. Only by becoming men can they enter into membership.

It is possible to consider the problem of women and leadership in terms of the ways in which organizations as purposive and rhetorical entities define themselves in counter-distinction to notions of the feminine and madness. Lacoue-Labarthe (1989: 129), for example, tracing his line of argument back to Plato, speaks of the major threat to 'the city' as being women and madness. This fear of women and the supposed disorder they bring remains a crucial element in understanding the role of women in organizations and contributes to an understanding of women leaders. The fear of women and their ability to rob men of their potency has a long history and plays a key role in psychoanalytical theories of male sexuality. 'The male subject has great difficulty reconciling himself to his lack of wholeness and so he projects it onto the female when he becomes aware of her anatomical difference: he needs to see woman as castrated' (Modleski, 1989: 35–36) in order to reassure himself that he is whole.

What can a woman do?

A woman can do battle with the mother, seize phallic power and become a man but in so doing, she renders all relationships with men homomorphic. However, to do otherwise or to seek to be other or different requires the *patronage* of men. As Eagleton (1990: 58) argues, 'The law is male, but hegemony is a woman; this transvestite law, which decks itself out in female drapery is in danger of having its phallus exposed'. This is apparent in the familiar ways in which organizations seek to create the lost *feminine*. This is rather similar to the idea put forward by Baudrillard in his critique of rationality in which he argues that the reduction of male and female to categories has produced an artificial distinction which *objectifies* the feminine. By this line of argument, the feminine is now constructed as a category of the masculine and, by implication, the power of the feminine to manifest itself in ambivalence is lost. Baudrillard sees *feminism, per se,* as ensnared within the construction of a phallic order (Baudrillard, 1990). In organizational terms, these constructions of the feminine are intended to console. The vicarious and representational has more seductive power than the physical and disordered other. These emblems function as an anamnesis to register what is no longer present as representation. For this reason alone, the emblem of loss is melancholic and pervades the organization with melancholy. It cannot offer consolation because it can only recall that there is a loss. It cannot reassure because it arises from a mere *erection*. This is only a shadow of the feminine and it is a travesty. It is the feminine constructed in the image of masculine desire to meet the needs of sterile perfectionism and rationality. It is a feminine which in this form is tidy, logical, entirely representative and without power, ambivalence and sexuality.

Converted to reason

In the organizational world, women's deficiencies can, it seems, be corrected by reason. In this sense, conformity requires submission to *psychology* (regulation of the psyche by the logos). If that which is defined as deficient will only submit to superior logic she will *realize* the extent of her disorder. She can be saved by surrendering to the logos, by abandoning her threatening femininity. When she is truly converted she might be permitted to play a role as long as she plays it in compliance with male expectations. When she does this, she will be rendered impotent as the price of membership. She will then be conformed to psychology: 'the wisdom of the master. And of mastery' (Irigaray, 1985: 274). If the logic of organization can convert women to the power of the logos, it is able to demonstrate control over hysteria and disorder. In other words, women are permitted entry precisely because they are no longer women.

It is clear that despite the many changes in the organization of work over the past 20 years or so, and not least the equal opportunities legislation of the past 30 years, women are barely visible in senior positions. While it is relatively easy to demonstrate areas of work where women *have* achieved success, for example, in finance and accountancy as an area of specialization where women appear to be able to demonstrate their mastery with metrics, it is extremely difficult to assess the degree of achievement, motivation and sacrifice which enable such 'successes'. In part, this is due to the fact that the notion of 'success' is traditionally defined in male terms. In this context, a commonsense notion of success might be usefully linked to career viewed as a normal and rational project which involves a linear progression and which is marked by stages of achievement and, not infrequently, by tangible and personal rewards.

It is difficult then to become a member of the organization. 'A woman will only have the choice to live her life either *hyper-abstractly* (original italics)...in order thus to earn divine grace and homologation with the symbolic order; or merely *different* (original italics), other fallen...But she will not be able to accede to the complexity of being divided, of heterogeneity, of the catastrophic-fold-of-"being"' (Kristeva, 1983 in Moi, 1986: 173). What Kristeva is saying here is that women must either live as a male construction or *be found wanting*. In this sense, to lack a phallus is a very serious deficiency from the point of view of the male subject. It induces anxieties that the same fate might befall him.

Consequently, the reward of membership is given for being more fully conformed to the symbolic order, for homologation. This is a bizarre transgression by which the appropriation is by what is conferred rather than by what is taken. She is given a metaphorical member in order to become a member. If the feminine threatens to subvert male order, then the move to confer the honorary penis, the metaphorical phallus, marks the reversal of the potential for transgression. The feminine is, thus, *incorporated*, and given membership by being made to conform to the phallogocentric order. This is regulation via homologation and arises from the fact that men *can* only reproduce themselves hyper-abstractly. The apparent autonomy of language, therefore, gives men the means of achieving quasi-reproduction in language. A woman cannot be a *member* and *a mother*. She must give up the embodied matrix in favour of the metaphorical phallus. Women's actions will lack propriety within male frames. Therefore, by virtue of their mere presence, women threaten to deconstruct male reality definitions. Generally then, women are excluded from male action unless a common, that is to say, male, rationale can be demonstrated. Men diminish women in order to protect themselves from the threat of alternative definitions. In short, it is always a question of membership. Women can never be full members because they lack the *membrum virile*.

Signed in

Some years ago, I won an award for a paper I had written about women in management. The awards were being presented at a special lunch at a London gentlemen's club. I arrived in good time with my deckle edged invitation and presented it to the imperious man on the desk by the front door. 'I'm afraid you can't come in', he said having read over the invitation. I was distressed. I had traveled down from Lancaster specially. He eyed me up again and with a face devoid of feeling and a voice equally devoid of caring he continued, 'I'm not saying that you can't ever come in. However, you can only come in if you are signed in by a male member'. The idea has amused me ever since.

References

Baudrillard, J. (1990) *Seduction*. London: Macmillan.
De Certeau, M. (1986) *Heterologies, Discourse on the Other*. Manchester: Manchester University Press.
Dourley, J. P. (1990) *The Goddess, Mother of the Trinity*. Lewiston: The Edwin Mellen Press.
Eagleton, T. (1990) *The Ideology of the Aesthetic*. Oxford: Blackwell.
Firth-Cozens, J. (1995) *To Have and to Hold: Men, Sex and Marriage*. Basingstoke: Pan Books.
Höpfl, H. J. (2007) 'Maternal Organization'. In Hansen, H. and Barry, D. *Sage Handbook of the New and Emerging in Management and Organization*. London: Sage.
Höpfl, H. J. and Matilal, S. (2007) 'The Lady vanishes: Some thoughts on women and leadership', *Journal of organizational Change Management*, 20(2): 198–208.
Irigaray, L. (1985) *This Sex Which is Not One*. Ithaca, New York: Cornell University Press.
Knights, D. and McCabe, D. (1997) *Innovate to Subjugate: The Self-Reconstituting Manager and the Reconstitution of Employees in a Motor Manufacturing Company*, Proceedings of the EIASM Conference, Organizing in a Multi-Voiced World, Leuven, Belgium.
Kristeva, J. (1991 [1988]) *Strangers to Ourselves*, trans. Leon Roudiez, New York: Harvester Wheatsheaf.
Lacoue-Labarthe, P. (1989) *Typography*. Stanford: Stanford University Press.
Lyotard, J. F. (1989) 'One of the things at stake in women's struggles'. In Benjamin, A. (ed.) *The Lyotard Reader*, pp. 111–121. Oxford: Basil Blackwell.

Modleski, T. (1989) *The Women Who Knew Too Much*. New York: Routledge.
Moi, T. (1986) *The Kristeva Reader*. Oxford: Blackwell.
Sartre, J-P. (1989 [1943]) *Being and Nothingness: An Essay on Phenomenological Ontology,* trans. H. E. Barnes, London: Routledge.
Whitmont, E. C. (1991) *The Symbolic Quest: Basic Concepts of Analytical Psychology*. Princeton: Princeton University Press.
Žižek, S. (2003) *Organs without Bodies: Deleuze and Consequences*. London: Routledge.

3
Pregnancy Centre Stage, Please: Contesting the Erasure of Pregnant Bodies from Workplace Space

Caroline Gatrell

The notion of women as either visible or invisible (but never 'the norm') within workplace space has been much debated within the context of research on gender and employment (Simpson and Lewis, 2005). In this chapter, I focus specifically on the erasure of the pregnant body from both workplace 'space' and management texts. Drawing on a netnographic study of pregnant workers, I show how the absence of the pregnant body in management scholarship is mirrored by the abjuration of the pregnant body at work.

I begin by highlighting and evaluating the absence of the female and especially the pregnant, body, from academic perspectives such as sociology, philosophy, medicine and management. This erasure of women's bodies from scholarship has been identified by feminist academics as significant in relation both to theory and practice (Gatrell, 2008; Haynes, 2008; Nettleton, 2006; Tyler, 2000). Contemporary feminist writers observe how the exclusion of women's reproductive, or what I describe here as women's 'maternal' bodies from 'scholarly' space is symbolic, and spills over into other aspects of social life including the workplace (Gatrell, 2008; Höpfl, 2000). In the context of this paper, my interpretation of 'maternal body' encompasses the pregnant and the post-birth body. I have circumscribed my definition of 'maternal body' in this manner partly because, as I have shown in earlier research (Gatrell 2005, 2007a and b, 2008), it is during pregnancy and post-maternity that the embodied nature of motherhood is at its most visible. Pregnancy has also been shown to herald the moment when discrimination against women in management and professional roles rises sharply (Equal Opportunities Commission (EOC) 2005) as pregnant women are excluded from the arena of 'career'.

The absence of women's bodies from mainstream scholarly debates has the effect of discounting women's contribution, and women's place within, the external social world. The invisibility of the maternal body within social scientific scholarship is subtle and long-standing, and it occurs because traditional and theoretical explorations of 'the body' and productivity have historically been presented as apparently neutral, and ungendered (Turner, 1996). Thus, for example, within sociology, early studies of the body and 'work' (such as Taylorism) centred almost exclusively upon the employed bodies of men. The male body was treated as 'universal' (Grint, 1998: 192) and the female body as 'other'. Where the social and embodied role of women in Western society *was* considered within sociology, this was usually in relation to heterosexuality and motherhood within the context of the home (Gatrell, 2005; Parsons and Bales, 1956). Prior to the second wave feminist movement (when writers such as Rich (1977) began to consider issues of maternity, production and gender inequality) the assumption that only the male body 'counted' in relation to paid work went unchallenged by all but a select group of pioneering feminists: 'the concentration upon men within sociology [was] so common that it was seldom perceived to require an explanation' (Grint, 1998: 192).

To some extent, feminist critiques of how women's bodies are disregarded within a scholarly context have begun to redress the balance by making visible the marginalizing and othering of women's bodies. Swan (2005), for example, explores, from the perspective of the sociology of learning, the pedagogical implications of being a woman teacher, educating managers. Similarly, cultural feminist Puwar (2004) examines the visibility/invisibility of women's bodies from the dual perspectives of race and gender, observing how women's bodies within public space are in practice either metaphorically invisible (and therefore ignored) or deemed out of place and 'other' (and therefore treated as highly visible, but in a negative sense), the white male body still retaining its privileged place as the 'norm'. Among others, Martin (1989), Haynes (2008) and Gatrell (2008) consider how women manage their reproductive bodies within workplace spaces, Gatrell (2008) and Haynes (2008) making specific reference to the absence of the pregnant and newly maternal body within management scholarship.

Equally, feminist writers have begun to highlight the erasure of the female body from philosophical scholarly space. Feminist evaluations of traditional malestream philosophy challenge claims that 'the body' is considered in a universal sense, when in practice the male body is the subject (Höpfl, 2000; Tyler, 2000). For example, in her desire to understand how power and social capital are manifested through the body, Pringle (1998) acknowledges the work of Pierre Bourdieu, but also points out that 'he overlooks gender as a crucial element in the constitution of [social] capital' (Pringle, 1998: 98).

The universalizing of the male body within philosophical space seems extraordinary because the maternal body, and the pregnant body specifically (perhaps containing more than one foetus), poses a serious challenge to apparently 'universalist' notions of the human form such as mind and body dualism. Tyler (2000) criticizes the manner in which women's 'troubling talent for making other bodies' (Haraway, 1991 cited in Tyler, 2000), is effectively erased from philosophical space. Moving from philosophy to the field of medicine, similar arguments have been made by Nettleton (2006) who observes how the healthy masculine body has for centuries been constructed as the 'norm', with the female body presented as an inferior version of male embodiment. Women's bodies in medical contexts are visible only in relation to their reproductive, or maternal, capacity (Kitzinger, 2003; Nettleton, 2006; Oakley, 1984; Rich, 1977). However, although the maternal body is visible once it becomes the focus of medical debate, this visibility is considered in negative terms. Thus, medical texts often use the opprobrious metaphor of 'malfunctioning machine' as a description for women's maternal bodies (Nettleton, 2006). Nettleton examines the way in which the maternal body is reduced, within medicine, to its reproductive status and is seen as unreliable and prone to breakdown and failure. Menstruation, for example, is described as 'failure' to produce a baby, and the end of menstruation as symbolic of the end of woman's useful and productive reproductive life.

Maternal bodies and management theory and practice

The relationship between medicine, masculinity and the body is relevant to the context of management theory and management practices. This is because the influence of the bio-medical model of the body (and associated notions of the male body as 'normal' and the female body as 'other') extends beyond the field of medicine, and into the workplace. The masculine form is seen by employers to represent 'ideal' traits of solidity, predictability and rationality, both physically and psychologically (Höpfl and Hornby-Atkinson, 2000). Healthy male bodies are regarded as the gold standard within workplace space and even the non-pregnant female body is thus excluded from this definition of the 'ideal' employee. The female body may be tolerated within management space on the basis that women manage to 'blend in' maternal bodily characteristics with predominantly male cultures. Thus, only women managers and professionals who succeed in rendering their maternal bodies invisible by keeping their reproductive capabilities 'off-stage' may be allocated the status of 'inferior men' (Höpfl and Hornby-Atkinson, 2000: 135).

For employed pregnant women, the requirement to erase the maternal from workplace space is almost impossible to meet – the pregnant body, after all, underlines women's bio-medical difference from the male 'norm'. In contrast to the comforting notions of 'male' solidity and rationality, the pregnant body incites fears, among employers, of unreliability, breakdown and failure. Bio-medical constructs of women's bodies as fragile and unreliable thus accord with the negative response to the maternal body in the workplace. Consequently, women's exclusion from what Martin (1989) describes as 'success in the public realm', appears to be related to women's potentially reproductive, or 'maternal' bodies' (Gatrell, 2008; Martin, 1989).

Given their obvious departure from male 'norms', the bodies of pregnant women are thus highly visible and treated as 'matter out of place' when they enter the 'public realm' of the workplace (Longhurst, 2001: 65). Longhurst (2001) and Gatrell (2008) suggest that the pregnant body is rejected within workplaces because pregnancy threatens to disrupt workplace conventions. Arguably, this is partly due to the literal and symbolic propensity of the pregnant body to 'leak'. The pregnant body, which expands to accommodate 'other bodies' within itself and which may leak fluid, is seen as unstable and therefore hazardous to workplace routine. Martin (1989), Longhurst (2001) and Gatrell (2008) further observe how the pregnant body and any pregnancy-related leakage is associated, by employers, with poor health and consequent unreliability. On this basis pregnancy may be treated by employers with suspicion and antagonism (Edwards, 1996; Makela, 2005). Negative responses to pregnancy on the part of employers may pressure pregnant women to conceal leakage of any kind. The physical symptoms of pregnancy – tiredness, nausea, vomiting, expanding waistlines, the threat of leaky breasts and breaking waters – must be rendered invisible within workplace space: literally kept 'off-stage'. As Longhurst (2001: 41) describes: 'Pregnant women's body fluids pose a threat to social control and order. [Others] may try to confine the pregnant woman to the private realm because of the threat that her leaking, seeping body...and her splitting self poses to a rational [male] public world.'

Extending the notion of the pregnant body as unreliable and prone to leakage, it has been argued that the women's bodies may be treated as disgusting, the maternal body inciting antipathy and revulsion. In a seminal observation which has been cited in relation to the employed pregnant body by Gatrell (2008) and Longhurst (2001), Grosz (1994: 203) observes how: 'Women's corporeality is inscribed as a mode of seepage ...The association of femininity with contagion and disorder, the undecidability of the limits of the female body (...in the case of pregnancy) leads to the social definition of women as liquid, irrational bodies and incites revulsion.'

The theoretical assumption that the pregnant body may be a source of social abjection and disgust (Grosz, 1994) and the notion that maternal bodies should be kept 'off-stage' suggests that the everyday experience of *being* a pregnant body at work might be challenging. This, and the relative scarcity of management studies on pregnant bodies, suggested the need for further research on how women experience being pregnant at work. In what follows, I discuss the findings from a research project in which, building on my previous research (Gatrell, 2007a and 2008), I sought to understand how employed pregnant women managed their maternal bodies within the workplace. Drawing upon data gathered from internet discussion sites (described as netnographic data) I show in this chapter how, despite decades of legislation supposedly offering protection and support, employed pregnant women are placed under pressure to disavow their pregnancy while at work.

Research method

Bearing in mind the sensitivity of researching pregnancy in the context of employment (given that pregnancy has been cited as a significant cause of gender discrimination, Edwards, 1996; Gatrell, 2008), I chose to undertake netnographic research (Eriksson and Kovalainen, 2008), rather than my usual method of qualitative interviews. This choice was made because research on internet use among pregnant women (Lagan *et al*, 2006) shows how pregnant users choose the internet as a source of collective support and advice which they feel unable to obtain elsewhere. Lagan *et al* (2006), state: 'for many women, the internet provides a new kind of safe haven. Often anonymous, it offers a never-ending source of information and reassurance...and can link individuals who...share common issues.' Netnography seemed appropriate as a research method to understand how employed pregnant women experience their maternal bodies, as well as identifying strategies upon which these women draw, in order to manage their pregnant bodies when at work.

Ethics and anonymity

Given the sensitivity of researching employment and the maternal body, the anonymity of participants was significant. Conventional rules on research ethics are difficult to apply in the context of research in cyberspace or 'netnography'. This is because participants have no personal involvement with the researcher, who does not know whether (or not) internet users would 'choose' for their message board posts to be researched. The internet is an 'open space', freely available to anyone with computer access and many users from different contexts read the messages posted on popular sites like 'Whattoexpect'. The openness of cyberspace is known to most users (Lagan *et al*, 2006) which is presumably why correspondents choose anonymizing internet identifiers. Nevertheless, the requirement to protect research participants remains paramount. In relation to netnographic research, the most helpful suggestions come from Eriksson and Kovalainen (2008: 106) who advise researchers to 'strip all identifying information' from netnographic materials in order to protect the privacy of those studied. Thus, in the context of this research, I have anonymized all posts cited, replacing chosen internet identifiers with pseudonyms. Where I have broad information about women's working circumstances, I indicate this. However, I have excluded specific personal details which might personally identify individual women.

This netnographic data considered in this chapter builds on a long term project (begun in 2006) to consider netnographic interactions between employed pregnant women. The data drawn upon in this chapter was collected between October 2008 and January 2008. In collecting this data I have focused mainly on commercial sites such as Babyworld, verybestbaby and whattoexpect, all of which offer message board facilities, but have also drawn upon smaller correspondant sites, which I do not identify.

Having gathered my data, I undertook a thematic analysis, identifying issues which related to the invisibility and visibility of the pregnant body at work. Having identified these themes, I then further analysed the data manually by cutting and pasting chat room posts electronically because, although this was time-consuming, it enabled me to handle and be 'close' to the data (Crang, 1997: 187). I then considered the data in the context of the pregnant body and work.

Research findings – Keeping the pregnant body 'off-stage'

The absence of references to the pregnant body within mainstream management debates has already been alluded to in this chapter. Here, drawing upon my netnographic data, I suggest that the invisibility of the pregnant body within traditional scholarship on management and the workplace is mirrored by a refusal to acknowledge the material pregnant body, in practice, in workplace space. I demonstrate how pregnancy at work may be treated as disruptive and unwelcome. Women's internet correspondance shows how, irrespective of employment policies allowing for risk assessment and attendance at ante-natal appointments, pregnancy is not permitted to interrupt workplace routines. Pregnant employees are, apparently, encouraged and/or compelled to conceal their pregnant state by presenting at all times a body which appears 'healthy', 'reliable', and 'sparky', thereby rendering pregnancy invisible (Gatrell, 2008). In effect, the erasure of the maternal body from scholarly space is accompanied by the social denial of pregnancy within the workplace.

Announcing pregnancy at work

Worries about negative attitudes towards the employed pregnant body, and the consequent need to conceal pregnancy, begin prior to announcing pregnancy at work. Knowledge that pregnancy will be unwelcome leads many women to fear revealing it to managers and colleagues. This is the case regardless of whether or not pregnant employees are already mothers, but it appears more of a concern for women who already have children, possibly due to negative experiences in the past. Betty, for example, who implies that she is an office worker, describes her fears about revealing pregnancy on the basis that line managers and colleagues have indicated that a second pregnancy will be unwelcome:

> *I am just so scared about telling work. As the time approaches where i am going to have to [tell] I am so scared of my bosses' reactions. I have had a few comments from colleagues and managers re: 'not going off to have another baby' and i know the stress of that is making me feel bad. Part of me thinks i'll just get it out of the way, say it was an accident and grin and bear their reactions. I know they can't do anything but they could make my life uncomfortable for a while...*

For those women who do announce their pregnancy at work, fears that their news will be unwelcome prove well-founded. In accordance with the arguments of Gatrell (2008), Martin (1989) and Longhurst (2001 and 2008), most internet correspondents record how their pregnant bodies are treated by employers with suspicion and distrust, as pregnancy threatens to alter routines and disrupt workplace practices. Regardless of the state of health of individual women, the pregnant body is viewed as prone to illness and unreliability. Pregnant employees are urged by line managers to minimize the impact of pregnancy on the workplace, sometimes (as in Maddy's case, below) to the point of being required to disavow their own pregnant state.

It is important to acknowledge, here, that positive responses from employers and colleagues were occasionally reported on the internet pregnancy sites which I investigated. Ella, for example, in response to chat room discussions about the dangers of revealing pregnancy at work, recalled how she had been nervous about sharing her news with colleagues, but states that she received mainly positive reactions. However, Ella also makes clear her determination to prioritize pregnancy, her assertiveness perhaps serving to moderate negative responses from colleagues. Through her observation that she received no unpleasant comments 'to my face', Ella also implies her sense that her pregnancy might have been discussed in negative terms behind her back:

> *I was pregnant with number 2 in July and told everyone in September. To be honest everyone seemed pleased for me and I didn't get any comments to my face although like you I was anticipating a negative response. I just thought I've got to be philosophical about this, and in terms of my age and where I am at in life babies were our priority. I didn't feel the need to explain myself in any way. After all when all's said and done its [only] a job.*

Ella's positive experience appears, however, to be in the minority. Most women sharing their experiences on pregnancy web-sites report unenthusiastic reactions from line managers and colleagues. Martha, for example, records feeling unhappy because since she revealed her pregnancy:

> *some members of work aren't talking to me any more.*

Many employers and colleagues appear to express antagonism to pregnancy. Often, antipathetic responses from line managers and colleagues compel pregnant employees to metaphorically erase their pregnant bodies from workplace space. Pregnancy, it is suggested, should not provoke interruption to workplace routines. Pregnant workers are thus required to continue their work 'as normal' no matter how they might be feeling and with no regard to workplace policies.

'Forget you are pregnant and just get on with it all'

Maddy, for example, having recently declared her pregnancy at work explains how, following her announcement:

> *I had my year-end appraisal. I have felt sick ever since. [My line manager has] basically told me that the next 6 months at work are going to be super pressurised and I am going to have to prove myself before I go on maternity leave in July. She said I am going to have to forget I am pregnant and just get on with it all. How on earth am I going to do that? I was left feeling really stressed out on Friday and all weekend its all I have thought about. I know its only work but I am the sort of person that takes things to heart. I have also had feedback via her from other managers that I come across as weak. This really upset me!*

Likewise, high-school teacher June found her pregnancy ignored by her school, which refused to allow pregnancy to affect June's teaching timetable. The directive that June's workload (and her associated responsibility for students' exam performance), should remain unaffected by her pregnancy, appeared to be applied even post-birth! June was thus expected to carry on managing her existing, demanding teaching load while also making detailed plans for lessons due to take place during her maternity leave. June reported that her school was making minimal effort to find a replacement to cover her maternity leave. In June's case (and in Maddy's case above), employer fears that pregnancy would disrupt workplace routines appeared to be manifested in a denial of the existence of the pregnancy and an expectation that June should carry on 'as normal', effectively erasing her pregnancy from workplace space. Writing just before her maternity leave was due to begin, June represented her situation as follows:

> *I teach a shortage subject in a secondary school and am due to start mat leave on 25th [of this month]. I informed them I am pregnant [five months ago] (at 13 weeks) and despite this they have [not yet appointed a] replacement... I have been asked to plan lessons for my year 11 classes with plenty of revision materials, practise papers and model answers for pupils to do in my absence. This is a lot of work in addition to a heavy teaching timetable.*

> *I have already had one baby and know I read something then that says something along the lines of employers having to cover your responsibilities whilst you are off. I am prepared to do a reasonable amount of handover ie topics my replacement should cover but not plan lots*

of lessons. I have asked for two periods off timetable for myself and a colleague so that we can spend time moderating the huge amounts of coursework my subject generates and have been refused this.

Changes to workplace practices

Perhaps unsurprisingly, given the workplace antipathy towards pregnancy recorded by many website correspondents, pregnant employees are nervous at the prospect of asking for changes to workplace routines due to pregnancy-related health problems. For example Meg, who seemed even before pregnancy to have been working unreasonably long hours, was reluctant to assert her need for proper breaks even though she was feeling the strain of standing for long periods in her work, and was struggling with the beginnings of varicose veins. Rather than approach her line manager directly, Meg sought advice from other women on the internet about how to prevent the further development of the veins. She writes:

> *I'm 13 weeks pregnant, the veins at the back of my knees are becoming more noticeable and one actually looks like it's starting to protrude!! I'm worried cos...at work I'm on my feet all day. A typical shift for me is 10am til 5pm...with no break at all...my boss doesn't give one even though I know I'm entitled to one and she frowns upon anyone If they are caught sitting down!!! Some days I work from 10am til 10pm and only get 1 hour break! The last thing I want is varicose veins...is there anything I can do to help this? Has anyone got any advise?* (sic)

Similarly, desk-based worker Emma seems afraid to ask for changes to her working routine despite her evident exhaustion. Her organization is resisting the possibility that she might require lunch breaks or exercise, and appear to be ignoring basic human needs. On Emma's part there appears to have been little attempt to negotiate proper breaks. The messages from Emma's line manager about continuing work without interruption have presumably dissuaded Emma from requesting consideration at work. Instead, Emma asks the views of other internet correspondents about whether she should continue working, and whether a doctor might be able to help her by signing her off sick.

> *I am 31 weeks pregnant and was trying to work till the end. Lately, I really feel like crap at work. It's hard for me to keep my eyes open during the day, I just want to nap!!!!! My feet are huge and hurt because they are swollen and numb. My back hurts so bad. I work in an office so I get to sit*

> *all day, however, I commute 1½ hours each way to work and work an 8 hour day, most of the time with no lunch break! I try to get up from my desk as much as I can, but then I get in trouble for walking around and not working. I am entitled to a lunch break, but sometimes there is so much work, that it's impossible to even take a break. I feel so worn out already and am wondering if I should continue working? Do you think it's possible for my doctor to take me out of work?*

For women who do attempt to alter daily routines by negotiating directly with line managers, so as to accommodate pregnancy-related health issues, success rates appear low. For example, Annabel, who did seek changes to her working conditions because she was pregnant with twins and had experienced a urinary tract infection, was denied the opportunity to be home-based during some of her working hours. Additionally, Annabel faced hostile treatment from colleagues, some of whom appeared to feel that the foregrounding of Annabel's pregnancy, due to her poor health, reflected badly on other women in the workplace. Annabel said:

> *I went to see my GP, I told him I was struggling...(I'm carrying twins) and he signed me off for 1 week. I went back to see him yesterday and he found a UTI and signed me off for another week. I have asked to be set up from home as my job is mainly emailing but this has been refused. In the meantime...my colleague...[she has] told the boss [that] I'm the kind of person who gives women a bad name.*
>
> *My worry is – what can they do [to me]?*

Annabel is not alone in fearing the possible consequences of requesting changes to working practices in order to help her combine pregnancy and employment. Maddy, the woman told to 'forget' about her pregnancy, explains that she is seeking advice from internet message boards about how to cope with workplace problems due to fears about her employment prospects (both immediately and post maternity-leave) should she fail to achieve the goal of 'forgetting' pregnancy at work. Maddy explains she is worried because:

> *I can't help think[ing] they are planning something*

Likewise, pregnant employee Joanna, who fears she might not be able to continue her work 'as normal' (and might therefore be seen to fulfil employer fears about unreliability and the breakdown of the maternal body), seeks advice from other women on: 'Can they make me redundant?', expressing her fears that her manager is thinking of '...giving me the boot'.

Pregnant employees who do disrupt workplace routines, for example by insisting on risk assessment, or requesting time off for ante-natal appointments, appear to find themselves in one or both of two difficult situations. This seems to be the case even when the changes to workplace routines sought are in line with 'official' workplace policy. When pregnancy-related requests are put forward, many line managers are either discouraging to the point of rudeness, and/or they take steps to exclude pregnancy disruptions from the workplace. Thus, for example, when women ask for 'risk assessment', this may be refused outright, or undertaken in such a manner that the assessment is intimidating to the pregnant employee and/or exposes lack of knowledge on the part of the employer. For example, Evangeline, a school teacher, reports being 'bullied' by her Head Teacher, whom she describes as:

making a huge stink over the risk assessment when I mentioned it, saying amongst other [things] 'women have babies all the time, look at the women in Africa'. When she conducted the risk assessment (thankfully, with the deputy there), she made a huge fuss over everything, saying e.g. tiredness should not be an issue or put on the risk assessment.

The head teacher's response suggests that Evangeline's pregnancy is viewed with hostility and suspicion. The statement invokes racialized and sweeping visions of supposedly primitive 'natural' and hardy African maternal bodies which are assumed to give birth with minimal intervention, no interruption to routine and, presumably, no requests for risk assessment. This statement about 'women in Africa' implies that Evangeline is being precious and making unreasonable demands on the school by requesting the risk assessment to which policy entitles her. The universalist implication that 'African women' cope with pregnancy and birth without disrupting work, further suggests a lack of knowledge on the part of the head teacher. The Head Teacher's statement fails to recognize both the range of social backgrounds among women in Africa (a vast continent!) and obfuscates issues of high maternal and infant mortality rates in some poorer parts of Africa. The comment about erasing 'tiredness' from Evangeline's risk assessment also obligates Evangeline to control and conceal tiredness while at work – she is required, presumably, to present a 'healthy' 'sparky' body (Gatrell, 2008), and to render invisible any symptoms of poor health which might interrupt work.

The idea that the pregnant body is associated with illness (and therefore with potential disruption to workplace routine) also affects women who seek time off for ante-natal appointments, even if these are supposed to be permitted within workplace policy. Women who request to attend ante-natal clinics during the working day may receive a discouraging response. Janet and Martha report respectively:

I had my Antenatal Day yesterday 9am to 4pm. (in this area we do a full day of the class). I told my Line Manager as soon as I had found out when the class was…and he was fine about it all (he's a lovely man and not the problem!). But when I sent the email around the office on Friday afternoon stating that I wouldn't be in until Tuesday, the Commercial Director…went into a right paddy over it and didn't believe I was entitled to paid time off for this…I printed off the web page from direct.gov.co.uk which clearly states that employees are entitled to [attend] antenatal classes etc and left this on his desk but I was still told to bring a copy of my letter about the class in today which I have done and he has still muttered about not being convinced over paid time off for this. This man has done nothing but cause hassle for me…(Janet).

I have an appointment with my midwife next tuesday (sic). *I told my team leader today…that I'd be needing time off to have this appointment. He said I didn't give him much time (isn't a week enough?!?) and that he can't cover that time so he can't let me go. I told him that…I'm allowed to go to these antenatal things within working hours if needed…He then started suggesting maybe it would be a good idea to change my working hours and I should work afternoons or nights in future. …I got…upset and told him I don't think it's fair he's changing my working conditions because of my pregnancy – before storming off to the loo to have a little cry ☹. What he said wasn't that bad, it was more the way he said it. As if I was being unreasonable and difficult requesting a couple of hours off. This was the first time I've needed time off, all my other appointments have been on my days off (Martha).*

The refusal on the part of employers to support attendance at ante-natal classes concurs with the notion that women are expected to keep pregnancy 'off stage' (Höpfl and Hornby-Atkinson, 2000: 135). Women who seek risk assessments and/or time out of the office for ante-natal clinics have summarily failed to 'blend in' with workplace routines. By drawing attention to their pregnant bodies (through discussing pregnancy and seeking time away from the office to attend pregnancy-related appointments), Martha and Janet had rendered their pregnant bodies 'visible'. The pregnant body had disrupted workplace routines and this was unwelcome, despite the existence of official policies intended to support the health needs of pregnant women. Martha's manager thus attempted to change her hours, rather than allow her to interrupt workplace schedules due to ante-natal commitments.

Janet's boss appears to be lacking in knowledge about the entitlements of pregnant employees, requiring Janet to prove that she is permitted to take 'a couple of hours off' to accommodate pregnancy in the context of the 'public realm' of the workplace (Longhurst, 2001: 65). It is notable that he leaves Janet the responsibility for proving her case, rather than taking steps himself to find out more about national guidelines, and policy within his own company.

Supra-performing pregnant bodies

Building on the notion that the pregnant body is required to be erased from workplace space so that it does not disrupt workplace routines, some pregnant women report being under such scrutiny that they feel compelled to work harder, and to a higher standard, than before they were pregnant. This phenomena is something which I observed during an earlier phase of this research project. I have termed the need to perform above and beyond the norm as 'supra-performance' (Gatrell, 2008). Maddy, who is quoted above, was informed that she must 'prove herself' prior to going on maternity leave by forgetting about her pregnancy and working under 'super pressure'. Likewise, Patsy, (who singles out schools as especially unsympathetic to pregnant employees) shares her experiences of being expected to demonstrate supra-level performance:

> *my school have been cr*p! I have been told that if I have made the choice to become pregnant then I must accept the consequences!...I am having to prove that being pregnant is not affecting my performance, therefore meaning I have to actually be better than an ordinary employee. Unfortunately I've heard quite a few others who have had problems in teaching too so it is common. I know it's illegal for them to be so awful but I've never found a good way of dealing with this kind of discrimination. It just seems most people get away with it.*

Evidently, Patsy feels that her performance is to be judged in a manner which does not apply to non-pregnant employees. She implies that, because she is pregnant, her employers have placed her under constant watch as they search for signs of unreliability, failure or breakdown. Patsy, like many other women in this sample, seems intimidated by her employer's antipathy, to the point where she feels compelled to accept the requirement of 'having to prove that her pregnancy is not affecting [her] performance'. Due to her employers' wish to erase pregnancy from the workplace, Patsy is obliged to disavow her own pregnant body.

In sickness and in health...visibility and the pregnant body at work

Women whose pregnancy does interrupt workplace practices are left in no doubt that this is inconvenient. Failure on the part of a pregnant employee to minimize the impact of pregnancy at work, by taking time off sick or attending medical appointments, is barely tolerated. For example, Angela, who is unwell and has had to take time away from the workplace to see her midwife and hospital consultant, has found herself under pressure to make this up at work by doing without lunch:

> *Im* (sic) *classed as High Risk due to growth problems with my other 2 in the womb...so I have to see the consultant alot. I try to get apts [appointments] as late as I can in the day but [my boss] still moans. I had an apt at 2pm last wk and I was at work from 8.50am to 5.30. I was told that im not entitled to any form of break as I would be out for the apt for around an hr [seeing] (midwife and consultant)...I have to drive there and then apts are straight after each other so I didn't get time to sit and eat anything apart from a banana all day.*

The pregnant body appears to be both threatening and inconvenient to workplace routines in case it fails the requirement to carry on working as normal. Pregnant employees like Angela are required to take personal responsibility for minimizing workplace disruption by (in this case) doing without lunch. The idea that Angela should be coerced into forgoing lunch at a time when her body most requires rest and nutrition could be seen as punishment for Angela's failure to keep her pregnant body 'off stage'. Employers' fears that the pregnant body might break down and prove unreliable seem to be manifested in a refusal to acknowledge any sign of compromised health on the part of a pregnant employee. Some employers seem prepared to pressurize pregnant women into working at or above 'normal' standards and deal harshly with women who fail to manage this because they are unwell. For example, Jess, who suffered severe morning sickness, was struggling to manage her 'massive' workload. Her request that her line manager might reduce this was ignored and subsequently, having been signed off on sick leave, Jess found that her employers questioned her own doctor's judgement that she was unfit for work, requesting that she should be re-assessed by a doctor of their choice. One can only speculate whether they would have meted out similar treatment to a non-pregnant employee who was signed off sick, due to workplace stress. In Jess's case, her employers seemed to expect that Jess should ignore her symptoms and return to work:

> *Im 23 weeks…and since the start of being pregnant have found it very hard, morning sickness was terrible the first few months,…[and]…I became…extremely emotional, I do work in quite a high pressure young office environment,…I explained to my Manager…that I wasnt* (sic) *happy, as the workload was massive, but she did nothing about it. Finally…I walked out feeling sick and in tears. I went to see the doctor who has signed me off with anxiety and stress, Im* (sic) *still a bit of a state some days crying all day, feeling extremely anxious, and dreading any contact with work, who are really pushing for me to come back, but I really cant* (sic) *cope with going back. They want to refer me for a health assessment [with a doctor of their choosing]…why can't they take my GP's word? After 5 years working there I feel so let down, and now every time they contact me I feel sick and stressed.*

Irene has also experienced severe morning sickness and writes how she has just returned to work following a period off sick due to the severity of her symptoms. Irene explains how she is struggling to conceal her continuing poor health from line managers because she is scared that if she requests changes to her workplace routine, she will lose her full time post. Irene's fears mean that, despite fainting on the train home, she is still making the daily journey to work for 8.30 am, standing for over an hour as she travels. Irene wants to ask for flexible hours so she does not need to travel to work in the rush hour. However, she is frightened to admit that she still feels unwell because poor health might be regarded by her employers as a sign of incompetence. No one in Irene's workplace has pro actively offered any help on her return: her pregnancy and weakened state following severe sickness is ignored, and she is expected to carry on working as normal.

> *I'm 15 weeks pregnant and have had quite a rough time of it, I've suffered with hyperemesis gravidarum (severe morning sickness) and been off work*

for the last 6 weeks. I went back to work on Monday and was very tired but ok, then yesterday (tues) I passed out on the train to work, have a little bump but stil no one gave up their seat and I'm too polite to ask, dont like to draw attention to myself (hence found fainting mortifyingly embarrasing).

Went to the hospital with the paramedics yesterday and gynacologist checked me over and both me and baby were Ok. She said because I was so ill I'm weak and need to gets lots of rest and not stand for too long. Am worried now about commuting in rush hour (I work 8.30–5.30) as trains are always packed by the time I get on. Also I dont (sic) *want to be off sick too much as scared my boss will think I'm not capable and try and make me work part time when I cant* (sic) *really afford to.*

Abjuring the visibly pregnant body

So far, I have established that the pregnant body is either ignored and/or treated as unwelcome in the workplace. Pregnancy is associated by employers with fears about ill health and unreliability. Employers are quick to indicate to pregnant workers that any disruption to workplace routines will not be tolerated, and may even be punished. At no point in my web search did I find any incidence of employers proactively seeking to adapt working practices so they could accommodate the pregnant body, and the health and social needs of pregnant women. Employed women are, apparently, required to manage their pregnant bodies so that they appear to be as operating 'as normal'.

Women are thus expected to render invisible the physical and physiological changes brought about by pregnancy within workplace settings: pregnancy, if women are to avoid criticism from colleagues and employers, must be kept 'off-stage'. While it may be possible to conceal pregnancy in the early stages, especially if women are healthy, women in the second and third trimesters are inevitably going to find this increasingly difficult. While morning sickness may be wearing off, for some (though not all) women, the material leakage of body fluids continues to occur throughout pregnancy, unpredictably and in a variety of ways ranging from unpredicted bleeding to leaking milk. In the second trimester, the baby starts moving, pressing on women's ribs, back and bladder, causing discomfort and the need to urinate more often. At the end of pregnancy, the 'waters' break which, as Kitzinger (2003: 251) describes, may be unpredictable and 'may happen suddenly with a rush of water, or more likely with a slow trickle of water. You may not be sure whether the bag of waters has burst or whether you are wetting your pants.' As the baby grows the body changes shape, and expanding waistlines and swollen hands, ankles and feet become increasingly visible.

Longhurst (2001) and Gatrell (2005) have both observed how the boundaries of acceptable social behaviour change when women are visibly pregnant. Personal remarks are often directed at pregnant women in a manner which would be deemed inappropriate in most other situations. When pregnancy and its symptoms become patently visible at work, so apparently do the fear and revulsion towards the pregnant body felt by some colleagues and employers. Fear and disgust at the possibility of leakage are openly expressed: the barriers are seen to be down and women may be exposed to no-holds-barred criticism. Often, such remarks are made in a supposedly 'humorous' light and pregnant women are expected to accept this behaviour, even if they don't themselves find it funny. Jokes about lactation and breastfeeding could be seen to be symptomatic of others' anxieties not only about leakage, but about blurring of the boundaries, symbolized by the pregnant body, between the maternal and the sexual (Young, 2005). Whatever the explanation, the ridiculing of the pregnant body at work may be explicit, and very personal as described my Lynn:

> *As I was drinking a container of milk once during our office birthday celebration an intelligent (so I thought), older, male, co-worker said to me across the conference room table "Are you taking it in so you can give it out later" and he made a gesture from his chest area signifying where I would be "giving it out" from.*

Similarly, Belinda describes how a colleague reacted when Belinda rendered her pregnancy 'visible' by referring to her back pain within workplace space:

> *If I wasn't pregnant, I would have knocked the socks of this smart *** old lady that I work with. I am 18 weeks pregnant so i have a noticeable bump now. I was sitting at my desk and said "My back hurts" and this women that sits next to me said "Well maybe it hurts from laying on it too much. If you did less of that, you wouldn't be in the position you are now". She said it loud enough for the whole office to hear and everyone thought it was funny…except for me. That was so RUDE!!!! (and just in case you missed it, she was referring to me laying on my back and getting pregnant)!!!*

On entering the third trimester, employed pregnant women find themselves subject to the public gaze, as described by Longhurst (2001) and

Gatrell (2005). It is commonly suggested to women with singleton pregnancies that their large size must indicate the presence of multiple foetuses, with colleagues who make such comments being reluctant to let the subject drop, or to back down:

> *The man I supervised looked at me a few weeks ago (just starting month 7) and said "you're sure you're not having twins?" I was flabbergasted and thought he was joking until he persisted.*

Comments about the number of foetuses and the size of the visibly pregnant bodies are accompanied by an undercurrent of fear, sometimes bordering on horror, even if this is obscured by supposed 'humour'. Pregnancy is abjured in a material sense as employers and colleagues refer to the imminent birth, fear of leakage and the prospect of birth mingling with concerns that work-related tasks might be left undone when maternity leave starts. Jo, for example, (at seven months pregnant) was asked on the train home from work:

> *You're not gonna have that now are you?*

Office worker Liz, similarly, reports how colleagues made plain their views that her heavily pregnant body was abjured and considered to have no place within the arena of the workplace:

> *In the team meeting they were joking around and it was all 'oh you look enormous are you going to have it here then ha ha, lets bring on the towels and hot water then' and then this woman (well she's only a kid really) but she went eeew yuck, and then they were all: 'well when ARE you going to go home then its about time' and they don't want the work not to get done but I think there* (sic) *secretly scared I'll have it right there on the floor, its makes me so mad I'd love to try it and that and then see what they do.*

Anxiety about leakage, birth and the expanding pregnant body may thus be manifested in supposedly 'humourous' terms, through jokes about the size of the pregnant body, multiple birth, and leakage. However, the use of 'humour' as a way of dealing with the visible pregnant body at work is accompanied by more sinister attempts to erase the pregnant body from workplace space.

Despite government and workplace policies intended to facilitate the accommodation of pregnancy at work, it is apparent that pregnant bodies, and the associated needs of pregnant women (for example to be risk assessed) are abjured by employers from the outset. Although the embodied needs of pregnant women are embraced by policy, some pregnant employees are under extraordinary pressure to perform at 'super-pressurised' levels. Pregnant women are expected to 'prove' that their bodies are healthy and reliable by acceding to extraordinary surveillance, and rendering pregnancy invisible within workplace contexts. In order to meet the raised performance standards imposed upon them by some antipathetic employers many pregnant women thus feel obliged to abjure their own pregnant bodies or face punishment. So, for example, pregnant women report that they are complying with directives to forgo lunch to appease line managers if ante-natal appointments are scheduled during office hours. Some women feel intimidated to the point where they do not challenge such treatment, turning anonymously to the 'safe haven' of the internet for the support of other pregnant women rather than question unreasonable directives. As a consequence, workplace practices in which the abjuration of the pregnant body has become 'normal' seem unlikely to change.

It is difficult to disentangle the abjuration of the pregnant body at work from the relative absence of the pregnant body within management scholarship, which I observed at the start of this chapter and which feminist management scholars such as Haynes (2008) are gradually beginning to address. Possibly, the dual absences of the pregnant body from textual and material workplace space may be interrelated, and may both be linked to ideas that pregnant bodies should be kept 'off-stage' within the context of paid work.

The experiences of the pregnant women reported here indicate that sometimes, the abjuration of pregnancy at work can reach the point where pregnant women are reviled and basic human needs are ignored, perhaps due to fears about unreliability and the breakdown of the maternal body. Whatever the reasons behind employer abjection of the pregnant body, the resulting denial of the fundamental health requirements of pregnant employees (such as eating lunch) would seem likely to invoke illness even among non-pregnant workers. Thus, employers' tearful prophecies that pregnant bodies may be prone to poor health and failure would seem to be at the same time self-fulfilling, and self-imposed. If pregnant women are refused permission to eat, work flexibly and attend health appointments, it seems unsurprising that some do become ill, and require time away from work as a result.

Whether or not the abjuration of pregnancy at work is related to the absence of the pregnant body within mainstream management scholarship, the erasure of the pregnant body from workplace space and management debate suggests an urgent need to place the pregnant body at the forefront of management scholarship, as a legitimate topic for study. It is time the maternal body was acknowledged within both the academic and the workplace arena. In the context of employment, it is time for the pregnant bodies to take their position in a positive spotlight, centre stage.

References

Crang, M. (1997) 'Analyzing qualitative materials', in Flowerdew, R. and Martin, D. (eds) *Methods in Human Geography*. London: Addison Wesley Longman.
Edwards, M. E., (1996) 'Pregnancy discrimination litigation: Legal erosion of capitalist ideology under equal employment opportunity law', *Social Forces*, 75(1): 247–269.
Equal Opportunities Commission (2005) *Greater Expectations*. Manchester: Equal Opportunities Commission.
Eriksson, P. and Kovalainen, A. (2008) *Qualitative Methods in Business Research*. London: Sage.
Gatrell, C. (2005) *Hard Labour: The Sociology of Parenthood*. Maidenhead: Open University Press.
Gatrell, C. (2007a) 'A fractional commitment?', *International Journal of Human Resource Management*, 18(3): 462–475.
Gatrell C. J. (2007b) 'Secrets and lies: Breastfeeding and professional paid work', *Social Science & Medicine*, 65: 393–404.
Gatrell, C. (2008) *Embodying Women's Work*. Maidenhead: Open University Press.
Grint, K. (1998) *The Sociology of Work*. Cambridge: Polity Press.
Grosz, E. (1994) *Volatile Bodies: Toward a Corporeal Feminism*. Bloomington: Indiana University Press.
Haraway, D. (1991) *Simians, Cyborgs, and Women: The Reinvention of Nature*. London: Free Association Books.
Haynes, K. (2008) '(Re)figuring accounting and maternal bodies: The gendered embodiment of accounting professionals', *Accounting, Organizations and Society*, 33: 328–348.
Höpfl, H. (2000) 'The suffering mother and the miserable son: Organizing women and organizing women's writing', *Gender, Work and Organization*, 17(2): 98–105.
Höpfl, H. and Hornby-Atkinson, P. (2000) 'The Future of women's careers', in Collin, A. and Young, R. (eds) *The Future of Career*. Cambridge: Cambridge University Press.
Kitzinger, S. (2003) *The New Pregnancy and Childbirth, Choices and Challenges*. London: Dorling Kindersley.
Lagan, B., Sinclair, M. and Kernohan, W. G. (2006) 'Pregnant women's use of the internet: A review of published and unpublished evidence', *Evidence Based Midwifery*, 4(1): 17–23.
Longhurst, R. (2001) *Bodies: Exploring Fluid Boundaries*. London: Routledge.
Longhurst, R. (2008) *Maternities: Gender, Bodies and Space*. New York: Routledge.

Makela, L. (2005) 'Pregnancy and leader-follower dyadic relationships: A research agenda', *Equal Opportunities International*, 24(3.4): 50–73.
Martin, E. (1989) *The Woman in the Body: A Cultural Analysis of Reproduction*. Boston: Beacon Press.
Nettleton, S. (2006) *The Sociology of Health and Illness*, 2nd edition. Cambridge: Polity Press.
Oakley, A. (1984) *The Captured Womb*. Oxford: Blackwell.
Parsons, T. and Bales, R. (1956) *Family and Socialization and Interaction Process*. London: Routledge and Kegan Paul.
Pringle, R. (1998) *Sex and Medicine*. Cambridge: Cambridge University Press.
Puwar, N. (2004) *Space Invaders: Race, Gender and Bodies Out of Place*. Oxford: Berg.
Rich, A. (1977) *Of Woman Born, Motherhood as Experience and Institution*. London: Virago.
Simpson, R. and Lewis, P. (2005) 'An investigation of silence and scrutiny of transparency: Re-examining gender in organization literature through the concepts of voice and visibility', *Human Relations*, 58(10): 1253–1275.
Swan, E. (2005) 'On bodies, rhinestones and pleasures: Women teaching managers', *Management Learning*, 36(3): 317–333.
Turner, B. (1996) *The Body and Society*. London: Sage.
Tyler, I. (2000) 'Reframing pregnant embodiment'. In Ahmed, S., Kilby, J., Lury, S., McNeil, M. and Skeggs, B. (eds) *Transformations: Thinking Through Feminism*. London: Routledge.
Young, I. M. (2005) *On Female Body Experience: 'Throwing Like a Girl and Other Essays'*. Oxford: Oxford University Press.

4
'Mothered' and Othered: (In)visibility of Care Responsibility and Gender in Processes of Excluding Women from Norwegian Law Firms[1]

Selma Therese Lyng

> *I: But is there anything that could be done in a firm that in some way could make it easier to combine work and family?*
> R: Why would, like, the firm want that?
> *I: Well, if they want a higher percentage of women*
> R: Sure, but they don't want a higher percentage of women at any cost. And that really is the point. They make accommodations and want to promote women, but the women they want to promote have to make the same choice as the guys. (...) One can't be bothered to subsidize. That's kind of how it is.
>
> Male Senior Associate Lawyer

Introduction

In line with a pattern widespread in Western societies, Norwegian professions are characterized by a seemingly paradoxical situation regarding the female proportion: while generally representing the majority in several elite educations and professions, women still constitute a minority in senior and top levels. This gap is particularly conspicuous in increasingly commercialized, prestigious and high commitment segments (Gulbrandsen *et al*, 2002). In the legal profession, while women currently constitute more than 605 of law school students, and half of the recruits hired by Norwegian corporate law firms, the drop-out from these firms is highly gendered, leaving intact the male dominance (88%) in the most prestigious, powerful and economically rewarding partner positions (Halrynjo, 2008; Lyng, 2008; NSSDS, 2007; Norwegian Bar Association, 2008).

This chapter explores issues of (in)visibility of care responsibility and gender in processes of othering and exclusion of women from careers in

Norwegian corporate law firms. The data consist of 30 in-depth interviews; eight male and 17 female lawyers and five management representatives from the largest and most prestigious corporate law firms in Norway. The interviewees were recruited formally through firms as well as informally through social networks. To prevent the potential biases in such a small sample of subcultures in particular social cliques and work organizations, the interviewees were selected from several firms and different, non-related social networks. Informants were purposively sampled to represent a variety of positions and career trajectories. While all have at some point been on the 'A-team' in prestigious law firms, some have transferred to smaller firms or other forms of legal work. Additionally, I 'job shadowed' five women (one partner and four lawyers at associate and senior associate levels) one work day each. One of the firms also provided me with an internal manual given to junior employees on 'how to be a partner in this firm'.

In the first section of this chapter I will outline the normative 'up-and-go career contract' of Norwegian corporate law firms, including both explicit and implicit, material, practical and symbolic criteria for constructing oneself and being regarded as an ideal worker on the 'A-team', eligible for promotion and career track in these high commitment, 'up-or-out' work organizations. I then explore the accounts of male and female lawyers' experiences both before and after entering parenthood, and investigate the ways in which gender and parenthood are (in)visibilized through practices, strategies and dominant discourses. In existing studies on exclusion of women from the legal profession, care responsibility is studied primarily as one of many binary gendered characteristics rendering female lawyers as deviants from a male norm and code of professionalism. While the findings in this chapter demonstrate how the gendered othering of parents is (re)produced, they give reason to question whether a general masculine professional norm should still be the main focus when studying why women leave corporate law firms in disproportionate numbers. In conclusion, I discuss how the findings suggest that, though often empirically overlapping, there is a need for further research and policy making to separate analytically between barriers related to gender v. care responsibility.

Male and female lawyers on the A-team

For most corporate lawyers, being recruited to one of the prestigious firms represents one step further in a continued experience of being on the 'A-team' in allegedly meritocratic settings. They have been among the best in their class throughout the educational system. In interviews, managers made sure to explain to me that they recruit among the top 5% graduates of law. A brilliant law degree is merely an entrance ticket, however, to yet another competitive hierarchy. A few decades ago, the recruitment to a law firm was almost equivalent to a secure career path towards partnership. In line with international developments, however, the Norwegian sector of corporate law has, since the 1980s, been subject to an ongoing process of restructuring. One of the most marked changes is mergers, resulting in fewer and larger firms with substantially more billing and salaried employees creating an increasing surplus value per partner. Consequently, the present career structure of corporate law firms have both (neo)traditional and modern features. They have acquired the pyramidal, hierarchical structure of the traditional corporate bureaucracy, implying an increase in the number of positions on the career ladder.[2] On the other hand, the career structure has been 'modernized' (Rosenbaum and Miller, 1996) in terms of introducing the 'up-or-out' model characterized by the decline of the general company man; one either goes up fast and stays, or one goes out. Hardly anyone stays at lower levels for a long period of time; doing so is considered to entail stigmatization – both socially and in terms of career chances even outside the firm. The insertion of more levels implies an increase in the number of years and checkpoints on the track towards partnership, intensifying the individual competition with internal and external peers. Although there are substantial individual variations, the duration of the 'partner track' is considered to be approximately ten years. Consequently, the time frame of career launch for Norwegian corporate lawyers is similar to that found in several other high commitment professions across national labour markets: the age of 30–40 represents the 'make-or-break-years' (Mason and Ekman, 2007). During this period, staying on the A-team implies the continued accomplishment of reaffirming oneself as promising 'partnership material'.

Describing what is involved in an A-team membership, informants turn to an additional sports metaphor – the elite athlete. Moreover, partners and managers compare partnership to marriage, stressing that entering partnership is an important, personal decision implying a lifelong relationship for better or worse. The notion of a reciprocal give-and-take relationship between the firm and even junior employees is explicitly articulated – as in this motto from the official recruitment profile material of one of the largest Norwegian firms: 'It's about giving of yourself – and getting a lot more in return'. In order to conceptualize investments and rewards associated with staying on the A-team, I will utilize the analytic construction 'up-and-go career contract'. Both the input and output sides of the contract include explicit and implicit, material, practical and symbolic elements.

The 'up-and-go career contract' in Norwegian corporate law firms

Although the ultimate prize in the long distance race for a partner position is reserved for the few, there are rewards for candidates en route. Even if the wage is not high compared to the work hours, corporate law firms offer both higher salaries for juniors relative to other employers, as well as the opportunity for competing for bonuses. Apart from the monetary rewards, there is substantial prestige and social status related to being a member of the A-team in one of the largest firms. The clients are powerful and important national and international players, and the public attention further contributes to the notion of 'being where the action is' and making a difference in cases where there is a lot at stake. Moreover, informants express a strong sense of being highly privileged in having the opportunity to work with the best people – both peers and superiors – in their field of law. One of the most emphasized elements of the output side of the contract is learning a lot at a high speed, and working with exciting and challenging assignments. Staying on the A-team implies frequent and intense experiences of positive feedback and self-realization.

Urge, drive, loyalty, commitment, dedication and sacrifice are key symbolic concepts to the 'up-and-go career contract'. 'To have a career in this line of work you really have to *want* it' and 'Do what is expected – and a bit more' are frequently used phrases. Operationalizing the input side of the career contract, informants emphasize hard work, 'team spirit' and abilities to attract and cultivate clients – put concisely by a partner: 'show an entrepreneurial attitude: think like a partner, not like an employee'. Even if formal evaluation tools are used, firms do not clearly specify all promotion criteria, and this fuzziness allows managers and partnerships to redefine and adjust criteria to fit available information (London and Stumpf, 1982: 215; Rosenbaum and Miller, 1996: 358) when evaluating an employee in terms of promotion, pay increases and bonuses. However, senior and junior informants do unite on certain requirements needed to fulfil the career contract associated with staying on the A-team. The material and practical aspects of the contract is prescribed in terms of standards regarding billable hours:

1700–2000 hours a year, varying by law firm and position. Somewhat more informally, one is expected to put in a substantial number of hours in initiating and participating in internal non-billable activities ('internal services'), related to professional, technical as well as organizational development. Additionally, an A-team player should give him/herself as well as the firm a high profile externally through publishing and giving lectures in relevant settings as well as participating in significant networks. To meet these demands, informants estimate that their actual weekly work hours vary from 50 to 70, though frequently providing 'extreme stories' of the week in which they went beyond 100 hours. These long work hours are also *unpredictable* for corporate lawyers in subordinate positions. Even when clients and assignments are not of the kind considered to demand immediate attention, time predictability and planning are privileges reserved for partners.

As to self-presentation and impression management, maintaining a position on the A-team requires demonstration of client orientation and identification in terms of understanding their 'business imperatives' and preferably displaying enthusiasm and knowledge regarding the nature of clients' business as well as development in relevant markets. Moreover, it requires the capacity to construct one-self as self-confident, positive, energetic, enthusiastic, 'pro-active', assertive, on top of the situation and exceedingly available and flexible towards clients as well as superiors.

A masculine career contract?

Input elements of this 'up-and-go career contract' include total commitment and dedication; loyalty and single minded allegiance; and parallel demands related to the ideal worker norm identified in a number of studies on 'greedy' and high commitment professions and work organisations (Acker, 1990, 1998; Blair-Loy, 2003; Brandth and Kvande, 2002; Coser, 1974; Hochschild, 1997; Halrynjo and Lyng, 2009; Sommerlad and Sanderson, 1998; Williams, 2000). Within existing studies concentrating on the legal profession, these elements are interpreted as gender specific, and the persistence of the long-hours culture is associated with the notion that law continues to be seen as a 'masculine' profession (Collier, 2005). In a recent article, Bolton and Muzio (2007) argue that the continued exclusion of women is still, in line with Davies (1996), a matter of the legal professional professing masculine gender. Drawing on a number of studies (Bolton, 2004; Cockburn, 1991; Davies, 1996; Hanlon, 1998; Harrington, 1993; Segal, 1987; Sommerlad and Sanderson, 1998; Sommerlad,

2002; Wajcman, 1998), they assert that women are excluded from advancement by a process of continued binary gendered construction of occupational and social roles, in which the masculine norm represents elements like expertise, rationality, control, predictability, commitment, competitiveness, profit orientation, aggressiveness, ruthlessness, cold calculating logic and a 'loud, harsh and laddish culture'. From Bolton and Muzio's perspective, the continued exclusion of women thrives on an ideology of women's difference. In addition, gendered internal closure mechanisms operate in ways that restrict access to rewards and opportunities to a limited circle of eligible males.

My data from Norwegian law firms give reason to complicate these notions. Both male and female informants reject the idea that women per se lack characteristics required for A-team membership. Women are not seen as deviating from a *masculine norm* in ways that prevent them from fulfilling the 'up-and-go career contract'. When male lawyers give this description, this may, of course, be a result of men conforming to – and not being aware of – such a norm. Moreover, when female lawyers insist that gender is 'no big issue', this might be interpreted as a matter of making gender invisible in terms of women struggling to avoid being identified as different from the masculine norm (Lewis, 2006). Further, it may be suggested that ignoring experiences of othering is required of women in order to overcome them and avoid discouragement and disillusion. It might also be that specific elements traditionally associated with men, masculinity and male subcultures are still excluding women at the top levels where 'rainmaking' – bringing business in – and inclusion in highly restricted networks are vital criteria for obtaining as well as maintaining an important and powerful position (Blair-Loy, 2001).

In the law firm studied for this chapter, however, it seems that there are multiple masculinities and femininities (Connell, 1995; Kimmel *et al*, 2005) available that, similar to other social arenas, are actually blurring some of the binary oppositions traditionally associated with masculinity versus femininity (Lyng, 2007). Signifiers of expertise, rationality, control, predictability, commitment, competitiveness, profit orientation and cold calculating logic are produced by A-team members, regardless of gender, and are not conceived of as gender specific characteristics. Some men as well as women seem to identify with and present themselves in line with the stereotypical 'Rambo' lawyer (Pierce, 1995), representing traditional hypermasculine signifiers like ruthlessness, aggressiveness as well as a 'loud, hard and laddish culture'. Others – both men and women – are alienated by this style. However, conforming to such a traditional male norm does not appear to be required to stay on the A-team. The female lawyers in my sample seem to (re)produce versions of femininity compatible with fulfilling the 'up-and-go career contract' – until they enter motherhood.

Entering parenthood: 'Mothered' and othered

This is certainly not to say that gender is not at play in a variety of ways in the culture of Norwegian corporate law firms, or that women are not confronted with gender specific barriers. Informants do point out that the legal profession represents a particularly gender conservative subculture. Nevertheless, they draw a picture in which male and female peers are on an equal footing in terms of possibilities and career prospects. The female lawyers report that entering parenthood represents their first encounter with their gender as a barrier at work. Their first years in these prestigious firms have been filled with frequent experiences of (over)achievement, excellent feedback and evaluations, promotions, recognition and appreciation as well as explicit and unambiguous signals from partners and management of satisfaction and being counted in on the A-team of promising candidates for partner track. The picture of gender equal opportunities is altered, however, when they become mothers. They experience being 'mothered', categorized as the other(ed) gender, and discover that working life is not that gender equal after all. Some describe this as a shock; that doing something as common as having children is actually disqualifying in terms of career chances:

> I've always though that it's just a matter of not caring that much about being a woman. I've always loved male arenas, and I just think it's been extra cool to accomplish the things the guys accomplish, and I haven't cared about that (....) I'm very disappointed – I've always thought that I can do everything men can do, and then suddenly I become a 'mother' in other people's eyes. And whether that's down to me or to society at large, I don't know. And this happens to surprisingly many.
>
> Female Junior Associate

Being 'mothered' implies being visibilized as deviating from the career contract on symbolic, practical and material levels. The othering is experienced as an accelerating process, and the first signals that one's status is altered may start with the mere announcement of pregnancy. The fact that colleagues and managers are happy for those expecting a happy event does not prevent the sense that they are now perceived differently:

> *[When I became pregnant] one of the older partners came in and said in jest 'So are you going to ruin your career now?' It was actually a nice thing to say, because it implied that I had good prospects to begin with, but I do feel that it was also the case that I was viewed in a somewhat different manner as soon as I was expecting a child. You know, that I couldn't sacrifice everything for the job.*
> Female Senior Associate

Various elements of othering sum up a distinct feeling of being excluded from the A-team. These elements include decline in interest and initiatives from managers, partners and colleagues as well as implicit and explicit messages that expectations regarding their capacity and commitment to fulfil the career contract are lowered, tested and being questioned. Motherhood symbolizes reduced work dedication, long-term unavailability during parental leave and long-term unpredictability, inflexibility and instability regarding willingness and opportunities to pursue a fast track career after child birth. Women entering motherhood seem to be transferred to a limbo position, with uncertainty as to whether what comes out on the other side of maternity leave is a still-dedicated or defected A-team member.

The social and symbolic othering comes with highly concrete manifestations. Mothers are subject to the signs of unattractive workers: empty desks, exclusion from prestigious, demanding, motivating and meriting projects and potentially promising client relations:

> *Even though I've worked like a galley slave, I haven't been away from work a single day when I've been pregnant. But you become a bit written off in a way when you get that stomach that starts protruding. And then you don't get invited to meetings with new clients and things like that.*
> Female Senior Associate

It has been noted that in addition to representing imminent responsibilities and commitments outside the work sphere, the excluding symbolic effect of the pregnant stomach may be interpreted in terms of women being embodied and gendered in work cultures characterized by a gender neutral, disembodied rationality (Børve, 2007) or rather the inappropriate type of gendered embodiment. In a profession where the body of the female lawyer is frequently sexualized, the non-erotic materiality of the pregnant body is discomforting and hard to deal with for the men of law (Sommerlad and Sanderson, 1998; Thornton, 1996). My data suggest that as an othering signifier for women, the temporary *bodily gendering* related to pregnancy is minor to its function as a pregnant symbol of enduring incompatibilities with the career contract. Both employers and employees emphasize the 'natural' inconvenience of staffing high profile projects with team members whose participation might be both unreliable and short-term. Further, when pregnant lawyers are excluded from new assignments and client relations, it is rendered a consequence of the taken-for-granted assumption that they will take the bulk of both the parental leave[3] and family work.

When returning to work after parental leave, the process of othering continues with maintained lack of interest, offers and expectations from superiors as well as significant colleagues:

You're not some new and exciting manpower that people have great expectations of – you're just someone whose coming back, without anyone preparing for it.
Female Senior Associate

Moreover, the othering materializes as being passed over in terms of wage rises, bonuses and promotion. Competence and earlier achievements and merits are ignored and invisibilized:

Actually, I've received feedback that everything's going exceptionally well and that I manage to put in enough hours at work. (...). But I didn't get that promotion, and that's been an issue of sorts, because I feel I've been here for so long and it's about time. (...). I had the impression that I was on the senior associate level before my maternity leave, but that it wasn't opportune to promote me right before I was about to go on leave. But that when I returned the promotion would take place swiftly, presuming that working with two small children would work out fine. (...). But now the situation is suddenly that there are many other criteria that must be fulfilled, so now I'm still not there [at the senior associate level] in a way.
Female Junior Associate

The thing that was a bit weird was that I thought I deserved a promotion, roughly around the time I was on leave. But I didn't get it. (...). [That it was due to the pregnancy and the maternity leave], they were a bit too politically correct to say that out loud. But afterwards the management

made some statements that in effect implied that their assessment of the situation was that there was no danger of me quitting.
Female Senior Associate

Mothers in the commercial law firms discover that pregnancy and parental leave are not regarded as temporary and exceptional periods when efforts, achievement and billable hours are evaluated. On the contrary, instead of basing the evaluation on the part of the year that they have actually been working, the reduced billing, desk-emptying and assignment drought during pregnancy and parental leave are entered as red figures. For those whose pregnancy and/or parental leave disperse over two financial years, this may imply two years of being evaluated as unworthy of those kinds of rewards considered to be the tangible measure and affirmation of the status as a successful and promising worker. From being regarded as overachievers on the A-team, these female lawyers find themselves in a situation where they feel stuck and categorized as underachievers, while watching peers in their own heat of the A-team pulling away.

Invisibilizing motherhood: 'De-mothering' counter strategies

Confronted with experiences – or fear of experiencing – the stigmas of motherhood, female lawyers make use of a variety of counter-strategies in order to invisibilize and dissociate with symbolic signifiers of deviating from the career contract, typically ascribed to mothers. A general strategy is to make extra efforts to signal continued or even intensified work dedication. More specifically, working throughout pregnancy and evading sick leave is considered a strategy to appear 'less pregnant' and keep one's A-team membership:

What I think gets noticed is, first of all, how you act when you're pregnant. (…). Obviously, it is hard to work with this type of job and be nine months pregnant. But that's something I just put my mind to, I'm not going on sick leave. I'm just not going to do that. I'm not going to be that type of person.
Female Senior Associate

And, sure, I received a lot of positive feedback on being at work until the day I gave birth, and all that sounds really great, but it was because I was so healthy. But of course, there's no one here who says 'Oh no I really think you should, like, go home now and put your feet up for a couple of weeks and really take it easy', and 'Are you sure you've been able to relax now' (....). I think people would have totally understood that if I had done it. But you are very, like, oppositely honoured for hanging in there.

Female Partner

The accounts of this strategy take the form of passing a test; to make an exertion demonstrating dedication and capacity to overcome the physical conditions of pregnancy as well as resisting the temptation to make use of entitled welfare rights.[4] Avoiding sick leave during pregnancy is implicitly constructed as a matter of will and mentality. This strategy may be risky to employ, however, because over-estimation of physical conditions may backfire in the case of sudden withdrawal from a project, leaving already over-worked colleagues and partners with the hassle of covering highly personalized competence, tasks and responsibilities.

Another strategy is to work a certain amount during parental leave and keep in touch with colleagues and partners as well as cultivating client relations. Symbolically, this strategy also is associated with demonstrating the capacity, determination, devotion and ability to make room for work and to keep up the commitment to the career and firm despite the physical absence. Additionally, it signals the wish and will to refrain from making full use of the legally established welfare rights of parental leave.

When returning from parental leave to full-time work, a commonly used strategy is to minimize conversations on child-related and domestic topics, and to carefully select those people at work with which such conversations are 'safe' – that is people who do not render family commitment as an inherent signifier of compromised job dedication. To manage work demands with their new care responsibilities, many turn to the strategy of speeding up their already efficient and high-speed work routines, by cutting down on sociability at work, only to discover that this may have the contrary implication of fortifying the othering in terms of being categorized as a worker at the margins.

Yet another strategy is to arrange for a conversation with significant managers and partners, emphasizing the determination to continue on the career track after parental leave. A request can be made for an individual arrangement for career development towards partnership assessment at a somewhat reduced pace, with some slack in billing demands during the most intensive care period after parental leave. Among those who actually manage to obtain such an individual 'parent track' to partnership, several have found that the firm breaks the agreement. In some cases, employers explicitly withdraw the offer. In other cases, the time for partnership assessment is considerably pushed forward, implying that the period of slack is cancelled. In practice, no initiatives or measures are taken in order to implement the 'parent track' plan.

At one level, the purpose of these individual strategies is to arrange for career demands to be met during pregnancy, parental leave and the first period as a working mother, by attempting to manipulate oneself or conditions at home or at work. At a symbolic level, the 'de-mothering' strategies may be interpreted as signs of persistent commitment to the career contract and messages of not having defected to 'involved mothering'. The success of these strategies is variable, however. Based on the experiences of the interviewees, it seems as if these strategies are necessary but not sufficient to stay on the A-team. The only mothers who escaped being 'mothered' and obtained partnership or felt convinced that they were still on the partner track – met one or several of the following criteria: They were considered to be 'super girls' by virtue of unique and unrivalled competences in their fields,[5] and/or had brought in particularly attractive clients with which they have a highly personalized relationship. Moreover, these mothers made sure to communicate at work their dissociation from care encumbrance; they had managed to downsize their care responsibility compared to most other mothers by hiring au pairs or live-in-nannies and/or by practising a division of labour at home where their husbands shared or took the bulk of care- and domestic work.

The experience of being 'mothered' and othered entails a decrease in recognition, loss of self-confidence, professional demotivation, and disappointment in both superiors and mentors. In short, they feel that there is a gap between the input and output side of the career contract, and that to continue in the firm will be more trouble than it is worth. Additionally, they lose the faith that their employers will ever understand, acknowledge – and much less implement – changes needed to include involved parents in the partner track. This is coupled with feeling inadequate and unable to fulfil the demands for 'irreplaceability' of both career and motherhood (Halrynjo and Lyng, 2009). This negative spiral eventually leads to the strategy of leaving the firm for a job where the career contract comes with lower expectations – both on input and output sides – but where motherhood does not automatically represent a downgrading to a marginalized category of a second class worker:

> *Either I play for the A-team where I can be a part of doing fun things, or I can't be bothered working there, and then I'd rather play for the A-team at some other workplace.*
>
> Female Senior Associate

Visible mothers – invisible fathers: Gendered meanings of parenthood

To sum up, the othering of mothers in these prestigious law firms is accomplished through ambiguous mechanisms of both visibilizing and invisibilizing. When visibilized as (m)others, competence, capacities, efforts and merit are invisibilized. Conversely, in situations, like evaluations, where motherhood could have been visibilized in order to acknowledge that pregnancy and/or parental leave represent periods of reduced opportunities to assert oneself in the internal competition, motherhood is rather invisibilized and given equal status as any other reason for not making this year's A-team billing standards. When their membership in the category mother is explicitly or implicitly activated, this is perceived as overshadowing membership of the category A-team player. For some, the explicit visibilization of motherhood seems to imply an impregnable otherness that feels impossible to escape or challenge:

> *I'm surprised that a part of my career plan at work is supposed to be this role as a mother. (...) I feel that there are some norms or something there. So it doesn't help to try harder here, in a way.*
> Female Junior Associate

The experience of being othered when having children is perceived and described as a gender specific process of being 'mothered'. Male colleagues escape this automatic othering when entering parenthood; they are not 'fathered' in similar ways:

> *I've discovered that at work I very much become a 'mother', while the dads are not as much 'dads'. And I think – there are, of course, some dads with young children here – and I don't get it – perhaps the wives do more in the household?*
> Female Junior Associate

Fathers do not experience being othered upon having children. Membership of the category 'father' does not imply altered expectations in terms of reduced career dedication, capacity, willingness nor opportunity to fulfil the career contract and stay on the A-team. Rather, it takes explicit visibility-work for fathers to be associated with care responsibility. And even when such work is undertaken, the dominating non-encumbered meaning of fatherhood may be highly resistant. While fathers escape the automatic othering when entering parenthood, however, the gender stereotypes are not strong enough to provide immunity to men. When they engage in practices associated with involved parenthood even male lawyers run the risk of othering or entering into the limbo position of 'unpredictable worker'. This finding parallels studies showing that when fathers are encumbered in ways typical for mothers, this affects their career chances in corporate law (Collier, 2005) and other occupations and supports the notion that the unencumbered ideal worker is a vital structuring principle in the distribution of material privileges, regardless of gender (Halrynjo, 2009).

Work-family policies entailing incentives such as economic compensation, a sense of entitlement and even 'mild coercion' provide high commitment professionals in the Nordic welfare states with far better opportunities to take parental leave compared to their peers in other countries (Brandth and Kvande, 2001; Børve, 2007; Lewis, 1996; Sommerlad and Sanderson, 1998). Nevertheless, as demonstrated in the case of mothers in this sample, there is still room for symbolic distinction by settling for less than one is entitled to. The principle that the degree to which one makes use of parental rights may function as a signifier of degree of commitment to work and the firm also applies to fathers. Although the part of the 'father's quota' not used by the father is subtracted from the couple's total parental leave, it is far from taken-for-granted that male corporate lawyers make full use of their quota. Longer leaves are considered rare:

We have, you know, a co-worker who's at home on – well, he is a very nice guy – who's on paternity leave (...). He's going to muck around at home with a pram until Christmas.

Male Partner

The few fathers in junior positions that have taken up somewhat more than the 'father's quota' with their first child, considered that it took such an immense effort to get back on track afterwards, that they decided to minimize their parental leave with the second child to avoid a second time of running the risk of being excluded from the A-team:

You get those second-hand consequences where you feel that 'Oh crap, I'm lagging behind now compared to the others. Could I, you know, be bothered doing this anymore?' And I'm talking here as a man who hasn't had one of those long parental leaves. What about those who, yeah,

usually women, you know, who take a leave for a year – and maybe not only one year, but perhaps two years, because they've had two children.
Male Senior Associate

A few of the male partners in the sample had recently taken up several months of parental leave, related to setting up a family for the second time. These were highly merited and felt secure in their status within their partnership, however, and did not consider that they ran any career related risk by enjoying this opportunity to invest in the relationship with their youngest children – in contrast to their first-time fathering practices. One of them even called his leave 'my half-year sabbatical – which bears associations with 'deserved time for personal self-realisation after years of significant effort' rather than 'making use of entitled rights to tend to parental care responsibility'.

Dominant discourses: Individualizing and gender essentializing female drop-out

Regardless of positions, informants share the observation and evaluation that children affect men's and women's careers differently. The 'baby bar' is recognized as the main obstacle to enhancing the female proportion in the upper echelons. As this manager states becoming a mother is regarded as the beginning of the end of women's careers in corporate law firms:

The common way for women to leave is that they take maternity leave, then they come back for a short while, but then they quit.
Male HR Manager

Nevertheless, except from the few fathers with similar experiences, most of the male lawyers and managers seem oblivious to the othering mechanisms that the mothers are subject to. This is even the case with mothers who are partners or still regard themselves on the partner track. When explaining the gender specific drop-out and lack of female advancement, they rather employed essentialist discourses of sex/gender[6] differences and individual preferences. In these accounts, *attitude* is the magical word; given status as the vital distinction between stayers versus quitters. When entering parenthood, mothers are confronted with their 'mother's instinct' and children and family becomes more important to women than to men. Conversely, the drive for competing and the need for professional victories, rewards and recognition are generally stronger for men than for women, and are left unaffected by fatherhood. Moreover, women lack the 'guts' to believe that parenthood and career is compatible. In this manner, discourses of sex/gender differences and individual preferences are interwoven to an explanatory construction where losing the required, individual career attitude is something that naturally, and essentially, happens to women when having children:

All the way up to senior associate level there's probably an equal distribution. (...). At the partner level we have three female partners out of 23. And it's clear that this is historically contingent, and partially culturally contingent that it in a way – there are girls who don't want to make a commitment. (...) It is of course – it's about, you know, when you are at that level , or at that level at that age, then you have children and then instead of giving less priority to the children and the family, there are quite a few who actually prioritise their children and family. (...) It's mostly a question of attitude. And also a little bit the ability to in a way – to have the ability to make practical accommodations. An attitude and a will, kind of.

Male Partner

I believe that if one first sees that one enjoys being a lawyer, and would like to remain at a law firm, then there is nothing – it is really mostly a question of attitude, if one then says that this is something one wants and signals that, and works when one works, but that one takes leave and follows the child up, and so forth, but that one simply signals that one wants to have both things. (...) That one dares to say that one wants both things. As long as one does in fact want both things. Because I believe there are many who after they have had children think that it is too difficult to combine, and that they therefore suddenly don't want a career.

Female Partner

This explanatory construction allows for ignoring and invisibilizing the processes of othering related to motherhood, and frames the mechanisms that produce a gender unequal outcome as operating independently of cultural and structural features of work organizations. On the one hand, the disproportionate drop-out of women in their firm and line of business is situated within a wider and more general context of biological and/or societal and cultural sex/gender differences. On the other hand, the decision of whether to stay or quit is strictly personal, dependent on each individual's attitude.

Hence, when the 'up-and-go career contract' clashes with involved parenthood, what is made visible is neither the career contract nor the gendered division of care responsibility. Rather, gender is explicitly highlighted as a way of explaining – and legitimizing – an unequal pattern of exclusion that would otherwise emerge as illegitimate and potentially disturbing in organizations supposedly constructed as 'pure' meritocracies. While discourses of gender differences are not activated in terms of men and women per se possessing characteristics that are compatible versus incompatible with the career contract, these dominant discourses of gender specific impacts of parenthood reinforce the gender based 'othering' of parents: the taken-for-granted assumptions that mothers are ineligible for partner track while male workers may – almost safely – be regarded as exempt from the kind of care responsibilities that collides with A-team membership. In times of gender balance of workers in junior positions, gender as a sorting principle among workers with children represents implicit economization and simplification of the procedures involved when identifying 'ups' and 'outs'. Rather than having to deal with a situation where all workers – both women and men – entering parenthood must be viewed as in a limbo position from which it is uncertain whether what comes out on the other side is a still-dedicated or defected A-team member, the continued gendering of care responsibility provides stability and predictability to selection processes. What remains strikingly invisible and concealed in dominant discourses, however, is the continued *(re)construction* of the 'up-and-go career contract' as incompatible with involved parenthood as well as the premise that if you have a family, you need a partner to take main responsibility at home:

> *Obviously, no on goes in and starts as an assistance lawyer in a large law firm – or likewise starts as a broker in a large brokerage firm – without at some point or another having a bit of a rough patch in your relationship or marriage because of that. Because it sucks so much out of you, and it takes so much energy, and you're away so much, and you're at work so much, and you're supposed to juggle so many balls, and be on top in relations at all levels really, that there's a price socially and for the family person. And (...) if you haven't met the right lady – or man, if that's the case – then you're off and running, you know, grinding it out every evening, and then something can go awry. And it's very important that you plan ahead. (...). There's a lot that has to be sacrificed, and in many ways that's a part of the deal you have to commit to. (...) if you're heading toward the top it takes a whole lot, and then you should have*

things in order at home and try to surround yourself with positive people who back you up and don't suck your spinal marrow. (...) If I go to work at eight and come home 10–12 hours later, we can't have crying about it day-in-and-day-out. You have to have that sorted out.

Male Partner

Prospects of visibilizing and 'de-othering' care responsibility

As pointed out by Simpson and Lewis (2005: 1270), when positioned outside the norm, to be invisible implies lack of power. Hence, gaining recognition and challenging the normative state may require increased visibility. What are the prospects of the othered mothers (and fathers) making themselves visible and challenging the normative career contract? I find several factors counteracting such a process of making the invisible visible. First, these work organizations lack collective arenas and cultures for discussing employee interests and problems, that might have been channels and forces of voicing and negotiating the claim for care-compatible careers. Initiating or participating in informal discussions among colleagues where experiences of othering or criticism of the prevailing career design are articulated, entails the risk of being categorized and othered as the 'whiner'. Such a 'defensive' and 'problem oriented' self-presentation is considered devastating for future career prospects. Enacting the norm of the specific subcultures of these lawyers' work places as well as social circles and networks requires presentations of self as competent, resourceful, successful, high-powered, positive, results-oriented, independent, self-sufficient, energetic, self-confident and in control of the situation. Some women have been invited by the management to take part in *ad-hoc* committees set up to work out measures to enhance the female proportion and prevent the gender specific drop-out. Encouraged by the appointment to such committees, they nevertheless felt that their explication of problems and obstacles in the work culture and organization did more harm than good to their career chances: They were 'outed' as 'whiners'. Furthermore, none of these initiatives reported by informants had ever been brought to an end – much less resulted in implementation of measures. As described above, even a 'pro-active' request for an individual arrangement to combine motherhood with partner track is a highly risky endeavour. While the intention is to signal uninterrupted career dedication, visibilizing and drawing attention to one's 'special needs' as a mother may just as likely imply that one's professional merits and potential is invisibilized.

When mothers leave their firm, the experiences of othering are not communicated to superiors, not even in the cases where 'farewell interviews' are arranged. Preserving a positive relationship with their former employer – in case of a future business relation or maybe even re-employment when the children are older – is considered irreconcilable with voicing the experience of being excluded. In the research interviews for this study, despite giving detailed accounts of othering, the mothers nevertheless identify with dominant discourses and are reluctant to place responsibility on their employers. In accordance with their superiors, male colleagues and the mothers who have maintained a place on the A-team, they voice the discourse of the career contract being naturally and intrinsically incompatible with involved parenthood. Additionally, they draw on discourses of motherhood prompting a modification in their personal preferences when accounting for the reasons for finding a job more compatible with child care responsibilities (Halrynjo and Lyng, 2009).

Last but not least, the othered mothers' lack of faith in employers' commitment to improving the conditions for work/family balance is highly substantiated. While partnership and managers of these firms do acknowledge the pressure to increase the conspicuously low number of women at senior levels, they reject organizational changes that would imply downsizing the career contract to a version more compatible with involved parenting. Rather than acknowledging care responsibility as a norm for parents – regardless of gender – they favour strategies that help mothers 'de-encumber' and outsource family work:

> *Well, we're trying to do as good a job as we can; we're trying to make accommodations to increase the number of female partners. But that doesn't mean that we're going to lower our demands or things like that. But there's flexibility and there's opportunities. But this is now largely about having girls who are – who are willing to do it, you know. And who see the – who see practical opportunities and that you are willing to work a lot and buy help. And it also has to be in a way accepted that you – yeah, buy help.*
> Male Partner

Conclusion

This chapter has examined processes of (in)visibility of gender and care responsibility in the highly gendered othering of parents in Norwegian corporate law firms. When entering parenthood, female lawyers are subject to a process of being 'mothered': explicit and implicit categorization, practices and mechanisms implying exclusion from the A-team, despite their employment of counter-strategies in attempts to 'de-mother' themselves and demonstrate continued dedication to the 'up-and-go career contract'. When becoming visible as mothers, their professional competence, capacities, efforts and merits are invisibilized. Male colleagues escape this automatic othering: they are not 'fathered' in similar ways. The processes of othering of workers with care responsibilities are left invisible and unchallenged by dominant discourses. In these discourses gender is made explicitly visible when explaining why women – as opposed to men – 'choose' to leave the A-team for less demanding, less prestigious and less economically rewarding jobs when having children. This explanatory construction further preserves taken-for-granted assumptions that mothers are ineligible for partner track while fathers may (almost safely) be regarded as exempt from the kind of care responsibilities that collides with the demands of the career contract. Correspondingly, the ideal worker norm is reproduced as incompatible with involved parenthood.

The female lawyers in my study report that entering the reproductive phase of their lives represents their first encounter with gender as a principle of exclusion and as a barrier at work. They draw a picture of their first years in corporate law as a period in which gender is hardly experienced as an issue; where female and male lawyers in junior positions are peers on the same A team and on an equal footing in terms of prospective possibilities and career chances. This description contrasts with conclusions commonly drawn in studies of gender barriers in law. Whether the gender specificity of the ideal worker norm on both junior and senior levels has been blurred or diluted is still an issue in need for further exploration in high commitment work organizations in Norway as well as in other countries. However, it appears that the female lawyers in this Norwegian sample (re)produce versions of femininity compatible with fulfilling the 'up-and-go career contract' and staying on the A-team – until they enter motherhood.

Indeed, it certainly requires work of self-discipline as well as emotional and moral labour to accomplish a continued self-presentation demonstrating control, competitiveness, profit orientation, aggressiveness, ruthlessness and cold calculating logic. Unspoken pressure to assimilate (Sommerlad and Sanderson, 1998: 122) is directed towards lawyers of both genders. It is of high importance for research to make visible and challenge such taken-for-granted discourses and practices – as well as their consequences for individuals, social groups, organizations and societies. Notwithstanding this, the findings in this chapter give reason to raise the question of whether these elements traditionally associated with a male norm should still be the main focus when studying why career women leave corporate law firms in disproportionate numbers.

While the 'baby bar' is recognized as a significant factor in reproducing women's subordinate position in the legal profession (McGlynn, 1999; Sommerlad and Sanderson, 1998; Wass and McNabb, 2006), existing studies tend to subsume the exclusion of caregivers under a more general exclusion of the 'other' gender. Though often empirically overlapping, there is nevertheless a need to separate analytically between gender and care responsibility as principles of othering and exclusion. This is further emphasized by the observation that the few fathers that actually engage in practices associated with involved parenthood have experiences of othering similar to mothers. Such a division is a matter not only of analytical precision; it also carries significance for the design of institutional as well as intra-organizational policies. Measures that may enhance women's advancement do not necessarily increase the participation of involved parents. Rather, the strategies favoured by representatives of partnerships concentrate on 'de-encumbering' women in ways that work directly opposite to the inclusion of both male and female caregivers.

It has been suggested that the masculine norm represents a *symbolic* barrier while domestic responsibilities constitute a *practical* and *material* barrier to women's advancement within the legal profession (Bolton and Muzio, 2007). However, the analysis in this chapter shows that encumbrance related to reproduction represents a breach of the career contract on practical, material as well as symbolic levels. Hence, a fruitful analytic distinction must acknowledge the ways in which involved parenthood is symbolically (re)constructed as incompatible with career. In effect, I propose that care responsibility may even be understood as a more profound symbolic principle of othering and internal closure mechanisms in high commitment, commercial law firms. Inclusion in senior positions, of women assimilating to the norm of non-encumbrance, either by childlessness or outsourcing childcare, does not represent a severe challenge to privileges, rewards nor work- and lifestyles of the elite segments of these work organizations. In contrast, the inclusion of women – or men – with a more balanced work/family adaptation, holds potential for compromising both economically and symbolically distinguishing rewards, privileges and practices associated with partner positions. Implicit and explicit discourses, practices and strategies of contemporary Norwegian corporate law firms seem to reflect that for guardians of the prevailing 'up-and-go career contract', the fear of women is minor to the fear of involved parents.

Notes

1 This chapter is based on a research project financed by the **Norwegian Research Council (Programme on Working Life Research) and the Norwegian Bar Association**. I would like to thank the Editors, Jorun Solheim, Dag Album and Sigtona Halrynjo for valuable comments and suggestions.
2 The large firms may have up to five levels in the organization hierarchy: junior associate, senior associate, senior lawyer, junior partner and partner.
3 Norwegian parents are entitled to a total parental leave of 44 weeks with full wage compensation. Nine weeks are reserved for the mother (the last three weeks before estimated delivery date and six weeks after childbirth). A specific 'father's quota' was introduced in 1993 (four weeks) extended to five weeks in 2005, six weeks in 2006 and will be further extended to ten weeks in June 2009. The remaining weeks are to be divided between the parents at their own discretion. However, in line with the main pattern among Norwegian parents, the uptake of parental leave within traditional elite professions is highly gendered: The average is approximately one month for fathers, while mothers take the rest (Halrynjo and Lyng, 2009).
4 If a pregnant woman works until birth, the three weeks of maternity leave prior to estimated delivery date are lost.
5 Several of these 'super girls' had obtained a PhD degree in law, which is rare in the context of Norwegian law firms.
6 Some contend that these differences between men and women are biologically determined, while others specify that they believe that differences are shaped by gender specific socialization. However, all these discourses indicate that when having children, men and women – either by biology or socialization – typically and essentially have different preferences regarding care and career.

References

Acker, J. (1990) 'Hierarchies, jobs, bodies: A theory of gendered organizations', *Gender and Society*, 4(2): 139–158.
Acker, J. (1998) 'The future of "gender and organizations": Connections and boundaries', *Gender, Work and Organization*, 5(4): 195–206.
Blair-Loy, M. (2001) 'It's not just what you know, it's who you know: Technical knowledge, rainmaking and gender among finance executives', *Research in the Sociology of Work*, 10: 51–83.
Blair-Loy, M. (2003) *Competing Devotions: Career and Family Among Women Executives*. Cambridge, MA: Harvard University Press.
Bolton, S. (2004) 'Conceptual confusions: Emotion work as skilled work', in C. Warhurst, E. Keep and I. Grugulis (eds) *The Skill That Matters*, pp. 19–37. Basingstoke: Palgrave.

Bolton, S. and Muzio, D. (2007) 'Can't live with 'em: Can't live without 'em: Gendered segmentation in the legal profession', *Sociology*, 41(1): 311–326.
Børve, H. E. (2007) 'Pregnant bodies: Norwegian female employees in global working life', *European Journal of Women's Studies*, 14(4): 311–326.
Brandth, B. and Kvande, E. (2001) 'Flexible work and flexible fathers', *Work, Employment and Society*, 15(2): 251–267.
Brandth, B. and Kvande, E. (2002) 'Reflexive Fathers: Negotiating Parental Leave and Working Life', *Gender, Work and Organization*, 9(2): 186–203.
Cockburn, C. (1991) *In the Way of Women*. London: Macmillan Education Ltd.
Collier, R. (2005) *Male Lawyers and the Negotiation of Work and Family Commitments: A Report to the British Academy*. Newcastle: University of Newcastle Upon Tyne.
Connell, R. W. (1995) *Masculinities*. Cambridge: Polity Press.
Coser, L. A. (1974) *Greedy Institutions: Patterns of Undivided Commitment*. New York: Free Press.
Davies, C. (1996) 'The sociology of the professions and the profession of gender', *Sociology*, 30(4): 661–678.
Gulbrandsen, T., Engelstad, F., Klausen, T., Skjeie, H., Teigen, M. and Østerud, Ø. (2002) *Norske makteliter* [Norwegian power elites]. Oslo: Gyldendal Akademisk.
Halrynjo, S. (2008) *Kjønn, karriere og omsorgsansvar blant jurister. [Gender, career and care responsibility in the legal profession]*. Oslo: Work Research Institute/The Norwegian Association of Lawyers.
Halrynjo, S. (2009) Men's Work–life Conflict: Career, Care and Self-realization: Patterns of Privileges and Dilemmas', *Gender, Work and Organization*, 16(1): 98–125.
Halrynjo, S. and Lyng, S. T. (2008) 'Kjønnet permisjonspraksis, kjønnet arbeid familiemønster og kjønnede karrierestrukturer. Om konsekvenser av graviditet og foreldrepermisjon i høytutdanningsyrker' [Gendered parental leave practice, gendered pattern of work-family adaptations and gendered career structures. On consequences of pregnancy and parental leave in elite professions], in Egeland. C. et al, *Erfaringer med og konsekvenser av graviditet og uttak av foreldrepermisjon i norsk arbeidsliv*. [Pregnancy and parental leave in Norwegian working life: experiences and consequences]. Oslo: Work Research Institute.
Halryngo, S. and Lyng, S. T. (2009) 'Preferences, constraints or schemas of devotion? Exploring Norwegian mothers' withdrawals from high-commitment careers', *British Journal of Sociology*, 60(2): 321–343.
Hanlon, G. (1998) Professionalism as enterprise: Service class politics and the redefinition of professionalism', *Sociology*, 32(1): 43–63.
Harrington, M. (1993) *Women Lawyers: Rewriting the Rules*. New York: Alfred A. Knopf.
Hochschild, A. R. (1997) *The Time Bind: When Work Becomes Home and Home Becomes Work*. New York: Metropolitan Books.
Kimmel, M., Hearn, J. and Connell, R. W. (2005) 'Introduction', in Kimmel, M., Hearn, J. and Connell, R. W. (eds) *Handbook of Studies on Men and Masculinities*, pp. 1–12. Thousand Oaks, CA: Sage.
Lewis, P. (2006) 'The quest for invisibility: Female entrepreneurs and the masculine norm of entrepreneurship', *Gender, Work and Organization*, 13(5): 453–469.
Lewis, S. (1996) 'Sense of entitlement, family friendly policies and gender', in Holt, H. and Thaulow, I. (eds) *Reconciling Work and Family Life: An International Perspective on the Role of Companies*. Copenhagen: The Danish National Institute of Social Research.

London, M. and Stumpf, S. (1982) *Managing Careers*. Reading, Mass: Addison Wesley.

Lyng, S. T. (2007) 'Is there more to "antischoolishness" than masculinity? On multiple Student styles, gender and educational self-exclusion in secondary school', *Men and Masculinities*, Online First, May 18, 2007, doi: 10.1177/ 1097184X06298780.

Lyng, S. T. (2008) *Opp eller ut? En kvalitativ undersøkelse av kvinnelige advokaters vei ut av bransjen og utfordringer knyttet til a[o] kombinere karriere og omsorgsansvar.* [Up or out? A qualitative study of drop-out among female corporate lawyers and issues of work/family balance]. Oslo: Work Research Institute/The Norwegian Bar Association.

Mason, M. A. and Ekman, E. M. (2007) *Mothers on the Fast Track: How a New Generation Can Balance Family and Careers*. New York: Oxford University Press.

McGlynn, C. (1999) *The Woman Lawyer*. London: Butterworths.

Norwegian Bar Association (2008) *Rapport fra bransjeundersøkelsen 2007* [Report from the Norwegian Lawyer Survey 2007]. Oslo: Norwegian Bar Association.

NSSDS (2007) Student Statistics 2007. Information on Research and Higher Education (DBH), Norwegian Social Sciences Data Services http://dbh.nsd.uib.no/rapporter/nokkeltall/studenter_visning.action.

Pierce, J. T. (1995) *Gender Trials: Emotional Lives in Contemporary Law Firms*. CA: University of California Press.

Rosenbaum, J. E. and Miller, S. R. (1996) 'Moving in, up, or out: Tournaments and other signals of career attainments', in Arthur, M. B. and Rousseau, D. M. (eds) *The Boundaryless Career*. New York: Oxford University Press.

Segal, L. (1987) *Is the Future Female? Troubled Thoughts on Contemporary Feminism*. New York: Peter Bedrick Books.

Simpson, R. and Lewis, P. (2005) 'An investigation of silence and a scrutiny of transparency: Re-examining gender in organization literature though the concepts of voice and visibility', *Human Relations*, 58(10): 1253–1275.

Sommerlad, H. (2002) 'Women solicitors in a fractured profession: Intersections of gender and professionalism in England and Wales', *International Journal of the Legal Profession*, 9(3): 213–234.

Sommerlad, H. and Sanderson, P. (1998) *Gender, Choice and Commitment: Women Solicitors in England and Wales and the Struggle for Equal Status*. London: Ashgate.

Thornton, M. (1996) *Dissonance and Distrust: Women in the Legal Profession*. Melbourne: Oxford University Press.

Wajcman, J. (1998) *Managing Like a Man: Women and Men in Corporate Management*. St Leonards: Allen and Unwin.

Wass, V. and McNabb, R. (2006) 'Pay, promotion and parenthood among women solicitors', *Work, Employment and Society*, 20(2): 289–308.

Williams, J. (2000) *Unbending Gender*. New York: Oxford.

5
Organizing Entrepreneurship? Women's Invisibility in Self-employment

Deborah Kerfoot and Caroline Miller

Introduction

Entrepreneurship in the UK, advanced not least by the British government and other agencies, encourages enterprise and innovation. For example, the Department of Trade and Industry (DTI) claims to:

> Promote enterprise, innovation and increased productivity – in particular by encouraging successful business start-ups, and by increasing the capacity of business including SME's to grow, to invest, to develop skills, to adopt best practice... [it is] UK policy to promote enterprise...and is seen to be of key importance in terms of employment, and wealth creation, and poverty alleviation. (DTI Website, www.dti.gov.uk).

This is especially the case with respect to women, who are depicted as representing a hitherto largely 'untapped' resource for future economic growth and development. The OECD (1998), for example, claims that the growth and presence of women entrepreneurs in SMEs is increasingly important to the global economy. Similarly, in the United States, 'the concept of micro-enterprise has been widely praised in the public and private sectors as, one of the hottest anti-poverty strategies' (Gugliotta, 1993, cited in Ehlers and Main, 1998: 425).

The evidence for what appears to be women's reluctance to participate in self-employment seems to be overwhelming. In the UK in 2005, 3.6 million people were self-employed, equating to 12% of all those in employment: 16% of all men in employment were self-employed as opposed to only 7% of all women in employment. Approximately three quarters of the 3.6 million self-employed were male. This proportion remains largely unchanged since the 1980s.

Whilst theorists reviewing the position of entrepreneurship with respect to women have produced diverse explanations as to the persistence of women's minority position, there has been comparatively less challenge to the traditional definition of entrepreneurship. Recent scholarship has sought to stress the significance of gender in understanding entrepreneurship and has highlighted the extent to which the masculinity embedded in entrepreneurship has led to 'male' and 'entrepreneur' becoming synonymous (Ahl, 2002; Bruni *et al*, 2004a, 2004b). Entrepreneurs have conventionally been considered to possess masculine characteristics: opportunism, adventurousness, restlessness, pro-activity and the ability to innovate (Burns and Harrison, 1996). Entrepreneurship is also thought to require ambition, energy, flair, need for achievement, risk taking, positive attitude and adaptability (Phillipson, 1995), strong leadership qualities, competitiveness and confidence. These characteristics are stereotypically associated with men rather than women (Green and Cohen, 1995).

Carter suggests that 'the absolute rise in female self-employment appears to have been largely caused by the overall increase in the number of women in the labour market as a whole' (Carter, 2000: 167). UK figures for the proportion of women in self-employment appear consistent with other European states where, 'males in six countries have a higher probability of self-employment than women. The countries and effects are as follows; Spain (+7.8%), Ireland (+6.4%), Italy (+10.8%), UK (+5.3%), Austria (+4.4%) and Sweden (+5.8%)' (Small Business Service Report, 2003). A UK Federation of Small Business report (FSB, 2004) showed that 9% of businesses are wholly owned by women, compared with 44% owned by men and 42% owned by both men and women. Men are around two and a half times more likely to be self-employed small business owners than women (UK Global Entrepreneurship Report, 2001).

From these statistics, it is evident that men in the UK are much more likely than women to be self-employed although explanations for women and men's differential participation rates vary. Despite this inclusion of women in studies of entrepreneurship, less attention has been devoted to theorising the ways in which entrepreneurship takes place in the context of gendered work. Research evidence is grouped into three main strands of argument. Accepting that such research is not neatly categorized, broadly, the first identifies barriers to entry for women in business; a second considers women's orientation to business and entrepreneurship activity; a third explores entrepreneurship in the context of gendered work.

Barriers to entry

One group of academics (Birley, 1989; Allen and Trueman, 1993 and Carter, 2000) have cited a variety of reasons for women's low take up of entrepreneurship as a career option. A significant factor is argued to be finance. Most finance agreements that rely on joint collateral to raise cash require a husband or partner to act as signatory, especially when women borrow against property. Similarly, limitations on access to loans are imposed by institutions such as banks, finance houses, and venture capitalists, as women are reported to experience credibility problems when dealing with financial institutions (Carter and Rosa, 1998). Gender specific barriers to accessing both informal and formal business funding have been discussed in the work of Carter and Rosa (ibid) and Marlow (2002). A further factor is women's perceived lack of training, knowledge, business skills, personal capacities and relevant work experience (Schwartz, 1976; Watkins and Watkins, 1984).

Carter (2000) suggests that it can be difficult for women to accrue the building blocks of entrepreneurship such as management competencies in for example, marketing, finance, human relations, or the technical skills of product/service knowledge and market or industry needs as many women are more likely than men to experience discontinuous careers because of other commitments or by limitations imposed by institutions such as the family. Time and spatial mobility are often restricted because of other commitments such as child or elder care, 'an environmental restriction', which may limit the female entrepreneurs 'mobility' (Ardener, 1993). In a study by Eckenrode and Gore (1990) it was found that organizing childcare, household chores and professional responsibilities were a great source of stress and conflict for women who worked. This in turn was thought to impact on women's capacity to form networks of contacts that might advance their enterprise. Women are said to have few role models as there are, to date, few successful women business owners nationally to emulate (DTI, 2005), whilst locally, they are often invisible.

Social attitudes towards women entrepreneurs and cultural restrictions are said to further inhibit women's take up of small business (Fay, 2002), though it is suggested that there are exceptions to this. National intervention by central government has explicitly targeted the removal of entry barriers for women. Supported programmes such as Shell Livewire offer assistance to 16–30 year olds in developing business, providing mentors and advice (www.shell-livewire.org). The Phoenix Fund offers development funds, venture funds and loan guarantees (www.sbs.gov.uk/phoenix). The Women In Enterprise Programme aims to encourage new starters to seek advice and information, and acts as a signposting and networking service (www.womeninenterprise.com). Practical assistance is proffered by SBS Incubation who help access suitable premises, finance and 'hands-on' support, (www.iwight.com/isle_womens/funding_support), Train2000(www.train2000.org.uk) and Prowess (www.prowess.org.uk). These, in combination with equal rights policies and campaigns to reduce barriers to entry (for example: The Know Your Place Campaign which encourages women to consider working in non-traditional roles for women) in order to create a 'level playing field' such that women may become self-employed on the same terms as men.

One of the common barriers to entry cited by women who want to start-up in business is recounted as a conflict between work and family life (Liff and Ward, 2001). Often the focus of this dichotomy is on the physical aspects of managing a 'double day' (Hochschild, 1997). We return to this theme in our discussion of the interview data.

Women's orientation: bringing gender into entrepreneurship

Reliance on socialization as an explanation for women's orientation towards and differential take-up of entrepreneurship underpins the work of Goffee and Scase (1985) in delineating four types of female entrepreneur. Largely working-class women with discontinuous work histories, 'conventionals' were seen as committed both to traditional gender roles and to entrepreneurship. 'Innovators' were mainly professional women regarded as committed to entrepreneurship as a way of expanding their career opportunities but not committed to conventional gender roles. 'Domestics' were women attached to gender roles for whom entrepreneurship was an add-on to their domestic priorities. 'Radicals' had little commitment to either gender roles or entrepreneurship and women's attachment in these ventures was more political. Whilst Goffee and Scase's attention to women's entrepreneurship explicitly set out to challenge 'popular conceptions of the position of women in society' (1987: 62) the construction of gender roles and entrepreneurship as oppositional categories had the effect of reinforcing the masculine orientation of the entrepreneurial ideal (Mirchandani 1999).

Later work has sought to explore the ways in which women 'do business differently' favouring small and stable businesses above growth orientated enterprises (Lee-Gosselin and Grise, 1990) and has highlighted the way that women in business can challenge the enterprise model, for example in their attachment to service business, where service is conceived not as transactional exchange for financial reward but as serving through relationships that can facilitate long-term caring bonds (Fenwick, 2002).

Gendered work

Recent debate on gender politics and gendered work rests on the theoretical development of the concepts of gender identity where gender is used as a verb rather than a noun. From this perspective, gender is a 'cultural performance' (Gherardi, 1995). 'Doing gender' is of salience where gender and entrepreneurship are culturally produced in everyday social practices. This theoretical turn illuminates a means by which gender difference and gender inequality are reproduced and sustained. The theoretical development of work on subjectivity and identity, influenced by the work of Foucault (1984, 1997) and poststructuralist theorizing has further opened up the field of enquiry. A result has been a marked shift in the debate on gender identity away from essentialist positions whilst simultaneously recognizing that predominant behaviours described in terms of masculinity can be enacted by both women and men. Whilst entrepreneurship remains associated with men, the construction of entrepreneurship and its relationship to masculinity is not simply enacted through male bodies. Entrepreneurship and gender are intertwined as representations of masculinity, some of which evince personal gain whilst others are more altruistic (Bruni *et al*, 2004a: 409). Here, subjectivities are to be understood as symbolic categories (Saco, 1992). In Bruni et al's work (2004a, 2004b) for example, a variety of subject positions born of a discourse of gender were sustained about what it means to be a 'real' entrepreneur. Their research found that definitions of entrepreneurship differed according to the organizational setting and to the people who took up, and in so doing transformed, entrepreneurial activity.

Revealing the extent to which gender can be seen as a cultural performance, this move away from essentialism further problematizes the existing concept of 'hegemonic masculinity' (Carrigan *et al*, 1987) as men's collusion to dominate women. Moreover, emphasis on the performative aspect of gender allows movement away from such universalism, whilst at the same time, recognizing the political and power effects of gender in organizational settings wherein masculine behaviours are privileged (Fenwick, 2002). In the case of self-employment business start-up under discussion in this chapter, the definition of entrepreneurship as a masculine domain is sustained by processes that position women and men differently in relation to the attributes and behaviours required of the successful entrepreneur. In addition, in responding to gender stereotypes of femininity, the women are, often unwittingly, active in sustaining definitions of entrepreneurship as 'men's work'.

As Bruni *et al* express it:

> If, in the classic literature, the features defining entrepreneurial figures are intrinsically connected with masculinity (the entrepreneur as the conqueror of unexplored territories, the lonely hero, the patriarch), more recent studies – even those examining female entrepreneurship – have also involuntarily contributed to a process of 'othering' the non-male, making masculinity invisible and sustaining a model of economic rationality alleged to be universal and agendered (2004a: 407).

Uncovering the mechanisms and processes by which gender is maintained in everyday practices, in the here and now, so to speak, creates the conditions under which change can be facilitated. This is to align with a political position on gender and with entrepreneurship, recognizing how such insight can show the ways that gender is both reproduced and sustained at the level of everyday practice. From such a perspective, gender is performed, enacted and constituted in intersubjective dynamics: 'Consider gender, for instance, as a corporeal style, an "act" as it were, which is both intentional and performative where "performative" suggests a dramatic and contingent construction of meaning' (Butler, 1990: 139).

The 'material actuality' of gender (Ransom, 1993) requires that gender difference be investigated by way of uncovering the conditions of its existence. For example, elsewhere in a case study of employment, Morgan and Knights (1991: 183) similarly found that 'although there was no formal bar, the culture developed...and social networks through which support was mobilized all ensured that women were unlikely to [seek opportunities] except in isolated cases'. In exploring the Self-Employment Access and Learning Programme under discussion, it is not our purpose to privilege the Programme as the *only* space in which entrepreneurship was sustained. Rather we draw on the Programme as a site for empirical research on entrepreneurship as gendered work.

Research context

In the vignette of a self-employment access and learning programme that follows, we present some discussion of a workshop for a would-be self-employed workforce. The research is part of a larger, three-year programme of work into self-employment. The research draws upon a number of methods including the use of documentary evidence, questionnaire data, participative and non-participative observation, and semi-structured in-depth interviews of between one and three hours conducted over one year with a total of 42 research respondents from a variety of self-employment programmes, including the Programme described here. For reasons of space, we present a brief selection of extracts from transcribed interviews on themes which came out of the research. The empirical research took place in the Midlands with subsequent follow-up interviews conducted throughout the Midlands, north and north-west of England. Ethnography generally 'implies fieldwork involving a sizeable amount of onsite observation' (Prasad, 1997: 102) yet is used in many different ways, and also applies to research undertaken in a local community which seeks to show how social action in that setting can be understood from the perspective of someone unused to that particular culture. Baszanger and Dodier (1997) consider ethnographic studies are carried out in order to understand the world as a field of emergent properties and suggest that this type of methodology calls for: an empirical approach; the researcher to remain open to elements and to code them in retrospect; and a concern for grounding the phenomena observed in the field. Briefer periods of exposure to the empirical material are currently sometimes denoted as ethnography (Atkinson and Hammersley, 1994; Silverman, 1997). 'Silverman [1997] goes furthest in this direction, describing ethnography as any research involving observation of events or actions in natural contexts, and which acknowledges the mutual dependence of theory and data' (Alvesson and Skoldberg, 2000: 45). Recognizing this mutual dependence of theory and data, our attraction to ethnography for the purposes of this study was the capacity for ethnography to introduce the reader to a new set of practices, values or beliefs, a result of which is that the reader is then able to make sense of something which might otherwise seem illogical.

Holliday (2002) suggests that a micro-ethnography or ethnographic type study could be carried out when there is insufficient time, access or opportunity for saturation. Willis considers that, 'In treating cultural experience as inherently formed through art...the ethnographic imagination recognizes that there are few unadorned "social messages" written on the surface of everyday cultural forms [and that] the latters embedded and localized meanings work through observable but often non-verbal modes of being and expression – that which only ethnographic techniques can record...' (Willis, 2000: 10).

In the research under discussion in this paper, a full ethnography was impossible due to the lone nature of the self-employed or small business starter and the lack of a geographic space in which to be situated in order to observe a given entrepreneurial community. Observing the self-employment programme provides a sense of place, as many of those interviewed were often merely contemplating start-up, were newly self-employed or doing occasional business informally 'on the side' accompanying paid employment in their employers' workspace. Many of the respondents were operating transitorily from places not normally conceived as workspaces. One woman did business on her computer in a cupboard under the stairs at home, surrounded by coats and shoes. Others had mobile businesses such as photography, webdesign, beautician and alternative therapy. Some worked from rooms at home designed for another purpose such as the bedroom, garage or dining room. Still others traded from their place of formal paid employment, covertly building an 'invisibusiness'.

Our analysis suggests that the conduct of the workshop and the construction of entrepreneurship deployed therein had the effect of sustaining gender division and reconstituting the entrepreneur as self-evidently male. Women participants in the research felt in no doubt as to their status as outsiders to the domain of entrepreneurship and, even before their self-employment could be further contemplated, the women had largely internalized their own exclusion from prospective entrepreneurship.

The case of a self-employment workforce

The Self-Employment Agency (hereafter, the Agency) is billed in its literature and publicity material as 'an Equal Opportunity Organisation committed to Lifelong Learning'. It forms part of a consortium of employment agencies in the UK providing free advice for those wanting to go into business on their own or to assist existing businesses who want to expand or who are experiencing problems of varying persuasions. The Agency was established in 1981, located in the UK Midlands and formed as an independent non-profit making organization sponsored by local businesses. The Agency is run by a Director with a support team of business advisors to provide business advice and training to prospective new and existing micro-business. The Self-Employment Access and Learning Programme, hereafter referred to as 'the Programme' forms the substance of our empirical research and consists of a programme of training for anyone considering starting a business. The Programme was chosen as a site for research insofar as it acts as gateway or entry portal for those wishing to begin self-employment. The Programme comprises a five-day course repeated at intervals for different cohorts of participants. Topics include markets, marketing and budgeting and the course culminates in a day-long session where participants are encouraged to present a business plan they have prepared during the Programme. The research took place at the invitation of the director of the Agency following a preliminary research interview. The course reported here took five day-long sessions, each from 9.30am to 4.30pm, spread over a two-week period and was located in a local business centre, owned by a major UK national bank.

Although the director of the Agency had previously stated that men and women usually attended the course in equal numbers, there were 13 men and five women on the Programme reported here. Later discussion with Agency employees and Programme tutors confirmed this ratio as not untypical of other cohorts, contradicting the director's information. Two of the women participants attended in the capacity of accompanying husbands wanting to start up a business, by way of offering support. One woman had left the Programme by lunchtime on the first day.

Day one

On arrival on the first morning, Sally introduced herself as tutor for the day and for an additional session where participants would cover marketing aspects of the course. The walls surrounding the seating and waiting area displayed accreditation certificates, Health and Safety regulations, approved training centre accreditation and various posters advocating the value of gaining new skills. Most featured men doing various tasks, for example, a man holding a wrench with machinery in the background entitled, 'I am happy to have started my own business', and a (male) electrician saying, he was now 'wired to self employment'. Sally explained that the Programme on small business start-up was informal and that the teaching style would be participative and relaxed with coffee breaks 'to allow for networking'. After stressing that the course was to be friendly and informal, participants were required to sign a register: Sally also gave a list of rules and regulations concerned with use of the building and facilities which caused some consternation amongst participants. She informed the group that the content of each session was pre-planned and that any informal discussion or 'disruption' was to the detriment of the planned agenda. There were no slides or visual aids as everything needed was in a pre-prepared printed workbook distributed on the first day. In discussion, Sally did not move from behind a desk nor shift her demeanour as tutor in charge. Questions were strictly controlled to half an hour at the end of the day. At no point did tutees venture to take either coffee or toilet break outside its correct slot in the Programme. Sally had provided a significant amount of paperwork to complete and pointed out that a number of Programme tutees had been sent from the Job Centre as they were 'over 45 years of age and were having trouble re-entering the job market'.

An afternoon session outlined the utility and relevance of the business bank account, premises, accountants and the business plan. Homework for the evening was to create a business plan for discussion on day three. A corporate video on marketing was also screened. This depicted men selling to men, and women shown were either in hierarchically subordinate positions assisting men or portrayed as stereotypically, 'difficult' in their behaviour. Though objectives were, on occasion, described as better if they were flexible, the main concern throughout the day was control of the business through planning, and that this planning should be supported by successive waves of plans drawn up, these having been assessed for faults.

Day two

Tutor Brendan was a white, middle class man aged about 50 years. Wearing a navy blue business suit, he explained that he had worked as a bank manager for 30 years before being made redundant. He had then worked as a business advisor for the agency for ten years. The day's topic was profit and loss and an overview of book keeping. Brendan stated that he did not like jargon, and promised an acronym-free day. He told anecdotes about business start-up and what he saw as its effects upon different sectors of the population. Brendan described what he regarded as young people's inability to get out of bed and that this was illustrative of the 'fact' that, as a business owner, 'you will only get out what you put in'. Brendan further underlined his views on the importance of reliability, inferring that this may be a problem for young people. Offering a lesson on the importance of dedication, he drew on the example of one business start-up that he said had forced a man to choose between his livelihood and his wife, as the wife liked to weekend away which was to the detriment of his business. Brendan also went through the pros and cons of different trading status, and problems of different choices of workplace. He discussed National Insurance, VAT, Tax and the necessity of employing accountants.

Legislation was described as able to invoke penalties, procedures and 'red tape' to make business start-up more complex. The tutor then went on at length to list extensive procedures required in setting up a business including taxation and VAT. He also listed the personality traits and personal qualities required of a small business owner. These were: confidence, optimism, drive, competitiveness, boldness, goal orientation, and the ability to innovate.

There was little or no discussion at the end of the session. At the close of the day, tutees quietly gathered their belongings and left.

Day three

On arrival the group discussed the previous sessions, the rules and regulations and the content of the Programme. Tutee Alan, found the numerical parts difficult and said that he felt like giving up as he knew his numeracy skills were 'not up to scratch' and had no-one to help him. Another, Liz, said that she was having problems with the language of business and had not felt able to ask for clarification for fear of exposure and embarrassment. Further, two women and one man had not arrived at all for day three and did not complete the rest of the course. Dave, John and Liz agreed that they had not recognized all the rules and regulations that tutor Brendan had outlined as existing to regulate small business. Dave and Liz were having second thoughts about starting up a business by this point.

Day three began with a visit from the accountants. Two male accountants gave a closely structured presentation entitled 'Why You Need An Accountant' which they emphasized was 'for the performance of compliance'. They discussed allowable and non-allowable tax-deductible expenses, the process of book keeping and paying tax, and VAT returns. Keen to offer themselves as specialists to a group of prospective small business owners, the accountants' message was that the small business owner was, at all times, to abide by the rules and regulations and was to ignore or overlook legal stipulations at his *(sic)* peril. They talked about the power of the tax office and 'the VAT man' to 'close your business and take your profits'. At once both advancing the scenario they described and offering themselves as its solution, the accountants neatly underlined the ineptitude of course participants as mere novices in the world of small business. Tutees were encouraged to agree with the accountants that the latter could be usefully deployed as a protective 'buffer' for the small business, emphasizing potential sanctions to the hapless small business owner who inadvertently 'gets it wrong'. Recounting scenarios of marriage break-up, nervous breakdown and bankruptcy, the accountants further suggested that they could help small businesses save money and constructed themselves as mediators between the taxation authority of the Inland Revenue and the unwitting or inexperienced newcomer.

The accountants left and tutor Brendan closed the day by encouraging course participants to take an active interest in their accounts. Despite Brendan's encouragement, tutees described feeling dependent upon more people than ever for their financial security, and on accounting professionals in particular.

Day four

Tutor Gary was white, and in his early 40s, dressed in a shirt and tie. He used a participative style of speech and encouraged questions. His session was on marketing and advertising which included a briefing on how to research competitors and market unique selling points. A (male) employee from the local library came to discuss sources of information available and the resources that libraries could offer to small business owners. Gary summarized, as he saw it, what self-employment could mean for individuals:

> The route to self employment is whatever you want it to be, 25 hours a week, reasonable car, laid back lifestyle or 60 hours a week, a Porsche or a Bentley, beating your brains out.

Tutees found Gary less controlling and enjoyed his departure from the set workbook. The session became spontaneous and lively, although Gary's continued sexual innuendo in speech seemed at odds with his role as tutor. A verbal slip by the researcher when observing the group resulted in Gary making the following comment:

> So you are lying? What *are* we going to do with a naughty girl like you? Put you over my lap and slap your legs?! [laughs].

At lunchtime, two of the women had been having a sandwich together. Gary suggested that, on this occasion, he should join in and that all three should go to McDonalds instead. The women politely refused. There was less sexual innuendo in the post-lunch session.

Day five

The morning session consisted of a talk by Diane, a woman VAT inspector in her early 30s. She appeared keen to present the tax, VAT authority and government officers as friendly and helpful to small business, stressing that officers were there to help. She advocated use of pre-start-up services from the Inland Revenue and VAT, consisting of an information pack and one-to-one surgery on initial registration. Despite Diane's efforts, the group was antagonistic toward her and there was extensive discussion amongst the group about the VAT authority breaking into people's homes, terrorizing families and removing goods from someone's house. Diane assured us that this scenario was not impossible but unlikely and that VAT men visited usually by appointment. Once again, participants were not reassured, least of all by the fact that the VAT 'bogeyman' was, in this case, a woman. Questions to Diane from the floor led her inadvertently to compound the image when she recounted tales of horrors committed by her colleagues 'catching out' unsuspecting small business owners.

After lunch, representatives from a large national UK bank and a firm of insurance brokers talked about sources of funding for small business. Perhaps unsurprisingly, the bank representative concluded that the best deals on funding could be had from his own organization. Later, Reg from the Inland Revenue gave a presentation on how the Revenue can help small business. His likeable, easy going and affable style endeared him to tutees far more than had the VAT representative. Despite his helpful and friendly demeanour, Reg was adamant that tutees were to register with the Revenue, 'or else'. Non-registration would mean the Revenue would 'slap your hands'. Much like the naughty child being alternately rewarded and punished, tutees were reminded that compliance or non-compliance brought its own consequences. Reg was clear and unambiguous when, in closing the day's session, he specified precisely what this would mean:

> *If you are a good tax payer and send money in on time the Revenue doesn't have to worry about you. [...] If you don't pay the Revenue on demand then we send the bailiff.*

> *If you don't send in the self assessment form then the Revenue send their demand just before Christmas, to spoil your Christmas.*

Then you have to fill in a form which is 17 pages long and complex.

Making sense of self-employment: themes from interview data

Of the 42 people that were interviewed, 30 of them had approached an outside agency for help. Many of the women who had been on a business start-up programme felt the negative effects created by using stereotypes to promote enterprise but had difficulty in articulating this as such. Elsewhere in the literature, Professor Barres, a female-to-male transgendered person, suggests that women do not talk about their experience of being treated differently to men: '...women do not recognise that they are treated differently because, unlike him they have never known anything else' (Highfield, 2006: *The Daily Telegraph*, p.10). Louise who ran her own consultancy business felt her enterprise did not actually qualify as a business at all. She describes this in terms of, '*I felt like a bit of a charlatan really because, I thought I'm not really setting up a business. I haven't got a business, I haven't got a truck, I haven't got a, it's almost like I haven't got me own business.*' It is interesting here how Louise draws on masculine imagery of the trucker to describe being in business. She uses the lack of a truck (male appendage) to signify her perceived powerlessness in the business arena. Other women like Liz in the vignette of the self-employment agency attended the self-employment programme but then felt start-up was not for them. They described this in terms of, '*I felt it wasn't for me*', or '*It wasn't meant to be*', or '*It didn't feel right*', and were often unable, or perhaps were unprepared to discuss, their feelings any further. What was clear was that the women had been subjected to, and subjects of, stereotypical representations of gender and work, the masculine symbolism of which had gone unremarked upon but had, nonetheless, impacted on their identity as women.

One of the main themes to emerge from the interviews with women contemplating entrepreneurship was their concern for its effects on family life, and how their engagement in self-employed work activity could potentially minimize time for family commitments. Lisa, already in full-time work but seriously considering realizing a long-held desire for self-employment, declined to follow up on her idea for a business. Her comments typified many of those who feared that the demands of self-employment and the associated long hours culture would spill over into domestic life. Having absorbed the image of the entrepreneur as stereotypically, and of necessity committed to the long-hours culture,

Lisa envisioned that setting up her own business would potentially undermine the order she has created at home:

> *I don't want to ruin my relationship with the worry of working long hours. If you have a business, if you are a business person and you run your own business then the stereotypes are that you've never got time for your family, your house, you'll never have time to clean your house, you'll live in chaos.*

Further, concerned to 'protect' her relationship and home life, Lisa reinforces the idea of the entrepreneur as a male who is supported by the service functions of a wife at home, and positions herself as the one who maintains responsibility for domestic harmony.

She continues:

> *I haven't [started a business]. Why? I haven't because I've had to get my daughter off to university [laughs]. I've had to support my other daughter who goes to university [laughs] because she's had a break up with one boyfriend but has taken up with another. My husband's been ill and I had to support him. I went through a period of depression last summer when I was working through some emotional sludgy stuff which I've got through now [...] Then we've had Christmas and I did the family boxing day instead of my mother-in-law this year. Em, my boss has been ill at work so I've had to work full time instead of part time. So there's been a million things. Oh my God!*

Lisa presents herself as a provider of long-term emotional support for those around her, and discusses her primary contribution in life as helping repair the damage in the lives of others, including her boss. She fears for the consequences of her withdrawal should she pursue her business idea, and rationalizes the decision not to become self-employed as one of protecting her home and family, despite the continued cost to her own emotions and well-being. Lisa continually subordinates her own desire for self-employment (c.f. Fenwick, 2002) presenting this as, in her eyes, a well-founded concern for the success of the lives of others, even those of her employer as non-family. In so doing, Lisa reinforces her own (gender) identity as a carer, as a 'good' wife, mother and employee and further removes herself from the possibility of self-employment.

By contrast, Dawn did not join a start-up programme, but went on to start a business. She too carries guilt at the idea that she has, in some way, let down her family. Dawn's comment illustrates the dynamics of domestic relationships similar to many of the women interviewed and for whom, despite having a partner who was ostensibly committed to sharing domestic work, childcare and to his wife's move to self-employment, the labour of care inevitably now falls to her. Dawn expresses it as follows:

> *He'll promise to do something or promise to go somewhere and if he doesn't do it the kids will keep badgering me... I know it's a generalisation but I think women generally feel a stronger sense of guilt [...]. It's hard and I think if I'd been doing a straightforward nine to five job it might not have been so much of a problem.*

Since starting up as self employed Dawn feels uncomfortable about 'not being there' for her children. She acknowledges that her husband is, as it transpires, not there for them either but like Lisa, she rationalizes this as her responsibility and not his. She absorbs the burden of guilt not just for spending less time and expending less emotional energy with the children but also because the family's economic situation has changed such that her income in self-employment might potentially fluctuate. This is doubly problematic in that her guilt at not being able to offer a greater degree of certainty about her own financial contribution to the household prevents her from challenging her partner about his own (lack of) involvement with the children.

Another theme amongst those interviewed was the experience of having a partner who, unlike Dawn's husband who simply withdrew from childcare, was actively hostile to the woman becoming self-employed or who sought to actively discourage her from starting a business. Despite having a partner who had been self employed for some time and having already identified and explored the possibility of a specific business opportunity further with a self-employment agency on a previous occasion, Elayne decided not to go into business. She describes her situation:

> *he runs around after me, but, but I think [pause] in a previous time, when I took a voluntary redundancy where I used to work at, initially I was going to buy a shop, a sandwich shop [...] I looked at self-employment then. It was at that point that he said with all the requirements, the commitment, all of the bits that require you to get a business off the ground, if two of us were trying to do that in one house, I can't see it working. One person needs to be able to sit on the back burner.*

Here, for his own reasons, Elayne's husband chooses to reinforce the perception of self-employment as difficult, of necessitating overly complex and time-consuming paperwork to satisfy 'the authorities', undermines her wishes and her confidence in her own ability, and eventually talks her out of realizing her long-held ambition. For her part, Elayne internalizes her husband's resistance to her desire for self-employment in terms of 'one person', that is Elayne herself, needing to sit on the 'back burner' rather than take up self-employment in her own right.

Neglect was a common theme amongst interviewees, particularly with respect to children. Lesley explicitly states childcare needs as her single motivation for seeking out self-employment:

> *I know I wanted to do a business, something that would fit in with Georgina when she was little [...]. I didn't want to go back to work full time. I've always said I should be at home with my children I'm a bit old fashioned I suppose [...] I was desperate to find something that would fit in.*

Discussion and conclusion: visibility, invisibility and entrepreneurship

Existing research has rightly called attention to the ways in which organizational structures and occupations are themselves gendered (Mirchandani, 1999). Our research underscores the need to pay attention to the practices within specific organizational sites where gender definitions are produced and sustained. The Self Employment Access and Learning Programme is one such site. As Acker contends, we need to conceptualize gender not as an addition to existing processes but 'rather as an integral part of those processes, which cannot be properly understood without an analysis of gender' (1990: 146). The methodological injunction for research on gender and entrepreneurship is to seek out where and how gender is constructed in everyday interactions and in the minutiae of everyday life.

Our research findings support the perspective of gender as a social practice rather than a biological property and calls for the pursuit of further research on gender and entrepreneurship without an essentialist 'woman' at the core. Moreover, the research presented here highlights the way in which women's place in, and relationship to entrepreneurship, becomes marginalized. Women are thereby rendered largely invisible in the construction of entrepreneurship as a gendered practice. The processes of gender differentiation in the specific site we have detailed constitute women as outside of what it means to be a 'successful' entrepreneur. The discursive construction of the entrepreneur as 'inevitably' masculine entails a celebration of particular forms of behaviour seen as required of the successful entrepreneur. In this respect, a (masculine) norm of entrepreneurship is reinscribed, elevated *and is made visible*, as a seemingly inevitable outcome and measure of small business success. Set against this norm, other expressions, forms and possibilities for a fuller, alternative or simply different way of doing things as an entrepreneur are rendered invisible. In this respect, entrepreneurship is experienced by the participants in our research study as particularly monolithic in its capacity to define the reality of their daily work.

As a consequence, it is perhaps not surprising that many women find themselves unwilling to engage in, or simply uncomfortable with, entrepreneurship and, in so doing, distance themselves from setting up in business. Of course this distancing is not just symbolic in that they shy away from or avoid the language and behaviours associated with 'being an entrepreneur'. Their distancing ultimately has real material outcomes at the level of their (potentially reduced) economic independence, (low) participation rates in business start-up and in maintaining their continued social and financial dependence on other, less satisfying arrangements.

It follows then that one reading of our data could be that women merely select themselves out of business start-up: that the women make themselves invisible in relation to small business. On the contrary, our discussion here should not be read as women *choosing* to avoid business start-up: rather, we are concerned to make visible the power effects of entrepreneurship as a discourse and to demonstrate that these power effects have a gendered dimension. In this regard, an aim of our chapter has been to render visible to the reader the processes by which many women become invisible in business start-up. The way that entrepreneurship was defined, described and enacted in our study made visible a masculine norm that had the effect of excluding many women from small business start-up. Moreover, the womens' life experiences and their perceived invisibility in work, family and domestic life for example, simultaneously compounded by their wider social invisibility, reinforced the perception of entrepreneurship as men's work. Clearly some women do indeed set up a business. It is not our purpose to suggest that entrepreneurship is always wholly and inevitably men's domain or that subjects lack the capacity to resist and transform discourse. Yet even those women interviewed in the study who do go on to small business start-up carried with them the expectations of entrepreneurship as a masculine domain, and regarded themselves, to varying degrees, as curiosities, mavericks or transgressors.

They saw themselves as visible, indeed, but not entirely on their own terms.

Our chapter has addressed the relationship between gender and entrepreneurship as enacted in a given organizational locale and has highlighted how entrepreneurship is reproduced as a gendered phenomenon. In combination with gendered imagery as to women's place, home, family and caring, the Programme constructed entrepreneurship as 'men's domain'. The Self-Employment Agency purported to encourage women to start-up in business but a different message was being received. The ethos of the Programme was to encourage assistance and informality for new starters in particular but this was not the experience of participants. As adults embarking on a voluntary programme for self-employment, tutees were at one and the same time, infantilized and overwhelmed by what was presented to them as the rules and regulations of small business; required to sit like schoolchildren and listen to, in some instances, recently redundant former managers, describe the ideal-type entrepreneurial personality. Visual material used gave a clear picture of the successful self-employed starter as white and male. Presentations by speakers reinforced the ideal that entrepreneurship meant being confident, bold competitive, innovative and a risk taker; being rational, hard working and reliable; putting profit before pleasure and being willing and able to sacrifice personal relationships.

Several points surrounding the womens' invisibility emerge from the research. The first is a paradoxical relationship between security and insecurity in self-employment. One of the motivations for considering self-employment on the part of participants in the research was a desire for what was perceived as the security of self-employment status and especially in the attraction of 'being your own boss'. Similarly, some of the women in Fenwick's (2002) study cited the desire to start a business as motivated by longing for more freedom and control over their lives. But the ideal of self-employment as freedom from insecurity, expressed in the demands and experiences of intensified work and precarious employment relations, contrasted with what was, for many participants, the unexpected presentation of self-employment as surrounded by rules, regulations and procedures that would trip up the unwary. This perception merely created additional insecurity rather than resolving it. The pursuit of greater autonomy and independence that had originally been a motivating influence in their seeking out self-employment as a career option was effectively undermined.

Second, and relatedly, in its presentation of the requirements of self-employment as administratively complex and time consuming, the

Programme constructed and reinforced the imagery of 'outside' professionals as possessors of the power to resolve fear and uncertainty in the hapless or inexperienced self-employed worker whose business, marriage or livelihood might otherwise 'go under'. Consequently, the self-employed and would-be self-employed were under pressure to cede more control over their work life to external paid professionals, and to accountants in particular. This dependency was in part a consequence of the requirement of the self-employed to be necessarily administratively accountable to the tax and VAT authorities, but was further constructed and capitalized upon, as a source of fear, by the professional bodies. The relationship between the 'raw recruits' to self-employment and experienced professionals was one of constructed dependency on professional services and on professionals who were active in constituting the problem, as well as positioning their own services as its ongoing solution. The lure of self-employment freedom was effective in its rhetorical value, in attracting people to the idea of self-employment and attendance as tutee on one of the Programmes. Once there, however, such ideals were drawn upon in enabling professional service providers to 'feed' from the anxieties and insecurities of the tutees. For some, the fear was such that they were put off self-employment entirely. For some women participants, the role of the (male) professional represented merely yet another extension of the controls they experienced elsewhere, from employers at work or from partners at home. This, coupled with uncertainty surrounding their confidence in their own abilities, was sufficient to put them off further consideration of self-employment as an option.

Third, women in the research recognized gender disadvantage and their being a woman was a problem for them in their desire to become self-employed. This finding is in contrast to other research suggesting that many women lack or refuse to acknowledge a self-conscious reflection of themselves as gendered actors 'believing that the "problem" of gender disadvantage has been "solved" and therefore that gender is no longer an issue' with respect to entrepreneurship (Lewis, 2006: 453). Considering the intertwining of entrepreneurship and gendered power structures, many women also faced power relations in economic structures that are shaped by their position with respect to childcare and domestic work to a far greater extent than many men, a feature largely ignored by the literature on entrepreneurship (Mulholland, 1996). Women interviewed were cognizant as to the role that caring work played in their lives and were always mindful of 'their' domestic responsibilities, even in households where there was a husband or partner present.

Conventional, often prescriptive, managerialist literature has turned on entrepreneurship as grounded in economic rationality and assumes entrepreneurial practices to be agendered (Ahl, 2002). In the self-employment agency which formed our case organization, together with interview data, we have charted the construction of entrepreneurship as a masculine domain which had the effect of excluding women as 'other' and reinscribing the visibility of the entrepreneur as self-evidently male. Perhaps in its very mundanity, bordering on at times outright crudeness, the self-employment agency Programme was most seductive at the level of reinscribing entrepreneurship as the province of men. As an empirical site for research on gender and entrepreneurship, we regard the self-employment agency as but one site for the construction and reproduction of entrepreneurship as a gendered activity.

The Programme at once both reproduced and reinforced the visibility of entrepreneurship as quintessentially masculine territory and the 'natural' domain of men. In five days, the Agency had created the impression that women were indeed outsiders to, and invisible from, the world of small business. From the use of sexist jokes and innuendo, deployed in presentations as 'icebreakers' (Cockburn, 1991) or 'banter' in presentation (Collinson, 2002); depictions of men in business in Programme literature; the construction of dependency on (often) male professionals and fear of the relevant authorities, women participants in the research felt in no doubt as to their status as outsiders to the domain of entrepreneurship. Even before their self-employment could be further contemplated, women had largely internalized their own invisibility and exclusion from prospective entrepreneurship.

By the end of the five-day Programme reported here, Liz as the only remaining woman, had decided to apply for a job at Tesco. She said she felt it was 'preferable' to starting her own business.

References

Acker, J. (1990) 'Hierarchies, jobs, bodies: A theory of gendered organizations', *Gender & Society*, 4: 139–158.

Ahl, H. J. (2002) 'The construction of the female entrepreneur as the Other', in Czarniawska, B. and Höpfl, H. (eds) *Casting the Other*, pp. 52–67. London: Sage.

Allen, S. and Trueman C. (eds) (1993) *Women in Business: Perspectives on Women Entrepreneurs*. New York: Routledge.

Alvesson, M. and Skoldberg, K. (2000) *Reflexive Methodology*. London: Sage.

Ardener, S. (ed.) (1993) *Women and Space Ground Rules and Social Maps*. Oxford: Berg Publishers Ltd.
Atkinson, P. and Hammersley, M. (1994) 'Ethnography and participant observation'. In Denzin, N. and Lincoln, Y. (eds) *Handbook of Qualitative Research*. Thousand Oaks, CA: Sage.
Baszanger, I. and Dodier, N. (1997) 'Ethnography: Relating the part to the whole'. In Silverman, D. (ed.) *Qualitative Research: Theory, Method and Practice*. London: Sage.
Birley, S. (1989) 'Female Entrepreneurs: Are they really any different?', *Journal of Small Business Management*, 27(1): 32–38.
Bruni, A., Gherardi, S. and Poggio, B. (2004a) 'Doing gender, doing entrepreneurship: An ethnographic account of intertwined practices', *Gender, Work and Organisation*, 11(4): 406–429.
Bruni, A., Gherardi, S. and Poggio, B. (2004b) 'Entrepreneur mentality, gender and the study of women entrepreneurs', *Journal of Organizational Change Management*, 17(3): 256–268.
Burns, P. and Harrison, J. (1996) *Small Business and Entrepreneurship*, 2nd edition. Edited by Paul Burns and Jim Dewhurst. Hampshire: Macmillan Press.
Butler, J. (1990) *Gender Trouble. Feminism and the Subversion of Identity*. London: Routledge.
Carrigan, T., Connell, B. and Lee, J. (1997) 'Toward a new sociology of masculinity'. In Brod, H. (ed.) *The Making of Masculinities: The New Men's Studies*. Boston: Allen and Unwin.
Carter, S. (2000) 'Improving the numbers and performance of women owned businesses: Some implications for training and advisory services', *Education and Training*, 42(4/5): 326–333.
Carter, S. and Rosa, P. (1998) 'The financing of male and female owned businesses', *Entrepreneurship and Regional Development*, 10: 225–241.
Cockburn, C. (1991) *In The Way of Women*. Basingstoke: Macmillan.
Collinson, D. L. (2002) 'Managing Humour', *Journal of Management Studies*, 39: 269–288.
DTI (Department of Trade and Industry) (2005) A strategic framework for women's enterprise.
Eckenrode, J. and Gore, S. (1990) *Stress Between Work and Family*. New York: Plenum.
Ehlers, T. B. and Main, K. (1998) 'Women and the false promise of microenterprise', *Gender and Society*, 12(4): 424–440.
Fay, B. (2002) *Contemporary Philosophy of Social Science*. Oxford: Blackwell Publishing.
Fenwick, T. (2002) 'Transgressive desires: new enterprising selves in the new capitalism', *Work, Employment & Society*, 16(4): 703–723.
Foucault, M. (1984) 'On the genealogy of ethics' In Rabinow, P. (ed.) *The Foucault Reader*. London: Penguin.
Foucault, M. (1997) 'Friendship as a way of life', in Rabinow, P. (ed.) *Michel Foucault – The Essential Works Volume One: Ethics, Subjectivity and Truth*. London: Penguin.
FSB (2004) Lifting Barriers to Growth in UK Small Businesses at www.fsb.org.uk/policy/overview/asp
Gherardi, S. (1995) *Gender, Symbolism and Organisational Culture*. London: Sage.

Goffee and Scase (1985) *Women in Charge: The Experience of Female Entrepreneurs.* London: Allen and Unwin.

Goffee and Scase (1987) *Entrepreneurship in Europe: The Social Processes.* Kent: Croom Helm.

Green, E. and Cohen, L. (1995) 'Women's business: Are women entrepreneurs breaking new ground or simply balancing the demands of "women's work" in a new way?', *Journal of Gender Studies*, 4(3): 297–314.

Highfield, T. (2006) 'Women are the victims of discrimination in science. I know – I used to be one', *The Daily Telegraph*, July 13th, p. 10.

Hochschild, A. (1997) *The Time Bind: When Work Becomes Home and Home Becomes Work.* New York: Metropolitan Books.

Holliday, A. (2002) *Doing and Writing Qualitative Research.* London: Sage.

Lee-Gosselin, H. and Grise, J. (1990) 'Are women owner-managers challenging our definitions of entrepreneurship? An in depth survey', *Journal of Business Ethics*, 9(4): 423–433.

Lewis, P. (2006) 'The quest for invisibility: Female entrepreneurs and the masculine norm of entrepreneurship', *Gender, Work and Organization*, 13(5): 453–469.

Liff, S. and Ward, K. (2001) 'Distorted views through the glass ceiling: The construction of women's understanding of promotion and senior management Positions', *Gender, Work and Organization*, 8(1): 19–36.

Marlow, S. (2002) 'Self employed women: Apart of or apart from feminist theory?', *Entrepreneurship and Innovation*, 2(2): 83–91.

Mirchandani, K. (1999) 'Feminist insight on gendered work: New directions in research on women and entrepreneurship', *Gender, Work and Organization*, 6(4): 224–235.

Morgan, G. and Knights, D. (1991) 'Gendering jobs: Corporate strategy, managerial control and the dynamics of job segregation', *Work, Employment & Society*, 5(2): 181–200.

Mulholland, K. (1996) Entrepreneurialism, masculinities and the Self made man'. In Collinson, D. and Hearn, J. (eds) *Men as Managers, Managers as Men: Critical Perspectives on Men, Masculinities and Managements.* London: Sage.

OECD Report (1998) *Women Entrepreneurs in Small and Medium Enterprises*, pp. 155–167.

Phillipson, I. (1995) *How To Be An Entrepreneur. A Guide For The Under 25's.* London: Kogan Page.

Prasad, P. (1997) 'Systems of meaning: Ethnography as a methodology for the study of information technologies'. In Lee, A. (ed.) *Information Systems and Qualitative Research.* London: Chapman Hall.

Ransom, J. (1993) 'Feminism, difference and discourse: The limits of discursive analysis for feminism'. In Ramazanoglu, C. (ed.) *Up Against Foucault.* London: Routledge.

Saco, D. (1992) 'Masculinity as signs: Post-structuralist feminist approaches to the study of gender'. In Craig, S. (ed.) *Men, Masculinity and the Media.* London: Sage.

Schwartz, E. B. (1976) 'Entrepreneurship: A new female frontier', *Journal of Contemporary Business*, Winter, 47–76.

Silverman, D. (1997) 'The logic of qualitative research', in Miller, G. and Dingwall, R. (eds) *Context and Method in Qualitative Research.* London: Sage.

Silverman, D. (2001) *Interpreting Qualitative Data*. London: Sage, Dehli: Thousand Oaks.
UK Global Entrepreneurship Monitor (2001) Executive Report at www.consortium.org
Watkins, D. S. and Watkins, J. (1984) 'The female entrepreneur: Her background and determinants of business choice, some British data', *International Small Business Journal*, 2(4): 55–70.
Willis, P. (2000) *The Ethnographic Imagination*. Cambridge: Polity Press.
www.dti.gov.uk
www.eoc.org.uk
www.iwight.com/isle_womens/funding_support
www.prowess.org.uk
www.sbs.gov.uk/phoenix
www.shell-livewire.org
www.train2000.org.uk
www.womeninenterprise.com

6
'Mumpreneurs': Revealing the Post-feminist Entrepreneur

Patricia Lewis

Introduction

In Autumn 2008, a programme called This Morning on ITV, one of the largest commercial broadcasting companies in the UK, ran a competition for mothers with business ideas, calling the competitors 'Mumpreneurs'. In addition, a number of websites have recently emerged which also make use of this term including The Mumpreneur Directory (www.mumpreneurdirectory.com); London Mums (www.londonmums.org.uk) which invites women to join the London Mumpreneurs' Group; Babyworld which recently invited women to 'Meet the Mumpreneurs' (www.babyworld.co.uk) and Mumsclub (www.mumsclub.co.uk) which provides details of a range of women owned businesses referring to these as mumpreneur profiles. The increasing use of the expression 'mumpreneur' gives rise to the question of how we should interpret its emergence. Is the phrase 'mumpreneur' simply a play on words or is it something more significant?

In this chapter it will be argued that use of the term 'mumpreneur' is a significant development associated with processes of female individualization (McRobbie, 2009). This is directly connected to the idea of individualization developed by writers such as Beck and Beck-Gernsheim (2002). Individualization refers to the increased capacity among individuals to construct their own personal biography within a context where the power of traditional structures such as class, gender, family and community has faded. It is argued that as women are released from the traditional ties of family they experience an 'individualisation boost' providing new opportunities and chances for them (Beck and Beck-Gernsheim, 2002: 55). McRobbie (2009: 81) uses the notion of female individualization as a means of signalling her concern with this position. She argues that this viewpoint pays little attention to the continued existence of gendered hierarchies as manifest in the way women are encouraged to be both '...willing subjects of economic capacity while also undertaking to retain their traditionally marked out roles in the household...'.

The emphasis on personal agency and the decline of previously existing social forms connects directly to the emergence of the discourse of enterprise. Writers such as du Gay (1996, 2000, 2004) have claimed that enterprise discourse has entered all spheres of social life, reconfiguring individual identities and constructing workers both in the public and the private sector, as responsible, self-reliant, independent, risk taking entrepreneurial beings. The suggestion is that the desire and opportunity to create a self-reliant, independent, dynamic, enterprising identity is available to everyone (Fenwick, 2002). However, drawing on McRobbie (2009) this chapter starts from a position which views the process of individualization connected with enterprise as being inscribed with gender. 'Mumpreneur'[1] is a manifestation of this inscription and should be seen not as a quirky label or play on words but as an emerging identity with specific attributes within the enterprise discourse. However what is notable about this emerging identity is not that it seeks to emulate the long existing identity of 'entrepreneur' which du Gay (1996) argues has been given ontological priority within contemporary times and which feminist writers (e.g. Ahl, 2002, 2004, 2006; Bruni *et al*, 2004a, 2004b, 2005; Lewis, 2006; Mirchandani, 1999; Mulholland, 1996; Reed, 1996) have characterized as gendered masculine. Instead the chapter suggests that the emergence of the term 'mumpreneur' is connected to the juxtaposition of the discourses of motherhood and enterprise which is providing a new discursive articulation of women and business. This leads to the repositioning of (business) women within the domestic sphere, a repositioning which is presented as choice as opposed to imposition (Probyn, 1997).

In exploring the emergence of the post-feminist entrepreneur, this chapter will begin by outlining the conventional account of business women and the domestic sphere found in much of the literature on women business owners. This highlights the negative impact family and motherhood is perceived to have on business success and how efficient management of domestic responsibility is advocated as a means for women to *detraditionalize* and enter the norm of entrepreneurship. Following this, an alternative version of business women and the domestic sphere is outlined. This depicts a process of *retraditionalization* whereby the connection between business women and motherhood is understood not as a cultural imposition but rather as a positive choice purposefully made visible. From this perspective home is not something which women seek to escape but rather insert at the centre of their business and their lives. Media depictions of business women along with a consideration of the new 'mumpreneur' websites will be included here.

Women, enterprise and detraditionalization

Individualization refers to the disintegration of previously existing social forms and the requirement that individuals formulate and manoeuvre their own identities amid constantly changing circumstances and throughout successive periods of their lives. The consequence of this for women is that their normal life story has been brought closer to that of men (Beck and Beck-Gernsheim, 2002). This is particularly true within the economic sphere where transformations connected to individualization are most marked and where detraditionalization processes are visible in women's entry into the labour market (Adkins, 1999, 2003; McNay, 1999). Within the economic context enterprise is a significant manifestation of this phenomenon, being presented as a liberating force which will not only benefit the economy but also enable individuals to reinvent themselves in entrepreneurial terms. For women this means entering the entrepreneurial field, a domain which was previously off limits but is now held out to them as the way by which they can escape tradition and achieve autonomy, self-realization and freedom. As women-owned businesses are now one of the fastest growing entrepreneurial populations in the world (Brush *et al*, 2009), women have clearly responded to these new social conditions.

As the number of women business owners has increased over the past three decades, this has been matched by an expansion of research in this area. Much of this research is influenced by the overarching question of how gender impacts on the experience of independent business ownership. While this research has considered the impact of gender in relation to a range of issues such as access to finance and networking, a key concern is the connection between family responsibilities and female owned firms and the impact this connection will have on the success of the business. Establishing connectivity between family and firm is central to research on women business owners, though this is an issue which is largely ignored in the general entrepreneurship literature (Ahl, 2006). This association can be traced from the earliest typologies of female entrepreneurs, right through to the range of research on women business owners today. One of the first typologies of female entrepreneurs produced by Goffee and Scase (1983) looked at the intersection between two sets of variables i.e. commitment to entrepreneurship ideals and acceptance of traditional gender roles and produced a four-fold typology. The *conventionals* had a high commitment to entrepreneurial ideals and a strong attachment to traditional gender roles; the *innovators* had a high commitment to entrepreneurial ideals and a low attachment to traditional gender roles; the *domestics* were highly attached to traditional gender roles but had a low commitment to entrepreneurial ideals; and finally the *radicals* had a low attachment to both sets of variables. A second typology constructed by Cromie and Hayes (1988) identified three types of female entrepreneur based around the possession of childcare responsibilities. This included *innovators*, who had a strong commitment to their business and no childcare responsibilities; *dualists* whose main reason for setting up a business was the management of childcare responsibilities which were prioritized; and *returners* who saw business ownership as a means of returning to the workforce after raising their children. A third typology was developed by Carter and Cannon (1992) who identified five ideal-types of female entrepreneur which included *drifters* who opted for business ownership due to unemployment; *young achievers* who were well qualified and used education to make up for their lack of business experience; *achievers* who were also well-qualified and committed to their business; *returners* who used business ownership to get back into the workforce after a career break and whose businesses tended to be organized around domestic responsibilities; and finally *traditionalists* who had no other experience of work except self-employment, often through involvement in a family business. A fourth typology was devised within the context of an industry specific study of self-employed workers in the publishing industry in Britain. This typology was built around four categories including refugees, trade-offs, missionaries and converts with women strongly represented in the trade-off group where the main motivation is the combining of work and family responsibilities (Stanworth and Stanworth, 1997).

Embedded in all of these categorizations is a type of woman business owner who set up her business for reasons connected to her family situation. This is either because she sought a means to manage her home and work responsibilities with the former being privileged over the latter or because her family responsibility has eased and she has now sought a return to the labour force. Where family responsibilities exist, it is clear that the social expectations surrounding home and family are different for men and women within the entrepreneurship field. The conjecture is that women carry the responsibility for family and childcare contributing to a conflict between the needs of the business and the needs of the family with the business always suffering. Indeed, Hundley (2000, 2001) has demonstrated that marriage has a negative impact on the earnings of women business owners with income decreasing when family size and time spent on domestic work increases. More recent research completed by Jennings and McDougald (2007) has similarly sought to investigate the impact of family on the economic performance of a firm headed up by a woman. Based on a comparison of male and female business owners, this research explicitly compares the economic performance of business ventures run by men and women by focusing on the issue of work-family interface (WFI). The research develops a model entitled 'Proposed Effects of Gender Differences in Entrepreneurs WFI Experience and Coping Strategies on Business Performance' which demonstrated that differences between men and women around work-family interface can to a degree account for '...the smaller employment size, revenues and income level of female-headed firms' (Jennings and McDougald, 2007: 748). In addition to this, use of the home as a base for a business is perceived to have a particularly negative impact on female owned firms with women's home based businesses being more likely to suffer than those owned by their male colleagues (Rouse and Kitching, 2006).

This snapshot of the female entrepreneurship research illustrates quite clearly McNay's (1999) suggestion that notwithstanding the increased labour force participation rate of women, traditional gendered expectations around family and childcare still impact on women and may in fact have become more ingrained. What this means is that the process of individualization for women is highly complex as the detraditionalized notion of living 'a life of one's own' is in tension with the traditional requirement that women focus on 'living for others' (Beck and Beck-Gernsheim, 2002). The difficulties women experience in fully adopting a detraditionalized entrepreneurial way of life are connected to the lack of synchronicity (McNay, 1999) between the system of durable, transposable dispositions and behaviours associated with 'living for others' (female habitus) and the institutional arena (field) of entrepreneurship which previous research (e.g. Ahl, 2002, 2004, 2006; Bruni *et al*, 2004a, 2004b, 2005; Lewis, 2006; Mirchandani, 1999; Mulholland, 1996; Reed, 1996) has characterized as masculine. Within the field of entrepreneurship this masculinity assumes a natural status which is inscribed into the objective structure of the social world of entrepreneurship and '..is then incorporated and reproduced in the habitus of individuals' (McNay, 1999: 99). This is well illustrated by a recent quote from a newspaper article about the bra entrepreneur Michelle Mone who founded the firm Ultimo:

> In the utility room there's one white board for each child, saying what they need to do and where they need to go, how much the fees are for the dancing, the rugby. My house is run like a business. My staff, the kids and my husband have key performance indicators and every Friday we get together with a flip chart and mark how the week has been. That sounds hard but it keeps everyone focused. Children love routine and this house is run like clockwork. I manage everything, but the kids and my husband aren't allowed to mark me...every night when I come in it takes me 17 minutes to go round the house and make sure everything is where it should be, all the white shirts together, all the black shirts together (Wark, 2009).

Michelle Mone appears to have dealt with the lack of synchronicity between the feminine habitus associated with home and the masculine field of entrepreneurship by conceptualizing and organizing her home space in terms of the vocabulary and practices of (masculine) business. In other words she has 'enterprised up' her family and the way in which she practices motherhood to facilitate a high level of co-ordination between home and her business. While the female entrepreneurship literature clearly demonstrates (through its focus on family), the disharmony between the female habitus and the masculine field of entrepreneurship, it tends to advocate the approach of Michelle Mone, i.e. tensions between home and business can be dealt with through efficient management and planning ahead. However, such an approach contributes to unevenness around experiences of entrepreneurship not only between men and women but also between women and women as not all women coordinate their home and business in the same way as Michelle Mone.

Women, enterprise and retraditionalization

According to McNay (1999: 103) there are aspects of identity which are more ingrained and deep-rooted, making them less amenable to modification and moulding, than theories of Individualization allow for. Though the detraditionalization associated with individualization may have led to a renegotiation of particular facets of gender relations such as the gender division of labour or marriage '...men and women have deep-seated, often unconscious investments in conventional images of masculinity and femininity which cannot easily be reshaped (while the) destabilizing of conventional gender relations on one level, may further entrench conventional patterns of behaviour on other levels'. The notion of enduring aspects of identity is certainly applicable to considerations of the experience of women business owners, particularly for those writers who have argued that female entrepreneurs challenge the conventional definitions of what it is to be a successful entrepreneur through their commitment to an enterprise model which centres around 'small and stable' business.

This model of business is presented as a means of achieving some balance between work and domestic roles. This balance is achieved by rejecting the prioritization of the business secured through the efficient management of family life and instead tries to accomplish a more equal balance between the demands of the business and the demands of home. Though Lee-Gosselin and Grise (1990) acknowledge that it is not only women who hold this business orientation, they argue that women '...are a group who unashamedly call for recognition of the legitimacy of their views. The vision women entrepreneurs have of their business...may bring a refreshing alternative to the "greater than life" models of entrepreneurship which are widely diffused in the popular press and so foreign to many women entrepreneurs' (Lee-Gosselin and Grise, 1990: 432).

A further study by Fenwick (2002: 719) adopted a similar stance arguing that many self-employed women are resistant to conventional entrepreneurship models which emphasize size, growth and profit. Instead their preference is to create models of enterprise which 'interweave desires of relationships, being and production, in spaces not limited by conventional notions of labour and knowledge that can be commodified and exchanged'. This type of research links women business owners with a range of attributes e.g. nurturing, caring, focused on relationships associated with an idealized notion of femininity. Though the attributes of idealized femininity are not conventionally connected to entrepreneurship which is normally represented as congruent with idealized masculinity, the research of authors like Lee-Gosselin and Grise (1990) and Fenwick (2002) can be seen as a challenge to the connection between masculinity and entrepreneurship. From this perspective the visible enactment of what is claimed to be a feminized form of entrepreneurship (small and stable) is presented as the contestation of the dominant masculine model of entrepreneurship

(Lewis, 2008b) based on the notion that '...even the smallest acts may transcend their immediate sphere in order to transform collective behaviour and norms' (McNay, 2000: 4).

However though the femininity of 'small and stable' may be interpreted as contesting the masculinity of entrepreneurship, it has certainly not 'overthrown' it and a second post feminist interpretation of research which visibly links femininity to entrepreneurship can be presented. This linkage is not about 'challenging' the masculinity of entrepreneurship but seeking an accommodation with it. From a post-feminist perspective, the process of female individualization can be understood as women who want both a successful career and a good family but recognize that within certain contexts (e.g. Britain where childcare provision is marketized) it is difficult to have both simultaneously. Wanting to avoid the 'supermum' stress of trying to be both a mother and a full-time worker, or fearful of ending up with a broken family and problem children, or not being prepared to relinquish having a family, women relocate back within the terms of traditional gender hierarchies by staying at home with children as a matter of *choice* rather than obligation (Yang and Rodriguez, 2009). Nevertheless women's care responsibilities and the limits that these impose on the way they participate in the labour force should not obscure the fact that younger women expect and set out to build organizational careers. Current statistics indicate that in Britain '...well-qualified young women with children under five are the fastest growing segment of the labour force' (Crompton, 2002: 548). While the emergence of the notion of post-feminist choice was originally associated with choosing between home *or* career, family *or* successful job (Probyn, 1997), choice has now become synonymous in Britain with a type of feminism characterized by a social compromise. This compromise sets limits on patterns of labour force participation and gender equality to enable women to fulfil domestic and childcare responsibilities (Crompton, 2002). This suggests that women who seek independence and self-reliance through entrepreneurship do so by setting limits on their participation in entrepreneurial activity. Thus domestic and childcare responsibilities are not something which have to be overcome on the way to entrepreneurial success in a manner similar to Michelle Mone referred to above, but rather determine the limits of entrepreneurial endeavours. While this compromise means that women are active in the public world of work as well as holding primary responsibility for children and the home, this is not about 'having it all' but 'having just enough' i.e. '...a reconfiguring of normative femininity, this time incorporating motherhood so as to accommodate with masculine domination. In the social compromise there is...a process of gender re-stabilisation' (McRobbie, 2009: 79).

Choosing between work and home is an issue which has been taken up within recent media reports with claims being made about a new trend among women of giving up work and staying home with their children (Yang and Rodriguez, 2009). Of particular interest here are those reports (e.g. Austen, 2008; Barrow, 2006; Dodds, 2008; Rose, 2008a, 2008b) which present business ownership as a way of building a career in tandem with motherhood. Within such reports entrepreneurship is presented as the means by which women can be involved in the public world of work without having to put their family in second place. This is a sentiment represented on one of the emerging websites which promote 'mumpreneurship' as follows:

> *Mumpreneurs at London Mums is a forum for modern women who want to fulfil their professional dream while doing the best for their children. Instead of going back to a permanent job after maternity leave, many mums decide to start their own business to enjoy more flexibility and time with the family. Women have the ability to run a business while multi-tasking and looking after a baby.*
> (www.londonmums.org.uk)

However what is notable about media portrayals of women who set up their own business is not only the emphasis that is placed on balancing the demands of home and family but also that the product or service being provided often tends to be associated with motherhood. Newspaper stories with titles such as 'Mothers of Invention', 'Million Dollar Mum' (Rose, 2008a, 2008b) or 'Women who mean Business' (Dodds, 2008) emphasize this association as follows:

> *Mandy Haberman, a Hertfordshire housewife and mother, invented the non-spill Anywayup Cup after watching a toddler chuck Ribena over a pale carpet. The cups now make more than £5million a year.*

> *Thirteen years ago, Sarah Tremellen was pregnant and unable to find pretty bras in her burgeoning size. She set up lingerie store Bravissimo and is now worth £13 million.*

> *Fed up with the logos and garishness of many children's clothes, mum of three Lucy Enfield (wife of Harry) set up ilovegorgeous with a friend. It's now sold in Selfridges.*

Mother of four Chrissie Rucker, founded the White Company after struggling to find plain white sheets. She now has 23 stores and for the year to March 31 2007, sales rose to £61.3 million.

Justine Roberts and Carrie Longton, who met at an antenatal class, envisaged a website which shared information among mothers. Mumsnet.com now has one million visitors a month.

(Rose, 2008a, 2008b)

From humble beginnings in her own kitchen, Jennifer Irvine's company The Pure Package now has its headquarters in New Covent Garden Market, a team of nutritionists and chefs, 3,000 clients on its books, and a turnover of £1.57 million a year.

Clare 37, started her business at the kitchen table. Concerned that the traditional spouted beakers for toddlers would damage her young son's teeth and gums, Claire designed a sturdy spoutless cup five years ago. From small plastic beakers, great things have grown. Claire's company SteadyCo.com now supplies Boots, Asda, ToysRus and Argos and has gone global. Well over a million of the original SteadyCups have been sold and the range has been extended to include plates, dishes and cutlery, designed to help children feed themselves without so many of the usual spillages.

(Dodds, 2008)

What is striking about all these representations of 'mumpreneur' businesses is their location within the traditional world of home and family. The range of products and services are reflective of an ethic of care, where women's focus is on what will not only fill a market gap but also connect to women's traditional caring responsibilities of looking after home and children. In addition, what is often emphasized is the low level of finances required with the following being typical comments about the resources needed to get started: 'I've never had a single loan or investor and the business is growing constantly' (Dodds, 2008). Allied to this, all of the accounts above can be characterized as 'success stories' with substantial sums of money earned through the business, marking a significant difference with the 'small and stable' representation of female owned businesses in much of the formal research on this issue. What such representations do, is make starting a business appear accessible to all. There appears to be little financial risk involved and much to be gained in terms of money earned and time spent with family as the following suggests: 'I work long hours because I'm so driven but I'm very protective of my time with my husband and daughters – our family time doesn't suffer' (Dodds, 2008).

In terms of business profiles, the mumpreneur directory (www.mumpreneur directory.com) contains similar types of businesses as those included in the media reports above as can be seen from the categories of business which the directory lists. Except for the categories Business Services and Property and Travel, all of the businesses listed under the various types identified in Table 6.1 below have two things in common. First, they are all mainly directed at a female consumer. If we look at the category Clothing and Fashion which has five subgroups within it, all of the businesses provide products which women are more likely to be interested in or to buy then men. The sub-category 'For Children' provides a list of businesses which produce designer or at the very least 'different from the norm' clothing for children; 'Just for Babies' list businesses which provide baby clothes; 'For Grown-Ups'

Table 6.1 – The Mumpreneur Directory (www.mumpreneurdirectory.com)

Categories of Business
Clothing & Fashion 　– for children 　– just for babies 　– for grown-ups 　– maternity 　– accessories
Toys and Gifts
Mother & Baby
Jewellery
Occasions
Arts & Crafts
Books and Magazines
Activities and Education
Food and Catering
House and Home
Property and Travel
Business Services
Working from Home
Seasonal Gifts

has one lingerie and swimwear business listed and though arguably men may buy this type of product, the end user is likely to be a woman; 'Maternity' is targeted at pregnant and new mums; and while the last category 'Accessories' contains only one business which produces baby changing bags for men stating that it '...sets the new standard for changing bags by not looking anything like one', this is likely to be a product which a woman purchases for her husband or partner to facilitate outings with children.

The second characteristic of the businesses is that they provide products and services which promote a highly-styled approach to motherhood and family matters. Designer clothing, designer stationery, innovative activities for children, educational books which support child development, ethical products – all comprise what McRobbie (2009) refers to as a re-ordering of femininity where the products and service you purchase are presented as reflecting the type of mother you are and the level of care you provide to your family and friends while also signalling submission to some invisible authority.

Conclusion

A central issue in any consideration of women's experience of business ownership is the opposition between the identity of mother and the identity of entrepreneur. Whether entrepreneurship is seen as a gender neutral or an inherently gendered activity, most research on female entrepreneurs treats family and home as responsibilities to be concealed and invisibilized through substitute care and competent management, similar to Michelle Mone, as a means of entering the (masculine) norm of entrepreneurship.

In contrast, this chapter has sought to explore the emergence of the post-feminist entrepreneur who does not seek to conceal the responsibilities of motherhood but rather to make them visible and central to her entrepreneurial activities. However, what is key to any understanding of the post-feminist entrepreneur, is that exposure of her mothering responsibilities along side her business responsibilities, is not about establishing what Fenwick (2002: 719) refers to as 'a transgressive path in entrepreneurship' rather it is abandoning criticism and censure of masculine hegemony in entrepreneurship in favour of compromise (Crompton, 2002; McRobbie, 2009). In the entrepreneurial sphere, this compromise requires that women undertake the dual role of mother and business owner i.e. being economically active through entrepreneurship while also being primarily responsible for children and domestic life, summed up beautifully in the label 'mumpreneur'. However three important characteristics of this post feminist entrepreneurial experience must be highlighted: first, though women adopt a dual role of mother and business owner this does not entail seeking an equal division of labour within the home but rather undertaking full responsibility for their traditional roles within the household. Second, maintaining this dual role involves reducing the ambitions for the business, placing instead an emphasis on coping with the demands of two different spheres (home and business), largely singlehandedly. Finally, the explicit incorporation of motherhood into women's entrepreneurship is presented as choice. Within what Probyn (1997: 130) refers to as 'a new age of choiceoisie' there is no coercion, no obligation around decisions about staying at home, having a career or combining both – all such decisions are put down to a matter of individual choice. While choosing to explicitly combine business ownership with motherhood signals opposition to the masculine norm of entrepreneurship, the retraditionalizing consequences of this choice must also be recognized.

Notes

1 Though I am using the term 'mumpreneur' in this chapter, elsewhere (Lewis, 2008a, 2009) I have made a similar argument around the label 'female entrepreneur'. This work suggests that the adjective 'female' before entrepreneur does not only signal difference from the masculine norm of entrepreneurship but also the emergence of a new feminized entrepreneurial identity. In this chapter 'mumpreneur' is the term being used for this new identity.

References

Adkins, L. (1999) 'Community and economy: A retraditionalization of gender?', *Theory, Culture and Society*, 16(1): 119–139.
Adkins, L. (2003) 'Reflexivity: Freedom or habit of gender', *Theory, Culture and Society*, 20(6): 21–42.
Ahl, H. (2002) 'The construction of the female entrepreneur as other'. In B. Czarniawska and H. Höpfl (eds) *Casting the Other: The Production and Maintenance of Inequalities in Work Organizations*, pp. 52–67. London: Routledge.
Ahl, H. (2004) *The Scientific Reproduction of Gender Inequality: A Discourse Analysis of Research Texts on Women's Entrepreneurship*. Liber: Copenhagen Business School Press.
Ahl, H. (2006) 'Why Research on Women Entrepreneurs Needs New Directions', *Entrepreneurship, Theory and Practice*, 30(5): 595–621.
Austen, A. (2008) 'Mum's the business', *BBC Money Programme*, 8 August.
Barrow, B. (2006) 'Boom in business tycoon mums', *Daily Mail*, 15 September.

Beck, U. and Beck-Gernsheim, E. (2002) *Individualization*. London: Sage.

Bruni, A., Gherardi, S. and Poggio, B. (2004a) 'Entrepreneur-mentality, gender and the study of women entrepreneurs', *Journal of Organizational Change Management*, 17(3): 256–268.

Bruni, A., Gherardi, S. and Poggio, B. (2004b) 'Doing gender, doing entrepreneurship: An ethnographic account of intertwined practices', *Gender, Work and Organization*, 11(4): 406–429.

Bruni, A., Gherardi, S. and Poggio, B. (2005) *Gender and Entrepreneurship: An Ethnographical Approach*. London: Routledge.

Brush, C., de Bruin, A. and Welter, F. (2009) 'A gender-aware framework for women's entrepreneurship', *International Journal of Gender and Entrepreneurship*, 1(1): 8–24.

Carter, S. and Cannon, T. (1992) *Women as Entrepreneurs*. London: Academic Press.

Cromie, S. and Hayes, J. (1988) 'Towards a typology of female entrepreneurs', *The Sociological Review*, 36: 87–113.

Crompton, R. (2002) 'Employment, flexible working and the family', *British Journal of Sociology*, 53(4): 537–558.

Dodds, S. (2008) 'Women who mean business', *Daily Express*, 4 October

du Gay, P. (1996) *Consumption and Identity at Work*. London: Sage.

du Gay, P. (2000) 'Enterprise and its futures: A response to Fournier and Grey', *Organization*, 7(1): 165–183.

du Gay, P. (2004) 'Against "enterprise" (but not against "enterprise" for that would make no sense)', *Organization*, 11(1): 37–57.

Fenwick, T. J. (2002) 'Transgressive desires: New enterprising selves in the New Capitalism', *Work, Employment and Society*, 16(4): 703–723.

Goffee, R. and Scase, R. (1983) 'Business ownership and women's subordination: A Preliminary study of female proprietors', *The Sociological Review*, 31(1): 625–648.

Hundley, G. (2000) 'Male/female earnings differences in self-employment: The effects of marriage, children and the household division of labour', *Industrial and Labour Relations Review*, 54(1): 95–114.

Hundley, G. (2001) 'Why women earn less than men in self-employment', *Journal of Labour Research*, 22(4): 817–829.

Jennings, J. E. and McDougald, M. S. (2007) 'Work-family interface experiences and coping strategies: Implications for entrepreneurship research and practice', *Academy of Management Review*, 32(3): 747–760.

Lee-Gosselin, H. and Grise, J. (1990) 'Are women owner-managers challenging our definitions of entrepreneurship? An in-depth survey', *Journal of Business Ethics*, 9: 423–433.

Lewis, P. (2006) 'The quest for invisibility: Female entrepreneurs and the masculine norm of entrepreneurship', *Gender, Work and Organization*, 13(5): 453–469.

Lewis, P. (2008a) Reproducing and Resisting the Female Entrepreneur: An Exploration of the Identity Work of Women Business Owners presented at the *26th International Labour Process Conference*, University College Dublin, 18th to 20th March.

Lewis, P. (2008b) 'Emotion work and emotion space: Using a spatial perspective to explore the challenging of masculine emotion management practices', *British Journal of Management*, 19, S130–S140.

Lewis, P. (2009) 'The female entrepreneur: A new entrepreneurial identity and a new gendered challenge for women business owners', presented at *European Academy of Management Conference,* University of Liverpool, 11th to 14th May.
McNay, L. (1999) 'Gender, habitus and the field: Pierre Bourdieu and the Limits of Reflexivity', *Theory, Culture and Society,* 16(1): 95–117.
McNay, L. (2000) *Gender and Agency.* Cambridge: Polity.
McRobbie, A. (2009) *The Aftermath of Feminism.* London: Sage.
Mirchandani, K. (1999) 'Feminist insight on gendered work: New directions in research on women and entrepreneurship', *Gender, Work and Organization,* 6(4): 224–235.
Mulholland, K. (1996) 'Entrepreneurialism, Masculinities and the self-made man', in Collinson, D. L. and Hearn, J. (eds) *Men as Managers, Managers as Men: Critical Perspectives on Men, Masculinities and Managements,* pp. 123–149. London: Sage.
Probyn, E. (1997) 'New traditionalism and post-feminism: TV does the home', in Brunsdon, C., Acci, J. D. and Spigel, L. (eds) *Feminist Television Criticism: A Reader,* pp. 126–139. Oxford: Clarendon Press.
Reed, R. (1996) 'Entrepreneurialism and Paternalism in Australian management: A gender critique of the "self-made" man', in Collinson, D. L. and Hearn, J. (eds) *Men as Managers, Managers as Men: Critical Perspectives on Men, Masculinities and Managements,* pp. 99–122. London: Sage.
Rose, H. (2008a) Mothers of Invention, *Magazine, The Times,* 19 July.
Rose, H. (2008b) Million Dollar Mum, *Magazine, The Times,* 19 July.
Rouse, J. and Kitching, J. (2006) 'Do enterprise support programmes leave women holding the baby?', *Environment and Planning C: Government and Policy,* 24(1): 5–19.
Stanworth, C. and Stanworth, J. (1997) 'Reluctant entrepreneurs and their clients: The case of self-employed freelance workers in the British book publishing industry', *International Small Business Journal,* 16(1): 58–74.
Wark, P. (2009) 'Has it damaged me? Probably', *The Times,* 15 January.
www.babyworld.co.uk/features/work/mumpreneurs1.asp, accessed on 20 May 2009.
www.londonmums.org.uk, accessed on 20 May 2009.
www.mumpreneurdirectory.com, accessed on 20 May 2009.
www.mumsclub.co.uk, accessed on 20 May 2009.
Yang, P. Q. and Rodriguez, E. (2009) 'The case for staying home: Myth or reality', *International Sociology,* 24(4): 526–556.

7
Masculinities in Practice: The Invisible Dynamics in Sports Leadership

Irene Ryan

Introduction

Contexts such as sport can shed light on cultural constraints and contested spaces. New Zealand (NZ) is a small, geographically isolated country where the presence of sport is difficult to avoid. In particular, the imagery of male dominated team sports is exceedingly visible in a nation that advocates it is 'passionate about sport' (Obel *et al*, 2008: i). In saying this, localized gender regimes in sport have rendered gender invisible because of the overpowering presence of a dominant form of masculinity as hegemonic discourse (Shaw and Cameron, 2008). The privileged position given to institutionalized sport conceals continuing gender based disadvantage and is underpinned by ideologies that link men to power and political leadership. Women are largely absent from positions of power in these contexts. In a recent audit, initiated by the New Zealand Olympic Committee (NZOC) to quantify the extent of gender imbalance in leadership and decision-making roles at national level sports organizations, the invisibility of women was confirmed (see Cockburn *et al*, 2007; NZOC, 2008). Men hold 81% of national sport organization (NSO) full time CEO positions (NZOC, 2008), two-thirds of high performance coaching personnel working with senior women's teams are male as are 77% of national governance boards, a figure that has not changed since 1994 (Cockburn *et al*, 2007). Further, the NZOC (2007) survey noted that only one quarter of respondents (26%), proportionally more men than women, perceived barriers existed for women to attain leadership roles in sport. This 'denial' may reflect implicit assumptions that characterize sports leadership as male – or may reflect a faith in meritocratic principles and equal opportunity that suggest gender is no longer an 'issue' in sports leadership careers.

Consideration of these issues, in the specific context of field hockey played by even numbers of men and women, frames the rationale for the discussion in this chapter.

Institutionalized sport, in contrast to the business and corporate environment, does have an influential role in local (organizations) and regional (society-wide) constructions of a dominant form of masculinity (Connell and Messerschmidt, 2005) and its association with 'heroic' models of leadership and national culture (Shaw and Cameron, 2008). This phenomenon is best demonstrated by the iconic status given to past and present 'great' All Black Rugby Union players, a team sport noted for its physicality, heavy-contact, mental toughness and aggression that holds a privileged socio-cultural position within NZ (Pringle, 2007).The relationship between the 'ideal' hegemonic-masculine male and contemporary practice in institutionalized sport is evident at a surface level in the positional power of groups of men from two generational groupings. The 'younger' group, elite athletes such as those mentioned above, are celebrated through sports performances (Pringle, 2007). Their presence is elevated by the imagery and rhetoric of the visual and print mass media (Bruce *et al*, 2007). The other, highlighted previously, is a generally 'older' mid-life group, and often ex-elite sportsmen, who hold decision-making power in sport. In both instances, hegemonic practices have separated the power each group has from privileged forms of masculinities created partly from NZ's colonial history, symbolically embedded (Pringle, 2007) and legitimized through specific forms of managerial practice now present in sport (Piggin *et al*, 2009; Shaw and Cameron, 2008). This suggests that congruence between the discursive practices of sport, athleticism and the 'doing' of managerial work in sport organizations described by Knoppers and Anthonissen (2005) is salient in NZ.

Added to this, the lack of open and critical dialogue, in other words, 'silence', has ensured the reproduction of existing gender systems (Messner, 2007; Shaw and Cameron, 2008) and that structures of male advantage in sport remain invisible. Indeed, as Hokowhitu (2007: 91) remarks 'the idealistic notion of the "level playing field" speaks to the inherent justice of sport, equal opportunities and is underpinned by egalitarianism'. This situation is further strengthened by an enduring societal discourse on equality (see Nolan, 2000) that historically has wide cultural currency in ANZ. The ideals of equal opportunity are clearly evident when policy issues are publicly debated and to an extent, underpin a state moderated, regulatory regime. This is evidenced in any gender equality policy discussions where the focus is substantially on women and equity, the ideal of fairness and social justice with gender equity initiatives promoted as 'best business practice'. The NZOC (Cockburn *et al*, 2007; NZOC, 2008) reports cited earlier are examples specific to sport. Connell (2005: 1806) highlights that one outcome of such discussions is silence on any explicit naming of men as advantaged despite their implicit presence as the normative group against which measures of women's disadvantage and exclusion from decision-making power are judged.

Juxtaposed with this 'silence' is a generation of 'third wave' feminists, born post 1980, who have adopted the tenets of liberal feminism. In contrast to their predecessors, Thorp (2008: 12) describes this group as 'a product of the contradiction between ongoing sexism and greater opportunities for women, individually focused, self-defined and self-orientated, it explicitly embraces hybridity, contradiction and multiple identities'. Described as 'entitled agents' who reject gendered binaries (Thorp, 2008: 10) young sportswomen do have an increased visible presence as participants and by doing so, contest narrow and limiting definitions of femininity (Messner, 2007). Yet, overall, their sports performance is marginalized and subordinate to that of male athletes and, as the NZOC (Cockburn *et al*, 2007; NZOC, 2008) audits highlight, women as a group have little organizational decision-making power over their sport experiences. Gendered organizational processes that readily links leadership with men goes unnoticed because of the belief in a gender-neutral social context (Simpson and Lewis, 2007) or are rationalized, individualized, justified and at times, denied. As a result 'one version of truth is privileged that argues gender equity is not a problem' [in sport] despite visible evidence to the contrary (Hoeber, 2007: 260).

This chapter explores some of the invisible dynamics of masculinities in practice that construct leadership roles in sport organizations. It draws on Martin's (2006: 255) proposition that 'gender in practice' is a product of both voluntary and involuntary actions of individuals and groups that define normativity in particular settings. It is however, the 'unintentional/non-reflexive practising of gender that is more prevalent at work than intentional practising'. Such practices are only visible to those 'who experience them. Improved understanding of non-reflexivity can reveal how and why well-intentioned people practise gender in ways that do harm'. As noted previously sport is one of the most visibly gendered institutions yet gender suppressive practices and a dominant 'male narrative' is invisible to many men and women (Shaw and Cameron, 2008). Moreover, Sinclair (2005: 37) notes masculinity as a point of analysis is almost non-existent in leadership research 'despite men being universally the subject of leadership studies'. Thus the aim of the chapter is to understand more of the 'involuntary, unintentional/non-reflexive' practice of masculinities that sustain male dominance in leadership roles in sport.

The chapter is organized as follows; firstly, the 'when' and 'where' questions of sport leadership are discussed to foreground government policy directed change to further show some of the interactional and situational context within which the narrative that follows, is placed. This narrative includes extracts from stories told by women involved in field hockey that have entered into roles which custom has reframed as male. Field hockey is an example of a sport where gender equity is assumed to exist because it is played by similar numbers of women and men. The analysis will highlight something of the tacit processes of masculinities in practice between well intentioned men and women. Over time, calls for equity and visibility of women in leadership roles within the evolving structures of field hockey have been silenced. In closing the chapter considers the future in a sector where normativity is indeed 'hidden by history' (Simpson and Lewis, 2007: 52).

The 'where' and 'when' questions of sport leadership

The 'when' and 'where' questions of leadership, in other words, the conditions and circumstances are central (Jackson and Parry, 2008) to analysis of deeper conceptualizations of invisibility within specific organizational contexts (Simpson and Lewis, 2007). In thinking of the 'where' questions of leadership, as noted, evidence of the importance of institutionalized sport is not hard to find in ANZ. In this context the majority of sport organizations at national, regional or local levels are located primarily in the not-for-profit or third sector. In an environment where both human and monetary resources are scarce the incompatibility between the 'taken-for-granted naturalness of sport' (Piggin *et al*, 2009: 89) and expectations of professionalism are 'stretching the 'old' sport model to breaking point' (Leberman *et al*, 2006: 410). Despite this, the altruistic wish for sport to be some how value-free and non-ideological (Collins, 2007) a perception reminiscent of the past, is popularized by the local print and visual media (Bruce *et al*, 2007). This conservative positioning alongside the many social interests embedded in organized sport, I would suggest, has negated any purposeful and change orientated social activism in the not-for-profit sport sector.

The invisibility of dissenting voices within organized sport could partly be explained by the timing of choices, the 'when' of leadership.

Changes instigated by direct government intervention in the sector has been profound in solidifying gender suppressive practices through a managerialist approach to sport administration (Leberman *et al*, 2006) and its masculine embodiment. As Sam and Jackson (2004: 218) outline:

> The image of a sport sector in crisis [by the mid-1990's under the Hillary Commission] became a mobilising myth with rationalisation, integration, reduction and amalgamation the tools for change appearing common-sense to predominately, male sport leaders. Subsequent 'rational' policy decisions were, therefore, underpinned by one core assumption, that uniformity across the sport sector should result in 'fair' outcomes.

The 'solution' proposed and subsequently actioned has been centralized government control of sport and physical activity provision that, in 2002, culminated in one Crown agency, Sport and Recreation New Zealand (SPARC). The outcome revealed a clear philosophical shift in the policy definition of 'public good' (Sport, Fitness and Leisure Ministerial Taskforce, 2001). No where is this more evident than at the high performance level and the quest to create a 'nation of winners on the international stage'. The message was made visibly clear to the sector, 'SPARC will assume a stronger leadership position. Investment and support will only be offered to organisations willing to engage in a performance partnership that assists SPARC to achieve its goals' (SPARC, n.d.). In an environment where alternative funding options beyond public money are very limited for many sport codes, the power and influence of Sparc has been significant (Piggin *et al*, 2009). In this instance the imposition of corporatist styles of management based on 'positivistic logic, the privileging of elite sport specific knowledge' (Piggin *et al*, 2009: 92) and a 'hierarchy of authority' (Collins, 2007: 226) has further institutionalized invisible forms of normativity. The result is that specific groups of men continue to retain legitimacy to control sport, so are in-effect, gatekeepers of any initiatives for change. Consequently, this group may see women as absent and initiate a variety of incremental adjustments to 'fix the problem' (Sinclair, 2005: 19). However, 'the factors that support the relative advantage of men go unnoticed'. 'As such the privileges that accompany masculinity go unremarked – hidden within the norm' (Simpson and Lewis, 2007: 54).

The preceding sections have provided an overview of leadership in a specific reception context, sport in NZ. Over time the tensions, challenges and problematic nature of policy-driven principles on people's experiences in sport are being examined through the research endeavours of a small group of academics in NZ (for example see Obel et al, 2008; Piggin et al, 2009; Sam and Jackson, 2004). The setting for the study upon which this chapter draws is the macro-policy driven principles where calls for rationalization have resulted in organized, traditional sports with male and female participants, to amalgamate or merge under the auspices of one national governing body (e.g. Bowls NZ – 1996; Golf NZ; Bike NZ; Gymsports NZ – 2003 onwards). This exercise in 'reduction' and uniformity across the sector is framed as 'common-sense' albeit long histories of separate and often successful autonomous development and leadership are rendered invisible. Any amalgamation or merger is political hence underpinned by ethical and moral arguments, more-so in the not-for-profit or third sector. To this extent, the amalgamation process may include assurances of gender equity but what exactly 'equity' means and how it will be adequately addressed, aligned or importantly, sustained over time may not be clearly articulated or quite possibly understood. Voiced concerns that recognize any change is in practice 'experimentation with the unknown' (Wilson, 2009: 419) appear silenced by the articulation of a particular type of knowledge. Policy-driven change therefore has had real consequences for localized communities over time (Sam and Jackson, 2004). It is to one localized community that the chapter will now turn.

In the next section an abridged version of an exploratory study will be presented. That one local story is used draws on the suggestion by Acker (2006: 442) to look at specific, local organizations to analyse how 'ongoing practical activities of organizing work, at the same time reproduce complex inequalities'. The data presented utilized two interpretive methods. The first inspired by the writing of Richardson (2000, 2007) is my own sense-making of a narrative that, from a feminist standpoint, makes visible my own 'slippery subjectivity, power interests, and limitations' (Richardson, 2007: 459). As such it recognizes a 30-year involvement as a player, supporter and current voluntary board membership at regional and national levels. Other characters appear within this narrative with whom I interrelate as I presuppose I can speak their thoughts and explain their behaviours (Duncan, 1998; Tsang, 2000). They, in turn, may perceive different truths (Rinehart, 2005). Melded with this, are the voices of five women who attained leadership through coach roles at the elite performance level. A selection of extracts from in-depth interviews show 'their unique realities' that in a similar manner to my personal reflections, are intertwined with 'outer contextual realities' (Aaltio, 2002: 25) gathered from secondary documents. Further, this section draws on what Aaltio (2002: 201) terms the 'paradox of hidden gender in interviews' and my role in revealing practices of masculinities as we 'read gendering processes from material in which gender is not explicitly mentioned'.

A history of female presence and ethos in leadership

Field hockey in Aotearoa/New Zealand celebrated its centenary in 2002 for both men and women (Watson and Haskell, 2002). It is one example of a sport that responded to calls for amalgamation, a process that began officially in 1988. Evidence suggests that men and women had played field hockey since the 1880s, either in an organized or informal manner (Watson and Haskell, 2002). While seen as a suitable game for young men, elements such as vigour and competitiveness challenged cultural representations of femininity so it is no surprise female participants, defined by their gender, struggled to get public acceptance of their sport performance. Despite overt criticism, a regional network of separate, volunteer-based administrative structures where women held the key decision-making roles evolved (Jackson, 1993; Watson and Haskell, 2002). Interestingly, men were never excluded as office bearers, a position that did run counter to the international governing body – the International Federation of Women's Hockey Associations (IFWHA) who in 1927 declared this as an organization to be run by women for women (Edwards, 2000). In the traditions of liberal feminism, the tenacity of early female administrators is not hard to find. For example, contestation with their male counterparts over ground allocations and persistent lobbying and fundraising led to the Auckland Ladies Hockey Association being allocated separate grounds in 1939. Melville Park, as it became known, was the first sportsground set aside for the exclusive use of sports women in New Zealand (Jackson, 1993). The symbolic importance of these achievements I would posit has now been lost to successive generations of younger women who as noted earlier, tend to situate themselves within a gender-neutral sport environment.

Also invisible I would suggest to younger generations of women is knowledge of the leadership shown by The New Zealand Women's Hockey Association (NZWHA), first established in 1908. New Zealand women's field hockey teams were regular competitors at international tournaments from the 1930s. In 1971 I recall the NZWHA hosting its first international field hockey tournament in Auckland, the largest such event (20 teams) held by any sport in ANZ up to that time (Jackson, 1993). The point is women's field hockey flourished because it was autonomous, a stance that facilitated a female enclave of amateur players, volunteer coaches and leadership shaped by a 'feminine ethos' (Simpson and Lewis, 2007: 30). However, as Messner (2007: 4) points out, 'the liberal quest for equal (but usually separate) opportunities for women in sport leaves men's sport largely intact and able to continue to reproduce hegemonic masculinity'. Convergence of two groups, one visibly defined by gender (New Zealand *Women's* Hockey Association), the other genderless (New Zealand Hockey Association), in an institution historically defined by men and privileged forms of masculinities is to understand the socially structured limits and constraints inherent in any negotiation of gender dynamics and the emergent contradictions. It is to this that the chapter will now focus.

As stated previously, the timing of 'choices' is critical. Growth of the women's game and female athleticism did, on reflection, exhibit many facets of resistant agencies and as such presented a challenge to the ideological basis of gender differences. The consequences of amalgamation between what were two distinct national governing bodies, however, were foreshadowed in a report published in 1987. As I read an abridged version of the report I note it was compiled by a committee of eight men and two women, on behalf of NZWHA and NZHA facilitated by a quasi government agency, the Hillary Commission for Sport, Fitness and Leisure. This agency, the predecessor to SPARC, had as one of its key funding targets, the professionalization of the management in NSO's (Hindson, 2006). The 'urgent' tone of the 1987 report is evidence of the creation of an image of a 'sector in crises' (Sam and Jackson, 2004: 218). For example, it makes it clear to the 'hockey fraternity' that if field hockey is to progress 'a continuation of the low key, ad hoc approach imposed on hockey by the current system will lead it towards obscurity' (Report of the NZ Hockey Review Committee, 1987: 9).

The timing alongside a persuasive argument was important. Constituents were reminded of bygone success, in particular that men's field hockey was the only New Zealand team sport, at that point, to have won gold at an Olympic Games. I was a spectator in Montreal and witnessed the success of the men's field hockey team in 1976. I also believed that to progress as an amateur sport and replicate this benchmark would require 'co-operative ventures' to enable the provision and financial viability of the new, expensive artificial playing surfaces. 'Far-reaching' administrative changes were advocated as a necessary precursor to ensure future success (Report of the NZ Hockey Review Committee, 1987). The argument exemplified the wider managerialist agenda outlined in the previous section with the recommended response a call for 'professional direction, administrative accountability, targeted volunteer participation, co-ordinated development and rationalised provincial associations' (Report of the NZ Hockey Review Committee, 1987: 8). McKay (1991) highlights the pervasiveness of the corporate-managerial argument, particularly the credence given to expert knowledge and 'trust our leadership' (Vickers, 2008: 566). The silencing or devaluing of any competing discourses does make it difficult for individuals, such as myself, to conceive alternative approaches or, as I recall, even appreciate the substance of the debate.

Invisibility and absence in leadership

To reflect back 20 years from when amalgamation began and review the social impact of what had been two distinctly separate organizational structures and institutional cultures is to indeed 'unmask the privileges and resources that accompany men and masculinity' (Simpson and Lewis, 2007: 54). Two organizational structures were melded into one administrative hierarchy.[1] Resembling the wider sport environment, described in the first section, field hockey, from 'body count' figures, is now controlled at national and regional levels, by predominately male decision-makers (Ryan, 2005). Yet, in spite of the visible presence of men in key structural roles at national and regional levels, field hockey is perceived as egalitarian compared to other New Zealand sports codes (personal communication – S. Simcock, August, 2008).

It is, on the one hand, understandable why the perception of equality exists given the dire under-representation of women at the higher levels of management and leadership in comparative sports (see Cockburn *et al*, 2007; NZOC, 2008). The National Governance Board of Field Hockey has had a constitutional obligation to ensure numerically even, male-female representation although as the NZOC (2008) audit shows a recent constitutional change now brings this commitment into question. Measurement using participation numbers also show field hockey is played by relatively even numbers of men and women (Hockey NZ, 2008). Further, unlike many other sport codes, male and female high performance field hockey teams are branded by the same name 'Black Sticks'. In addition, there is over a period of time, evidence that the principle of fair and equitable allocation of resources including money to the men's and women's high performance programme is enacted (e.g. Hockey NZ, 2009). One question does arise from the gap between the visible positional power of men and the perception of equality in field hockey. Do assumptions and beliefs of meritocracy and equal opportunities serve to conceal masculinities in practice that privilege men? To explore this question, one part of a wider study will be utilized: the impact on the visible presence of women in coach leadership roles subsequent to amalgamation set within centrally driven policy directives outlined in prior sections. As one interviewee recalls, 'the picture changed quite quickly'.

> *I had gained confidence as a player [represented New Zealand in field hockey] and as a coach so never thought anything of the 'step-up' to coach women at the national level. I felt comfortable. It was an era [1980's] when there were plenty of female role models in [field] hockey. I had a bad experience that caused a lot of pain but went forward although it was a huge step up. It was not until Barcelona [1992 Olympics] when I walked into a meeting of all the coaches in the New Zealand camp, it struck me, they were all men. After this I started to take stock of what was going on. I did not feel gender barriers; I was single, so never thought of issues for women. Over the years [1992–2008] it has puzzled me, how the few women who appeared [in field hockey high performance coach structures] seem to be cut out of everything. She [referring to one specific example] appeared to rub them [decision makers] up the wrong way. Now there are no role models. I don't really understand how this has happened. Unless outrageously confident, it is hard to break into the clique. Guys are 'ankle tapped', use their networks and are more confident. [Field] Hockey is a joint sport – there is a need to model this rather than all the visible experts being male.*

It is well documented in research from a variety of sources around the world that the visibility of female coaches at the high performance level of sport is declining (see Edwards, 2008; Cockburn *et al*, 2007; Sport Scotland, 2008). At the individual level, the obstacles aspiring female coaches face to move through the levels of a stratified and increasingly, professionalized coach hierarchy are also well researched (see Edwards, 2000, 2008). Not surprisingly, given the dominant managerialist approach of sport organizations in NZ the barriers for individual women are strikingly similar to those in the wider paid workplace environment. As signalled in the above interview extract female coach leadership in field hockey at the high performance level[2] 20 years after amalgamation is negligible. Is this surprising? Since 2002, the shape, form and expectations of high performance has been prescribed by SPARC who with a 'corporatist approach to investment'

(Piggin *et al*, 2009: 92) have exerted significant pressure on NSO's to get results. This model of high performance has had an impact on internal structures and importantly, the culture of a representative hierarchy in field hockey. At the top of a hierarchy of representative competitions is the National Hockey League (NHL).[3] The status of this competition recognizes its importance in the professional development of coach leadership at the national level. Coach appointments are made by each of the eight regional field hockey associations who compete. Female presence at this level has also diminished significantly.

In saying this, a few individual women have succeeded to some extent in negotiating the constructed hierarchy at regional level (NHL) and briefly at national level (Black Sticks), a point raised in the interview extract. The interviewee, however, is puzzled and looking for deeper explanations as to why, over time, dissonance between women and coach leadership has exacerbated given the hegemonic narrative of equal opportunity. In seeking answers the organizational structures in which individual women experience disadvantage will be used to make visible what is invisible, the dynamics of masculinities in practice that privilege men in high performance coach leadership.

Organizational structures and barriers to leadership

Research has shown that many paid work organizations have, in the face of change, become a 'patchwork of flexible, new, old and modified working practices' (Perry, 2004: 53) so, to an extent, offer 'choices' of work practice. In amateur sports, in this case field hockey, virtually all of the 'contact work' of a coach with a team is scheduled in nonstandard hours, week nights, between 6–10 pm and weekends. A common theme I have heard on several occasions and was raised by all interviewees was a lack of consultation when allocating training days/times, no acknowledgement of time external to training (e.g. – planning and game analysis) and little dialogue on expense reimbursement. As one interviewee describes;

> For me a double whammy. Not only a female but a single female with small children trying to juggle training times for elite teams. From a female perspective you can't just walk out of the house. Having to juggle and find people to baby-sit three, four times a week I could not afford to pay. Even if I had a partner it would probably be no different. At (regional association) a lot more work and time – I did not want to disclose my

finances, I never felt there was anyone I could confide in – it was not user-friendly – all male.

Another interviewee reflects;

It is expensive – the costs are quite high [petrol – travelling to practices]. I got told the money was not available – then find the men got more money for expenses – same the year before. Is it because they [male regional administrators] perceive we will do it for nothing [coaching] women are not hard enough – if I ask for money what will they think?

Each interviewee refers to the power, in the form of organizational logic (Acker, 2006) used by regional and national administrators to define and shape what is possible and permissible. High performance expectations set by the drive to create a 'nation of winners on the international stage' require a significant ongoing time commitment from coaches. To question this logic is to be categorized as 'difficult', 'uncooperative' and 'unreasonable'. A deeper analysis suggests the normalized, unintentional, non-reflexive practices of masculinities are 'at play here'. By highlighting their personal situations the vulnerability of women within an invisible masculine schema categorizes them as 'a problem' and in need of special treatment.

The outcome, whether intentional or not, is the construction of 'a glass ceiling'. This is demonstrated in practice where stereotypes of the coach roles for which women are 'naturally' deemed more suitable. Women are found in age-defined female regional representative sides (e.g. under 13; under 16; under 18) on a voluntary basis. 'Good experiences here can propel you to look beyond to the high performance level' (Interviewee). To look beyond and seek promotion in a constructed hierarchy based on normalized 'invisible' masculine values (shown in the previous extracts) is to take up heightened visibility – 'be exposed in a very public arena'. As one interviewee explains:

I remember my first year coaching men [the only female to take a men's side in National Hockey League – the top national premier competition] I was quite shocked at the response from the Media and other male coaches. I stepped into their territory, yet they had been stepping into ours forever. Not a problem to the guys in the team but certainly for those external – I stood out. If they lost – it was my fault because I was female – it wasn't that they [the team] just had not done what they were expected to do. At the end of games, the Managers and Coaches of the other teams *would come and shake my hand, as Manager. I had a male assistant coach – they would think he was the Coach. The Technical Delegates would give me the Match report to sign – as Manager – for three years this went on.*

This extract illuminates the unexpressed norm the Head Coach will be a man more so because the team is male. The Assistant Coach is attributed leadership by virtue of being a man. Simpson and Lewis (2007: 87) note that to be 'outside the norm, women are 'marked' as a devalued, deficient Other – an embodiment of difference'. The following extract reveals the personal cost of vulnerability because of gender, 'which is so highly salient to others, [so] can be quickly blamed for any failings' (Eagly, 2007: 7).

I certainly did not anticipate what I was going to encounter in terms of players, parents and even the assistant coach and xxx who had appointed me – they put you there and when your back is against the wall do not support you – all worked away in the background to undermine my role and credibility. On reflection I struggled when issues arose – a huge job particularly on a part-time voluntary basis – hard to keep on top of everything – no support.

The imagery of a 'glass ceiling' implies a single, invisible, structural barrier. Groups of women [and men], however, are differentiated by a raft of diversity categories, such as chronological age, availability of support networks, social class and stage of life-career, some of which may progressively change. Individual women may perceive and/or experience the 'coach glass ceiling' at different times, before or beyond motherhood and for different reasons as shown above. One interviewee who has been involved as a coach for a number of years at a variety of levels adds her perspective:

Women get into coaching through kids…at one stage I was taking eight teams. The further up you go [the coach hierarchy] the more politics involved. It is extremely frustrating, you have to have a very thick skin. That is why I feel so many women walk away, all the crap you have to deal with.

A further parallel theme between workplace literature and the literature that highlights the invisibility of female elite sport coaches is the liberal feminist call for gender equality and equity, fairness and justice, underpinned by the assumption that this will reduce female disadvantage. Equal opportunity initiatives are placed on an agenda to supposedly re-dress an imbalance, more often between the visible presence of men and the absence of women. It is useful to take note of interviewees' experiences of 'women only programmes' and the relationship between what is espoused, the purpose of the programme and what eventuates (Hoeber, 2007). Field hockey has sponsored individual women to be part of programmes that in the words of one participant 'just die a natural death'. This is indicative of the discussion in the first section on the dialogue between gender equality and policy decisions. Silence on any explicit naming of specific groups of men as advantaged despite 'all the visible experts being male' (Interviewee) enables the power held to remain 'invisible'. This in-turn leads to a cycle of marginalization and women's supposed need for 'development'.

Equally, an embedded belief in the gender neutrality of structures can lead to comments I have heard on several occasions by men; 'We try to help them [women] – xxx just asks for more – expects so much but as soon as the going gets tough they [women] give up'. When this idea was posed to interviewees, the following is reflective of their responses:

> *The (coach) pathway is a wee bit of a joke – there is always an out clause – we had done all that could be done. Women give up is totally rubbish [they] hit a brick wall and deviate, may take a year out, come in back through another door, figure out a different way. Women are tough. In our everyday lives we can't just walk away – have to deal with it and I think we are very good at doing that.*

The last sentence 'have to deal with it and I think we are very good at doing that' is indicative of the theme that was prevalent in the interviews. There is a sense of something deeper in other words a 'construct-centred explanation' (Sinclair, 2005: 24). It is here we see the interconnections between the unintentional/non-reflexive masculinities in practice evidenced in the interview extracts set against the wider dominance of managerialism embedded in public policy initiatives. The impetus for the amalgamation of two structures, the NZWHA and NZHA, each with a distinct history and culture, has over time, been shaped by a unitary approach formalized in strategy documentation (e.g. SPARC *High Performance Strategy, 2006–2012*: n.d) and the implementation of structures and processes to facilitate the stated objectives. Cementing prescribed hierarchical high performance structures have been a priority with 'investment' in National Sport Organizations dependent on the 'right' structure, 'right' people, proven need, strategic planning, and importantly, 'winning performances' (SPARC, n.d). The outcome after 20 years in field hockey is as one interviewee highlights 'no role models'.

In NZ field hockey elite players are amateur but the landscape has changed for coaches. One reason argued here is that as SPARC driven high performance structures have evolved, expectations of payment for 'professional services' have heightened. What this has fostered at all levels of the field hockey infrastructure is the dual possibility paid career pathway for men where they can coach either a men's or women's team whereas a single, voluntary, pathway continues to be modelled as the sole option for women. As a consequence and demonstrated by the few women who are selected to coach teams in the premier domestic competition, NHL, further negates possibilities to reach the high performance level. Hockey NZ has modelled the duality of career path available to men in their appointments of coach and assistant coach for the female Black Sticks and Junior Black Sticks teams. Clearly, the structures and managerialist driven ideologies now prevalent inside sport, invisible and taken-for-granted, have evolved and have effectively resulted in 'occupational closure' (Leberman and Palmer, 2008: 34) in one sport that espouses gender equality.

Two immediate concerns are apparent; firstly, a generation of young women, who, in their limited playing career have rarely been exposed to female coach leadership. Moreover, potential coaches who are ex-female Black Sticks also have little experience of being coached by their own gender. Secondly, it is becoming increasingly difficult for women to build the relationships and networks necessary to gain acceptance. As evidenced in the interviews, a select 'boy's network' of coaches, such as ex-Black Stick male players, now provide the benchmark against which any coach, male or female is measured. The point is, for women to 'infiltrate' and gain credibility in a structure that has an embodied male presence and associated culture and practices that such a presence creates, requires the male gatekeepers 'to end [their] privileges and remake masculinities to sustain [any hope of] gender equality' (Connell, 2005: 1817)

Concluding thoughts

The purpose of the chapter was to examine the invisible dynamics and practices of gender in sport leadership. It sought to shift the focus from viewing women as disadvantaged and the sole gendered subject to one where 'the privileges and resources that accompany masculinity are unmasked' (Simpson and Lewis, 2007: 54) – resources that advantage specific men in sport in New Zealand. The chapter has highlighted that context, both past and present, does need to be in the foreground to understand the 'when' and 'where' questions of gender and sport leadership (Jackson and Parry, 2008: 62). One abridged case was used to illustrate how policy driven 'solutions' underpinned by an ideological shift to managerialism, has resulted in high performance sport such as field hockey being redefined along narrower lines. As a consequence, key components of the hegemonic masculinity discourse that historically has permeated the sport landscape have been further legitimized (McKay, 1997). At the same time, gender has been rendered invisible through a faith in equal opportunities and through a dominant form of masculinity that links men to leadership and power. Even when an organization advocates gender equality and where individual men may act 'equitably', a dominant male narrative that is largely invisible helps to construct hurdles for women. As Acker (2000: 631) observes after reviewing the outcomes of three organizational equity projects in work organizations that 'unfortunately, it seems, this narrative cannot be written yet'. Connell's (2005: 1801) statement is also telling, 'It is women who are disadvantaged. Men are, however, necessarily involved in gender-equality reform [there needs to be] change among the gatekeepers'. Women who are in the minority in leadership roles in organized sport are vulnerable because of the salience of their gender. Thus, at this point in time and in this place leadership in sport organizations in New Zealand appears particularly resistant to doing leadership 'in a different kind of way' (Sinclair, 2007: 185).

Notes

1 Hockey NZ is the national governing body (approx. 20 paid employees) – eight large regional associations (with between 4–10 paid employees) made up of 32 smaller associations (mix of paid and wholly volunteer run organizations).
2 The structure has been subject to change but essentially involves the Black Sticks Men and Women (inclusion determined by player ability); Junior Black Sticks (based on player ability – age restriction under 21); Academy Group – promising players but not necessarily in the two elite teams.
3 In 2007, three regional associations appointed a female as Head Coach of their Women's NHL team while in 2008, only one was appointed.

References

Aaltio, I. (2002) 'Interviewing female managers: Presentations of the gendered selves in contexts'. In Aaltio, I. and Mills, A. (eds) *Gender, Identity and the Culture of Organisations*, pp. 201–217. London: Routledge.

Acker, J. (2000) 'Gendered contradictions in organizational equity projects', *Organization*, 7(4): 625–632.

Acker, J. (2006) 'Inequality regimes. Gender, class and race in organizations', *Gender and Society*, 20(4): 441–464.

Bruce, T., Falcous M. and Thorpe, H. (2007) 'The mass media and sport'. In Collins, C. and Jackson, S. (eds) *Sport in Aotearoa/New Zealand Society*, pp. 147–164. South Melbourne, Albany: Thomson.

Cockburn, R., Gray, K. and Thompson, R. (2007) *Gender Balance in New Zealand Olympic Sports*. Wellington: New Zealand Olympic Committee.

Collins, C. (2007) 'Studying sport in society'. In Collins, C. and Jackson, S. (eds) *Sport in Aotearoa/New Zealand Society*, pp. 2–22. South Melbourne, Albany: Thomson.

Connell, R. W. (2005) 'Change among the gatekeepers: Men, masculinities, and gender equality in the global arena', *Signs: Journal of Women in Culture and Society*, 30(3): 1801–1825.

Connell, R. W. and Messerschmidt, J. W. (2005) 'Hegemonic masculinity. Rethinking the concept', *Gender & Society*, 19(6): 829–859.

Duncan, M. C. (1998) 'Stories we tell ourselves about ourselves', *Sociology of Sport*, 15: 95–108.

Eagly, A. H. (2007) 'Female leadership advantage and disadvantage: Resolving the contradictions', *Psychology of Women Quarterly*, 31: 1–12.

Edwards, M. F. (2000) *Gendered Coaching: The Impact of Gender on Roles and Qualities of Elite Women's field Hockey Coaches*. Unpublished Doctoral thesis, Massey University.

Edwards, M. F. (2008) 'Gendered practice: The impact of gender on the coaching of women's sport teams'. In Obel, C., Bruce, T. and Thompson, S. (eds). *Outstanding Research about Women in Sport in New Zealand*, pp. 227–248. University of Waikato: Wilf Malcolm Institute of Educational Research.

Hindson, A. (2006) 'The evolution of sport management in New Zealand'. In Leberman, S., Collins, C. and Trenberth, L. (eds) *Sport Business Management in Aotearoa/New Zealand* (2nd ed.), pp. 24–41. South Melbourne, Albany: Thomson.

Hockey NZ (2008) *Black Sticks*. Retrieved September, 2008 from www.hockeynz.org.nz.

Hockey NZ (2009) *Top Australian Secured as Black Sticks' Women's Coach*. Retrieved January, 2009 from http://www.hockeynz.co.nz/news/index_dynamic/containerNameToReplace=Middle/focusModuleID=8091/overrideSkinName-newsArticle-full.tpl.

Hoeber, L. (2007) 'Exploring the gaps between meanings and practices of gender equity in a sport organization', *Gender, Work and Organization*, 14(3): 259–280.

Hokowhitu, B. (2007) 'Maori sport: Pre-colonisation to today'. In Collins, C. and Jackson, S. (eds) *Sport in Aotearoa/New Zealand Society*, pp. 78–95. South Melbourne, Albany: Thomson.

Jackson, D. (1993) 'New Zealand Women's Hockey Association 1908–1988'. In Else, A. (ed) *Women Together: A History of Women's Organisations in New Zealand*, pp. 425–427. Wellington: Daphne Brasell Associates Press.
Jackson, B. and Parry, K. (2008) *A Very Short Fairly Interesting and Reasonably Cheap Book about Studying Leadership*. London, Thousand Oaks, New Delhi, Singapore: Sage Publications Ltd.
Knoppers, A. and Anthonissen, A. (2005) 'Male athletic and managerial masculinities: Congruencies in discursive practices?', *Journal of Gender Studies*, 14(2): 123–135.
Leberman, S., Trenberth, L. and Collins, C. (2006) 'Sport management trends, challenges and the future'. In Leberman, S., Collins, C. and Trenberth, L. (eds) *SportBusiness Management in Aotearoa/New Zealand* (2nd ed.), pp. 401–422. South Melbourne, Albany: Thomson.
Martin, Y. M. (2006) 'Practising gender at work: Further thoughts on reflexivity', *Gender, Work and Organization*, 13(3): 254–276.
McKay, J. (1991) *No Pain, No Gain? Sport and Australian Culture*. Sydney: Prentice Hall.
McKay, J. (1997) *Managing Gender. Affirmative Action and Organizational Power in Australian, Canadian and New Zealand Sport*. Albany: State University of New York Press.
Messner, M. A. (2007) *Out of Play. Critical Essays on Gender and Sport*. Albany: State University of New York Press.
Nolan, M. (2000) *Breadwinning: New Zealand Women and the State*. Christchurch: Canterbury University Press.
NZOC (New Zealand Olympic Committee) (2007) *Gender Balance, New Zealand Olympic Sports*. Wellington: New Zealand Olympic Committee.
NZOC (2008) *Gender Representation in New Zealand Olympic Sports*. Wellington: New Zealand Olympic Committee.
Obel, C., Bruce, T. and Thompson, S. (eds) (2008) *Outstanding Research about Women and Sport in New Zealand*. University of Waikato: Wilf Malcolm Institute of Educational Research.
Perry, M. (2004) 'Organisations, organisational change and globalisation'. In Spoonley, P., Dupuis, A. and De Bruin, A. (eds) *Work and Working in Twenty-first Century New Zealand*, pp. 41–70. Palmerston North: New Zealand.
Piggin, J., Jackson, S. J. and Lewis, M. (2009) 'Knowledge, power and politics. Contesting "evidence-based" national sport policy', *International Review for the Sociology of Sport*, 44(1): 87–101.
Pringle, R. (2007) 'Sport, males and masculinity'. In Collins, C. and Jackson, S. (eds) *Sport in Aotearoa/New Zealand Society*, pp. 355–380. South Melbourne, Albany: Thomson.
Report of the New Zealand Hockey Review Committee. (1987) *Hockey: The Task Ahead. Executive Summary*. Wellington: The New Zealand Sports Foundation, Inc.
Richardson, L. (2000) 'Writing: A method of inquiry'. In Denzin, N. K. and Lincoln, Y. S. (eds) *The Handbook of Qualitative Research* (2nd ed.), pp. 923–948. Thousand Oaks, London, New Delhi: Sage Publications.
Richardson, L. (2007) 'Reading for another. A method for addressing some feminist research dilemmas'. In Hesse-Biber, S. (ed.) *Handbook of Feminist Research. Theory and Praxis*, pp. 459–467. Thousand Oaks, London, New Delhi: Sage Publications Ltd.

Rinehart, R. E. (2005) '"Experiencing" sport management: The use of personal narrative in sport management studies', *Journal of Sport Management*, 19: 497–522.

Ryan, I. D. (2005) *'Their Stories, Our Stories, My Stories'. The Intersectionality of Age and Gender through the Voices of Mid-life Sportswomen*. Unpublished Doctoral thesis, University of Auckland.

Sam, M. P. and Jackson, S. J. (2004) 'Sport policy development in New Zealand: Paradoxes of an integrative paradigm', *International Review for the Sociology of Sport*, 39(2): 205–222.

Shaw, S. and Cameron, J. (2008) '"The best person for the job": Gender suppression and homologous reproduction in senior sport management', in Obel, C., Bruce, T. and Thompson, S. (eds) *Outstanding Research about Women and Sport in New Zealand*, pp. 211–226. University of Waikato: Wilf Malcolm Institute of Educational Research.

Simpson, R. and Lewis, P. (2007) *Voice, Visibility and the Gendering of Organizations*. Hampshire, New York: Palgrave Macmillan.

Sinclair, A. (2007) *Leadership for the Disillusioned. Moving Beyond Myths, Heroes to Leading that Liberates*. Australia: Allen Unwin.

Sinclair, A. (2005) *Doing Leadership Differently*. Australia: Melbourne University Press.

Sport, Fitness and Leisure Ministerial Taskforce (2001) *Getting Set for an Active Nation: Report of the Sport, Fitness and Leisure Ministerial Taskforce*. Wellington, New Zealand.

SPARC (Sport and Recreation New Zealand) (n.d.) *High Performance Strategy 2006–2012*. Retrieved 18 July, 2008 from www.sparc.org.nz.

SPARC (2008) *SPARC Invests in Future Kiwi Sporting Success*. Retrieved 15 December, 2008 from http://www.sparc.org.nz.

Sport Scotland (n.d.) *Gender Equity in Sport and the Gender Duty*. Retrieved 16 December, 2008 from www.sportscotland.org.uk.

Thorp, H. (2008) 'Feminism for a new generation: A case study of women in the snowboarding culture'. In Obel, C., Bruce, T. and Thompson, S. (eds) *Outstanding Research about Women and Sport in New Zealand*, pp. 7–30. University of Waikato: Wilf Malcolm Institute of Educational Research.

Tsang, T. (2000) 'Let me tell you a story: A narrative exploration of identity in high performance sport', *Sociology of Sport Journal*, 17(1): 44–59.

Vickers, D. (2008) 'Beyond the hegemonic narrative – a study of managers', *Journal of Organizational Change Management*, 21(5): 560–573.

Watson, G. and Haskell, W. (2002) *Seasons of Honour. A Centenary History of New Zealand Hockey 1902–2002*. Auckland, Palmerston North: Dunmore Press in association with New Zealand Hockey Federation.

Wilson, D. C. (2009) 'Organizational change management'. In Clegg, S. R. and Cooper, C. L. (eds), *The Sage Handbook of Organizational Behaviour: Macro Approaches*, Vol 2, pp. 409–423. London, Thousand Oaks, New Delhi, Singapore: Sage Publications.

8
Leadership and the (In)visibility of Gender

Jennifer Binns

Introduction

> *Fundamental to patriarchy is the invisibility of women, the unreal nature of women's experience, the absence of women as a force to be reckoned with* (Spender, 1983, p. 13).

Why is gender rarely mentioned in articles, books and courses about leadership? Is it because gender is irrelevant to leading or is something else going on below the radar? Dale Spender's observation provides a useful starting point for exploring these important questions. However, we need to move beyond considering the invisibility of gender solely in terms of the invisible feminine or the absent woman.

This is because 'gender' is the product of the relationship between the categories of masculine/man and feminine/woman, categories which are socially constructed as opposites. Hence, the absence of women and the characteristics associated with women is predicated on (and essential to) the presence of men and the characteristics of maleness. But this invisible woman/visible man dualism still does not capture the complex nature of (in)visibility and leadership. Using interview material from a small empirical study of leaders I explore the processes of (in)visibility which, rather than being straightforwardly aligned to gender categories, often operate in ambivalent and contradictory ways.

In this paper, interview material from my study is analysed through a conceptual framework comprising three interconnected forms of (in)visibility. Firstly, conceptual or *discursive (in)visibility* refers to the absence of feminine values and characteristics from dominant (highly visible) understandings of leadership, and to the invisible nature of the links between the ideals of masculinity and the ideals of leadership.

A recognition of the material effects of discursive (in)visibility leads to my second category – *corporeal (in)visibility*. This term refers to the material or physical absence of women's bodies from leadership contexts (which are dominated by male bodies), but also alludes to the seeming anomaly of women being highly visible when they trespass on the 'masculine' world of leadership. This contradictory position shapes my third category, *(in)visibility as identity work*. Here, identity is understood as an ongoing and active process of crafting a leadership persona and practices from the cultural materials (norms, gender stereotypes, social values and expectations) made available to individuals as occupants of the category 'woman' or 'man'. A key point here is the inseparability of gendering practices – 'doing gender' (West and Zimmerman, 1987) – and leadership practices. Gender and leadership are 'done' (enacted/ practiced) in concert with each other, a *pas de deux* in which gender is sometimes showcased and at other times obscured.

The study

During 2003, I completed a small qualitative study involving a series of interviews with 16 leaders located in Perth, Western Australia. The interview group comprised women and men who held mid level management positions in the public and corporate sectors, or ran small businesses. There was a mix of 'formal' leaders (with the positional authority conferred by the title 'manager') and 'informal' leaders (facilitators and advisors, both internal and external to the organization).

A semi-structured interview process was used, comprising a series of guided conversations with each participant. The research topics were spread over three interviews, with two to three week intervals between each. At the first interview people talked about their understandings of leadership in the context of their own work practices. The second interview focused on the leaders' working relationships, while the third interview explored emotions, learning and gender. This chapter draws on nine (four male and five female) of the 16 narratives that form part of the research project. Pseudonyms are used and other identifying information changed to preserve anonymity.

As I write this it occurs to me that disguising the identity of the research subjects so that they can be safely presented (made visible) to the reader also makes them less fully visible as embodied, flesh and blood people. This is a paradox given the topic of this chapter, but one which underscores the complex nature of (in)visibility. The author, or the author's subjectivity, also risks invisibility within a text which 'reveals', analyses and presents others' lives. The invisibility of the researcher is a hallmark of mainstream academic inquiry. Dorothy Smith (1987) argues that, by denying his embodied masculinity, the male sociologist is able to present his intellectual work as gender neutral, objective and normative. Challenging the masculine orthodoxy means insisting that research and writing are highly personal endeavours (Frost and Stablein, 1992; Marshall, 1981).

Every text 'bears the traces of its author' (Lincoln and Denzin, 1998: 413), hence this text cannot be uncoupled from my own ontological and epistemological stance. The invisible hand of this author has taken apart and reassembled the leaders' accounts into themes and categories, making their lives visible in particular ways and through selected viewing points. Other assemblages and patterns remain outside the reader's view. Some meanings will perhaps never be visible to this author, looking through her particular lens. Recognizing the inevitability of this research, myopia means proceeding with caution, developing nuanced understandings and endeavoring to resist the seduction of simple gender categories.

Discussion: Dimensions of gender invisibility

In this section I interweave theory with empirical material in order to explore the gender (in)visibility of leadership – through discourse, corporeal practices and identity processes.

Discursive (in)visibility

Leadership ideals/images are synonymous with the normatively masculine values of heroic individualism, toughness and decisiveness (Sinclair, 1998). But, like the emperor's new clothes, it is not considered polite within mainstream leadership discourse to 'name' masculinity, let alone men (Collinson and Hearn, 1994; Hearn, 2004). Masculinity, maleness and men are, then, taboo subjects in most academic research on leadership, in popular management texts, and within leadership development programs (Sinclair, 2000). This conspiracy of silence – and of blindness – supports the pretense that leading is a genderless practice, except when women do it. The dearth of analyses of 'masculine' leadership contrast with myriad studies about women and leadership. These studies make the gendered construction of leadership visible, but only as a 'feminine' alternative to the main/male game.

The genderedness of leadership – as construct and as practice – has been made visible by feminist critiques (Blackmore, 1989; Eveline, 2004;

Sinclair, 1998), however such insights have not been a feature of mainstream and popular leadership texts. So-called soft or feminine conceptualizations of leading are often permeated by heroic ideals which operate invisibly to undermine the alternative being presented. For example, the highly influential writings on emotional intelligence (Goleman *et al*, 2002) have been criticized for refashioning the feminine qualities of emotional connection and sensitivity into the heroic techniques of control and rationality (Hatcher, 2003). It appears that, as Fletcher (2001) contends, the 'demise of heroic leadership' has been 'greatly exaggerated'.

The tenacity of heroic notions of leadership is evident in some of the accounts from my study. Peter, the head of a small manufacturing firm, described leadership in gender neutral terms but at the same time he evoked highly masculine concepts:

> *It's been drummed into us that equality is important, and it is to me. And I've had female bosses, doesn't bother me. So I don't draw those kinds of distinctions…When I think of male leaders I generally go to people who have an element of conflict around their leadership style, e.g. Churchill, Mandela, Gandhi, Hitler, Stalin, JFK.*

In Peter's account, women are visible within a discourse of gender equality while male leadership is constituted by the heroic archetype. But how can anonymous 'female bosses' compete for credibility and legitimacy with the great men of history listed here? Dan, an HR Manager for a non-profit organization, also shifted from gender neutral to strongly masculine concepts of leadership:

> *I've never been a female and I don't ever want to be a female. I like fast cars and watching violent videos, and all these other things that the typical bloke likes to do. My wife is very different and so are many of the other females I know. But, whatever those differences might be, we are judged by our behaviours. And, the way that we work as a leader in our community is totally based on our behaviours. There are underlying cognitions, thoughts and so on. I don't think it makes any difference whether you are male or female; it's the behaviour you exhibit that's the leadership…So, it's not whether you are male or female, whether you like V8 cars or knitting – sorry, I'm a very blokey bloke! [laughing] (note: 'bloke' is an Australian colloquial term for a manly man).*

While this account highlights the notion of leadership as a set of genderless behaviours, Dan's colourful language reveals the discursive power of the heroic masculine archetype. The reference to 'knitting' signifies the tasks that women do, or 'should' do – quietly, gently, and under the radar of the public world of formal leadership. When women operate in that public world they are expected to 'knit' people together, make connections and nurture relationships. But the dominant leadership discourse 'disappears' the relational practices (Fletcher, 2001), informal leading (Eveline, 2004) and liberating approaches (Sinclair, 2007) that fall within a more generous understanding of what it means to lead (Eveline, 2004; Sinclair, 1998, 2007). And because these alternative activities are associated with femininity and are done primarily by women, both the activities and the women who do them are symbolically and materially absent from what counts as leadership.

Lea, a middle manager from my study, described her difference from the male norm in terms of both visibility (she is seen as an anomaly) and invisibility (she is not recognized as a legitimate leader):

One of the things I like to do is create an atmosphere of difference. As a leader, sometimes I'm not taken as seriously as I could be. They'll say 'Lea's a bit weird.' People tell me I don't get the recognition I deserve but I'm too busy doing it to think about being acknowledged...

Being female is pushing against the tide...It's exhilarating knowing that you are venturing into unchartered territory and that you're setting yourself up as a role model for other women, including my daughters. But it hasn't been easy. You learn to be more cautious.

'Pushing against the tide' of the dominant discourse means that Lea's visibility as a leader is dependent on a different notion of leadership, that of the role model. She is a visible example to other women of how to do leadership differently. But this kind of visibility requires constant effort and vigilance to guard against the ever present risk of discursive disappearance from the leadership frame into the oblivion of 'weirdness'.

Corporeal (in)visibility

The disappearance of women (and non heroic men) from leadership occurs at more than the discursive level. Discursive invisibility constitutes, and is constituted by, corporeal invisibility. The absence of flesh and blood women from the roles and activities normally recognized as leadership reinforces the masculinity of leading. But women's bodies are, of course, not totally absent from mainstream leadership contexts.

Rather, they are present in small numbers, generally on the margins and only marginally tolerated. For this reason, gender is highly visible as embodied femininity. However, this very visibility can make women leaders vulnerable to removal from leadership contexts (the ultimate form of invisibility). This is the experience of Rachel, a senior public servant who took part in my leadership study:

> I've always had precarious relationships with guys in the workplace. They perceive a competitive relationship, although I don't consciously set this up. They perceive me to be awesome but not in the nice sense. I often have tricky relationships with men who often spend a lot of their time trying to work out how to do one-upmanship. I suppose, instead of ignoring them, I get engaged which probably encourages them...Apparently I'm seen as incredibly threatening to an awful lot of men. And I don't know what I do to be threatening other than try to get my job done and trying to make a difference. And it gets to the point where they get rid of me, which is very hurtful...Maybe I'm not properly deferent and I say it the way I see it...Maybe people feel disconcerted because I always assume that I have the ability to influence.

Being awesome, active, outspoken and powerful fits the heroic leadership ideal in all but one essential way – Rachel is not a man. Transgressing gendered norms makes her highly visible and therefore invites male hostility. Rachel is perplexed by such hostility towards her efforts to 'get my job done and trying to make a difference.' But it is *difference* that unsettles the organizational rhythms to a point where Rachel's symbolic exclusion/invisibility takes a material form. The signifiers of masculine leadership mark Rachel as aberrant and threatening. She is a marked woman, to be 'gotten rid of' at the first opportunity. The absence of her female body then becomes the final move in the invisibility game.

As visibility can be a risk for women leaders, especially those like Rachel who deploy power overtly, others use more covert strategies. Another research participant, Thea, described the strategic benefit to her change management project of making her leadership practices, and herself, invisible:

> I've been thinking about the leadership role and talking to...[change management consultant]. She says that all the women she's working with in government departments operate in the same way in that they have not been given an overt leadership role but are all driving this thing and making huge changes. They all have different personalities but are all

doing it by lurking around corridors and forming relationships. And all very primary in bringing in something that will be quite massive but doing it in a very non overt way...

This picture of idealized femininity – of unassuming and quiet achievement – is the template for *female* leadership but the antithesis of *real* leadership. Heroic leaders do not 'lurk around corridors' but are confident in using power in more direct and overt ways. However, as Rachel's experience shows, women who exercise power overtly are highly visible as threats to the masculine order and therefore risk disappearing from the leadership stage altogether.

While embodied femaleness is noted, scrutinized and barely tolerated within mainstream leadership, the mass of male bodies is simply seen as the body of leadership. Men are invisible *as men* but highly visible *as leaders*. This may seem contradictory, given that heroic leadership involves highly masculinized and none too subtle bodily performances (Sinclair, 2005a, 2005b, 2007). Due to force of numbers, as well as size and stature, men physically embody what is thought of as leadership (Sinclair, 2005a, 2007). For example, failed Australian entrepreneur Steve Vizard was described by a former associate as a born leader whose 'sheer physical appearance' meant 'you can't help but see him... he stands out' (cited in Sinclair, 2007, p. 9). However, these performances are seen as the doing of leadership, rather than the doing of masculinity.

An embodied understanding of gender (in)visibility situates flesh and blood leaders spatially and temporally. Women and men are expected to occupy different physical settings – women in the home and men in the workplace; women in secretarial pools and men in boardrooms. These are the traditional gender images reproduced through films, books, magazines and lived experience. Andre, a research participant, described this corporeal separation in the following way:

I don't see leader and man in the same context. I see man in a more traditional element that society establishes...Leadership has no gender at all. I come from a family where my grandmother was housebound, but...she was a leader because she had an ability to bring a family of thirteen kids into thinking the same. Whereas my grandfather had the ability to earn money to keep the family, so together it worked well. So, he was a leader in his own domain.

Although Andre declares that 'leadership has no gender at all', his grandparent anecdote foregrounds gender dynamics. It presents a gendered image of leadership based on separate but complementary masculine and feminine 'domains'. Here, women's leadership is visible as long as it is enacted in the right domain, the private sphere of home and family.

But what happens when women place themselves in the 'wrong' domain? Extending Marshall's (1984) view of women leaders as '*travellers* in a male world', the responses of the women leaders in my study suggest that female invisibility is an effect of women being *trespassers*, both figuratively and literally, on normatively male terrain. Because women in leadership lack legitimacy within the dominant heroic discourse, their experiences of leadership require a degree of corporeal maneuvering not required of men. As Lewis (2006) found in her study of female entrepreneurs, visibility (success and acceptance) *as a leader* entails disappearing *as a woman*. However, such a strategy can never be fully achieved, as demonstrated by my conversation with study participant Rose, a small business owner:

> *I believe that a good leader is a chameleon. I learnt that when I first became the director of a company. I was twenty-seven and I'd been a secretary and the next day I was going to be a director...So I thought, okay, the next day I'm going to get up and put a director's coat on. I've kept that analogy all through my business life. If I have to do something I'll put that coat on and that's the person I'll be.*

Rose was speaking both literally and figuratively. The director's coat is both a state of mind (psyching herself up) and an actual garment (dressing the part). The chameleon changes its physical appearance to become visible as a leader – the corollary is becoming invisible as a woman. But how successful is this physical transformation? Rose, again, later in our conversation:

> *I used to think – when I was at the Chamber of Commerce – that this is odd, there's no-one else here. I've heard about the glass ceiling...but in my case I didn't think much about being a woman. I was sometimes surprised that people commented on it. Because I just thought I was talking business. But the problem you do have being a woman, I recognize that it's a very uneven playing field in that if I got tough about something, then of course I'm a bitch. Whereas a man could walk into a meeting and quite easily say 'this isn't good enough'...Whereas if a woman does that, especially as at the time I was younger, attractive and*

had a nice figure. So people didn't expect me to have a business head on my shoulders.

Rose describes the literal absence of women from masculinized domains like chambers of commerce ('there's no-one else here'). She is wearing her director's coat (camouflaging her womanly difference from the norm) and 'talking business' just like all the other (male) business leaders. But Rose apparently cannot escape her highly visible embodied femininity which disqualifies her from being seen as a business leader. Her 'feminine' shoulders are all too visible in this milieu of 'masculine' business heads.

Susan, a management consultant and trainer, told a similar story of female invisibility within masculine settings:

I've been on boards where they're all high powered and financially oriented. So when I say that we should lower the steps on the buses for people with disabilities and mothers with prams, that takes huge effort, because they all sort of stop and look at you, nod, then go back to talking about money. I didn't want to be always raising the women's issues but that was all that was left. The men looked after the money and I looked after the little old ladies with sticks. But I always thought hard before I spoke and my heart was always pounding.

Susan is the imposter in the male boardroom. As a woman, she looks after the 'soft' issues – relationships and 'little old ladies with sticks' – but compliance with this feminine expectation makes her a less visible, audible and credible player in the masculine money game. And speaking from a position of invisibility is difficult and risky – little wonder that Susan's heart pounded!

Given that visibility *as a woman* may be the only form of visibility available to female leaders, it is not surprising that strategies of female empowerment sometimes play on embodied (visible) gender difference. As Rose put it:

The MD [Managing Director] of ABC Communications and I formed a good relationship – he saw himself as a god and me as his female version. He called me his goddess. I used to wear mini skirts, had a good figure and looked pretty good when I whacked on the makeup. At a trade party once he said to me 'if you wear a skirt like that to our next meeting I'll give you an extra percentage point', which is a woman thing [because] you wouldn't say that to a man. I could take that the wrong way but I wore the short dress so I guess I was asking for it.

The invisible chameleon transforms into a goddess whose power comes from foregrounding her embodied femaleness. Rose visibly and deliberately embodies the *femme fatale*, the seductress, even though she is aware that men are not required to make their embodied masculinity visible. But what are women leaders 'asking for' when they deploy this form of visibility? Because the rules of the leadership game are stacked against them, feminine visibility is inevitably coupled with leadership *in*visibility.

The identity work of (in)visibility

The chameleon becomes a metaphor for the operation of embodied (in)visibility – the presence/absence of actual men and women from leadership contexts and the presentation of bodies via gendered codes of dress and deportment – but it also signals the inseparability of the body from identity. Bodies matter but bodies are not just bodies; they are inscribed with gendered symbols, social expectations, cultural norms and experiences (Gatens, 1996). So, Rose's chameleon stands for the physical presentation, positioning and look of a woman's body (which make it visible in the world of men) *and* her self-perception (symbolically taking on the masculine identity of director).

In my study I was interested in exploring how people saw (or didn't see) themselves as leaders within a gendered context. At the end of the three-phase interview process, I posed the following question: 'What does it mean to you to be a man/woman and a leader?'. Although I did not at the time have gender (in)visibility in mind, the responses do seem to reveal the ways in which these leaders made their gender identity visible (of consequence) and/or invisible (of no consequence).

The responses from the men and women in the study are, I think, noticeably different. The question seemed to 'make sense' to the women leaders, who talked in detail about the ups and downs of being a woman and a leader. However, in common with Whitehead's (2001) study of men in education management, my male respondents were mostly puzzled or troubled by the question. Unlike the women leaders, the men had never needed to reflect on their gender identity. As Hearn and Morgan (1990: 15) put it, men 'generally have no more need to theorize their situations than fish need to theorize about water'.

This is not to present 'men' as a unitary category. As Connell (1995) has argued, there are different forms of masculinity and many men are located outside of what he calls hegemonic masculinity (the heroic archetype). Perhaps only one of the men in my study could be said to fit the masculine stereotype – this is Dan who described himself as 'a red blooded male'. Others were at pains to distance themselves from the stereotype.

But despite the differences amongst men, amongst masculinities and between men and masculinities, there are also unities (Collinson and Hearn, 1994). This is because the hegemony of masculine values in leadership discourse is inseparable from the hegemony of men in actual leadership contexts (Hearn, 2004). Male advantage is maintained through normalization processes that make men's advantage invisible (Eveline, 1994a and b). It is impossible to talk about masculinized subjectivity in isolation from the actual advantages that embodied men enjoy as leaders. And one of those privileges is the ability to be seen, and to see oneself, as just a leader (without the gender adjective which attaches itself tenaciously to *women* leaders).

Gender (in)visibility is produced through the crafting and presentation of identities, a process that involves both engagement with and resistance to the discursive categories man/masculine and woman/feminine. The notion of identity as 'work' (Linstead and Thomas, 2002) signals the effortful and ongoing nature of gender as gender*ing*. Similarly, the terms masculin*ized* and femin*ized* underline the socially constructed process of gender identity, as opposed to the fixed categories of feminine/masculine (Eveline, 2004).

In the identity work of women leaders a tension must be negotiated between playing down and highlighting gendered identities. If identities are conceptualized 'as masks that are created as resources for participation in an ongoing masquerade' (Linstead and Thomas, 2002, p. 1), it becomes clear that the mask of femininity is not always going to serve women as a resource for negotiating leadership positions. Thus, a feminized identity may need to be 'masked' through presentations of either genderless or masculine/heroic leadership. This is what Patricia Lewis (2006) found in her study of female entrepreneurs, many of whom did hard identity work to avoid being seen as different from the male norm.

The mask metaphor captures the possibility of gender identity being visible (on show) and invisible (masked) at different times and places in the leadership masquerade. Both female and male leaders can be said to have an investment in presenting their leadership as genderless (as just leading), but for women such a move is fraught. Male leaders can avoid naming themselves as men, whereas female leaders need to do effortful identity work to reconcile the embodied feminine with the masculine ideals embedded in the dominant concept of leadership.

The notion of gender switching (Bruni and Gherardi, 2002) is useful as a way of thinking about movement between gender visibility (*female* leader) and invisibility (just a *leader*). Rose's chameleon is a classic example of this, with the director's cloak being the symbolic and material mechanism through which the gender switch occurs.

The synchronization of masculine ideals with ideal leadership means that men do not need to engage in gender switching – there is no contradiction to reconcile. For women, however, the representation of femininity as the devalued opposite of masculine leadership means that becoming visible (recognized) as a leader often entails trying to be invisible as a woman. The strategy of gender switching is illustrated by the following excerpt from my interview with Susan:

Interviewer:	*Can you talk some more about your [earlier] comment that dealing with the Managing Director brings out your masculine side?*
Susan:	*Yes, I guess I matched him. I wasn't going to waffle around because I know what he'd do – stare out the window and look at his watch.*
Interviewer:	*How did you feel adopting that masculine style?*
Susan:	*Great, because it's actually part of me. It's just a different part of my personality. But with the women, it's like it is with you, just sitting and chatting.*
Interviewer:	*How easy is it to switch between these two modes of being?*
Susan:	*It's easy. I think it's a capacity a lot of women have because we have to do it all the time. For example, going from business mode to mum mode.*
Interviewer:	*Is there one mode or style that comes more naturally?*
Susan:	*The one that doesn't wear me out is the feminine one. I get really tired when I have to spend a day talking to blokes like that. It takes more effort to stay there.*

In Susan's account, the changing feminine and masculine masks is initially presented as unproblematic ('it's easy') and enjoyable ('great'). Switching from 'business mode to mum mode' is something that women 'have to do...all the time'. However, such identity work becomes hard labour. As Susan put it, 'it takes more effort to stay' in the masculine, to be an imposter in a male world. Conforming to the unwritten rules of heroic masculinity is effortful and risky, and for women it can never be completely successful.

Women cannot stay in the genderless identity position, because 'just' doing leadership entails alignment with a (hidden) masculine construct. As Rachel's experience shows, when women's leadership is seen to be aligned to the dominant mode, this invites accusations of 'managing like a man' (Wajcman, 1999). This is the ultimate crime against femininity (which ought to remain demurely in the organizational background), punishable – in Rachel's case – by removal from her leadership position.

Women's leadership is not just invisible to others, but often also to themselves. Although Rachel has held senior management positions (one step down from chief executive) and run large public sector divisions, she loses sight of her own leadership credentials:

> *Leadership in the public service probably isn't for me, unless I was going to run an organization. Like most women, I'm not sure if I could do that anyway...*
>
> *People have said that I've been a role model as a leader but I seem to have a hard time talking about it...My daughter says you have to be honest and not blow your own trumpet. In a way that's true because I see men doing that. But there must be a way for me to feel self confident. I've always been a leader and I presume I do fairly well. I don't know.*

Gendered expectations permit men to 'blow their own trumpet' but sanction women who do so. Even daughters urge their mothers to keep their leadership achievements under wraps! While female leaders may need to avoid drawing attention to themselves and their achievements, their male counterparts are engaged in a different invisibility game in which it is masculinity that is downplayed.

For many of the men in the study, the gender and leadership question only made sense when they were able to re-cast it as an issue of women's leadership styles, thereby rendering their own gender identity irrelevant and invisible. Consider the following excerpt from my interaction with Peter, CEO of a small manufacturing firm:

> Interviewer: *What does it mean to be a man and a leader?*
> Peter: *I have no frame of reference for not being that. I could speak for hours on that but where are you trying to get to? What's underlying it? I'm not wanting to be defensive.*

Interviewer: *I'm just interested in how you see the impact of you being a man on your leadership...*

Peter: *I lead differently to anyone else, because there's only one of me. I don't know whether there's a gender bias in that, I don't think there is. My belief is – talking about management – I think females are far better managers than men. Are they better leaders? My perception is that's where the question is going. What's a male perspective on female leaders? I know very little about female leaders throughout history – I can't think of too many. I think there has been an impediment to women taking up leadership roles. There's childbearing issues, glass ceiling type issues. So you can't compare because there's not the same history. Does that answer your question?*

Interviewer: *I'm not looking for a particular answer, just...*

Peter: *Watching people squirm!*

Interviewer: *...asking the question and seeing what people feel is the link between their gender and their leadership.*

Peter: *I don't think there is one. I think there's a link between the person Peter George is and leadership.*

Interviewer: *And Peter George is a man.*

Peter: *But he's also a unique individual. So I don't see there's a causal effect between Peter George-man-leadership. I think it would be wrong logic to say that I am a leader because I am a man.*

Peter made sense of the 'gender question' by casting it as an issue of *difference*; that is, how women's leadership differs from the (male) norm. Yet his own 'difference' (uniqueness) is secured by rejecting gender categories in favour of the genderless ideal of individualism. While Peter's response calls on the notion of the abstract genderless subject, it also contains an account of gender specificity. This paradox is resolved by the semiotic slide from 'gender' to 'female', a move that makes 'gender' visible *as a woman's issue*. A similar shift from 'gender' to 'woman' is evident in the response to the man-leadership question from John, a project manager:

I suppose I'm a feminist by nature...Adopting a macho image of a capital M man I believe has very little to do with leadership. From my days in the Army I've seen many superb women leaders, therefore I wouldn't attach anything gender-specific to leadership. You've only got to look around the world; some of the most male-dominated countries have women leaders...I enjoy being a leader and the fact I'm a man's probably got nothing to do with it.

In John's response, gender is visible in a specific way, through the example of 'superb women leaders' whom he has seen. John has also seen gender operating in 'macho' leadership practices – roughly equivalent to the heroic archetype. But gender is not visible in John's own leadership. His identity as a leader is secured by rejecting the gender tag. It 'makes sense' for men to claim that being a man has 'got nothing to do' with leading because the masculine norm obscures itself and its own effects. But for women leaders, the identity position of 'just a leader' is problematic.

Closing thoughts

Patricia Yancey Martin (2006: 270) argues that making gender visible is the first step in challenging the organizational power relations that privilege men at women's expense. This chapter is a contribution to the project of revealing gender processes, using leadership to explore the ongoing ways in which masculine/feminine and men/women are produced as (in)visible. I have proposed a theoretical framework comprising three interlinked forms of (in)visibility – discursive, embodied and identity work. While I have found this typology useful as an analytical device, I am also conscious of the artificiality of separating out three distinct forms of (in)visibility.

It is important to recognize that all the dimensions of (in)visibility coalesce in the daily experiences and practices of flesh and blood leaders. Perhaps this, then, should be the focus of feminist intervention. We need to go beyond academic texts, to 'catch gender in practice' (Martin, 2006: 254) and to encourage leaders, especially male leaders, to 'see' gender dynamics and effects. In Australia, Amanda Sinclair (2000) has been doing this with MBA students and corporate leaders. However, Kerfoot's (1999: 197) contention that '[m]asculine subjectivity is...unreflexive and unreflective in its unwillingness, or sheer inability, to challenge the conditions of its own perpetuation' reminds us that this is no easy task.

References

Blackmore, J. (1989) 'Educational leadership: A feminist critique and reconstruction'. In Smyth, J. (ed.) *Critical Perspectives on Educational Leadership*, pp. 93–130. London: Falmer Press.

Bruni, A. and Gherardi, S. (2002) 'Omega's story: The heterogeneous engineering of a gendered professional self'. In Dent, M. and Whitehead, S. (eds) *Managing Professional Identities: Knowledge, Performativity and the 'New' Professional*, pp. 174–201. London: Routledge.

Collinson, D. and Hearn, J. (1994) 'Naming men as men: Implications for work, organization and management', *Gender, Work and Organization*, 1(1): 2–22.

Connell, R. W. (1995) *Masculinities*. St Leonards New South Wales: Allen and Unwin.

Eveline, J. (1994a) 'The politics of advantage', *Australian Feminist Studies*, 19: 129–154.

Eveline, J. (1994b) 'Woman in the ivory tower: Gendering feminised and masculinised identities', *Journal of Organizational Change Management*, 18(6): 641–658.

Eveline, J. (2004) *Ivory Basement Leadership: Power and Invisibility in the Changing University*. Crawley, Western Australia: University of Western Australia Press.

Fletcher, J. (2001) *Disappearing Acts: Gender, Power and Relational Practice at Work*. Cambridge, Mass: The MIT Press.

Frost, P. and Stablein, R. (1992) *Doing Exemplary Research*. Newbury Park: Sage.

Gatens, M. (1996) *Imaginary Bodies: Ethics, Power and Corporeality*. London: Routledge.

Goleman, D., Boyatzis, R. and McKee, A. (2002) *Primal Leadership: Realizing the Power of Emotional Intelligence*. Boston: Harvard Business School Press.

Hatcher, C. (2003) 'Refashioning a passionate manager: Gender at work', *Gender, Work and Organization*, 10(4): 391–412.

Hearn, J. (2004) 'From hegemonic masculinity to the hegemony of men', *Feminist Theory*, 5(1): 49–72.

Hearn, J. and Morgan, D. H. J. (1990) *Men, Masculinities and Social Theory*. London: Unwin Hyman.

Kerfoot, D. (1999) 'The organization of intimacy: Managerialism, masculinity and the masculine subject'. In Whitehead, S. and Moodely, R. (eds) *Transforming Managers: Gendering Change in the Public Sector*, pp. 184–199. London: UCL Press.

Lewis, P. (2006) 'The quest for invisibility: Female entrepreneurs and the masculine norm of entrepreneurship', *Gender, Work and Organization*, 13(5): 453–469.

Lincoln, Y. and Denzin, N. (1998) *The Landscape of Qualitative Research: Theories and Issues*. Thousand Oaks, California: Sage.

Linstead, A. and Thomas, R. (2002) '"What do you want from me?" A poststructuralist feminist reading of middle managers' identities', *Culture and Organization*, 8(1): 1–20.

Marshall, J. (1981) 'Making sense as a personal process'. In Reason, P. and Rowan, J. (eds) *Human Inquiry: A Sourcebook of New Paradigm Research*, pp. 395–399. Chichester: John Wiley and Sons.

Marshall, J. (1984) *Women Managers: Travellers in a Male World*. Chichester: John Wiley and Sons.

Martin, P. Y. (2006) 'Practicing gender at work: Further thoughts on reflexivity', *Gender, Work and Organization*, 13(3): 254–276.

Sinclair, A. (1998) *Doing Leadership Differently*. Melbourne: Melbourne University Press.

Sinclair, A. (2000) 'Teaching managers about masculinities: Are you kidding?', *Management Learning*, 31(1): 83–101.

Sinclair, A. (2005a) 'Body and management pedagogy', *Gender, Work and Organization*, 12(1): 89–104.

Sinclair, A. (2005b) 'Body possibilities in leadership', *Leadership*, 1: 387–406.
Sinclair, A. (2007) *Leadership for the Disillusioned: Moving Beyond Myths and Heroes to Leading that Liberates.* Crows Nest, New South Wales: Allen and Unwin.
Smith, D. (1987) *The Everyday World as Problematic: A Feminist Sociology.* Boston: Northeastern University Press.
Spender, D. (1983) *Women of Ideas and What Men Have Done to Them.* London: Ark.
Wajcman, J. (1999) *Managing Like a Man: Women and Men in Corporate Management.* St Leonards New South Wales: Allen and Unwin.
West, C. and Zimmerman, D. (1987) 'Doing gender', *Gender and Society*, 1(1): 125–151.
Whitehead, S. (2001) 'The invisible gendered subject: Men in education management', *Journal of Gender Studies,* 10(1): 67–82.

9
'Now you see me, now you don't': The Visibility Paradox for Women in a Male-Dominated Profession

Jacqueline H. Watts

Introduction

Work has long been understood as central to male identity signifying personal/family responsibility and, more recently, commitment to the duties of citizenship (Lewis, 2004). With the rise in women's labour market participation, however, work is now increasingly influencing women's sense of self. Explanations for growing attachment to paid work include increasing economic needs or desires but also strengthening the sense of identity or self esteem provided by work and the opportunities it offers to engage in meaningful relationships with others (Lewis *et al*, 2003). Women who undertake professional work are still seen as stepping outside the traditional female stereotype and those who are employed in male-dominated professions remain as tokens in most sectors. As tokens, they are often in a position of representing their ascribed category to the majority group so that 'ordinary' group membership eludes them with the label of 'female-judge', 'female-plumber', or, as in this case, 'female-engineer' firmly assigned. Because of their obvious difference in relation to the dominant group 'tokens capture a larger awareness share' (Whittock, 2000: 177) which renders them highly visible and subject to intense scrutiny by others, often experienced as social exclusion. The choice by tokens of accepting isolation or taking active steps towards assimilation is risk-laden and complex and dependent on the occupational context.

In this chapter I am concerned with the experiences of women as professional civil engineers within UK construction and how they negotiate their place as minority workers in a masculine environment. This negotiation is complex and is centred on women having to establish a credible professional identity in ways not required of men. The challenges to women go beyond those experienced by men due to the double anxiety (Dryburgh, 1999) they face of being female in male terrain. McIlwee and Robinson (1992) conceptualize this as a double handicap with high visibility often resulting in a negative impact on job satisfaction and the enjoyment of a worthwhile life (Blair-Loy, 2001). It also requires women to compensate for their femaleness by being exceptionally competent at their work and encourages the self-imposed development and enactment of excessive work demands. This visibility extends to the work-family interface with women's identity in the professional sphere being tainted or compromised by expectations that work is a secondary commitment with home and family a priority (Lewis, 2002; Watts, 2008). Polarized perceptions of women *either* as hard-working professionals *or* as caring homemakers persist. The dilemmas and choices women face in developing a professional career are complex but for women in male-dominated professions these appear to be particularly stressful and subject to scrutiny with their visibility, due to minority status, rendering them as conspicuous but 'unseeable'. The framing of women's professional role in this context rests along a continuum of what Dellinger (2004) terms as 'safe' or 'embattled' workplace recognition that functions as a response to boundary heightening (see below) by the majority (Kanter, 1993). These ideas are discussed below to develop the theoretical framework of the chapter that focuses primarily on the work of Kanter (1993), Cohn (2000) and Kram and Hampton (2003) with their model of the visibility/vulnerability spiral serving as a key conceptual tool of analysis.

Gendered visibility of minority corporate actors

Kanter's (1993) work on the sociology of gender has long been recognized as a seminal text and, despite its longstanding presence in the literature, continues to provide insight into the general mechanics of corporate behaviour as well as the particular problems minorities face in achieving workplace advancement. In her discussion, the term 'minority' refers to any cohort that represents less than 50% of the total and, to which the feature of standing out as different attaches. Kanter argues that minority status always involves the attribute of visibility that can have both positive and negative effects. Central to this ambivalence is the issue of risk; high visibility can be enjoyed when things are going well and targets are achieved but, in the face of poor performance or costly errors, visibility becomes problematic under the watchful gaze of critical colleagues and superiors. When newcomers who are different (for example, in terms of culture, gender or ethnicity) join an established homogeneous group they can represent a potential challenge to the majority. One response to reinforce the dominant culture of the majority is what Kanter terms boundary heightening that can be understood as actions by the majority to emphasize their group characteristics to make the newcomer feel as different and 'outside' as possible. Thus, for example, when a woman enters a male-dominated workplace sexual jokes and crude language may become overt rather than repressed. In some settings, the physicality of the workplace can border on sexual harassment – this holds particular resonance for women working on construction sites where women and other highly visible minorities are the butt of lewd jokes and comic innuendo (Watts, 2007a). Similarly, in the setting of the boardroom where a woman finds herself in the minority of one within an otherwise all male team, talk before the main business begins may be centred on football and other male sport interests leaving her outside this social discourse (Cohn, 2000).

Cohn (2000) develops Kanter's (1993) critique to argue that boundary heightening behaviour on the part of the majority is intended to test the newcomer, to gauge their resilience, their willingness to conform and fit in and also to gain some sense of whether or not they can be trusted. This behaviour has as its primary effect the isolation of the entrant. If the newcomer is defiant or non-compliant this isolation is increased with their being further deprived of social support from colleagues. In these circumstances the likelihood that the newcomer will fail is increased. Within the business context being without friends is professionally dangerous (Cohn, 2000: 100) and can soon escalate into a profound handicap that cumulatively may result in a damaged reputation, a position from which it is difficult to recover. The consequences for women in a workplace where men define themselves as the norm are varied and contextual, but these can be usefully summarized as the necessity to overcome their 'otherness' (Davies, 2003). In a context where one group has the power to decree its own ideas and attitudes as the only meaningful ones this can be very challenging for the minority cohort.

The exclusion of women from powerful roles in male workspaces continues because high status men have the power to exclude them although, with the introduction of sex discrimination legislation in the UK, they do not have the power to restrict their entry. Thus, we see the highly visible female engineer, the female judge or the female surveyor threatening the identity of men because women, by invading the territory that defines male gender, challenge the male monopoly on corporate/professional success. In cases where women have the 'only woman' status they become tokens accruing, on the one hand, the advantage of being different and known but, on the other hand facing the loneliness of outsider estrangement from male peers. This is a complex dynamic that oscillates between visibility as an advantage and visibility as an obstacle to professional progression and is the principal theme of the discussion that follows.

The visibility/vulnerability spiral

Kram and Hampton (2003) offer a critique of women in corporate management and leadership roles that they argue is characterized by the visibility/vulnerability spiral. Although they apply this model specifically to leadership it has wider relevance for those who occupy token or outsider status within professional cultures. Their conceptual framework has its roots in Kleinian (Klein, 1959) object relations theory where the two psychological mechanisms of 'splitting' (coping with stress by separating the self from painful feelings) and 'projection' (distancing oneself from destructive feelings by disowning them and actively placing these onto someone else) are useful in explaining the threats to the success of women in minority/high profile organizational positions. The sequence of cause and effect operates with women in minority positions (particularly as leaders) made highly visible and subject to scrutiny and criticism. Kram and Hampton (2003) argue that this increases their vulnerability to the collective dynamics of splitting and projective responses that itself leads to closer surveillance. If the challenges that attach to this scrutiny can be overcome the pathway is clear for career advancement but carrying with it greater minority isolation, increased visibility and the continuation of the spiral.

The two strands of visibility and vulnerability merit closer interrogation to fully capture the relevance of this model for the analysis presented below. Women in some occupations and professions still have novelty value, particularly at senior levels. With this come a set of experiences that involve increased visibility, close scrutiny of performance and pressure to 'fit in' to the dominant majority culture (Kanter, 1993; Greed, 2001). As a minority worker, the requirement to 'overperform' to demonstrate comparable worth with majority members is anxiety-laden but necessary to gain acceptance. In some instances a particular type of performance is required of minority women to advance the cause of organizations and Wajcman (1998) argues that this can occur almost imperceptibly, as women are manoeuvred by male colleagues into roles or situations where it is their femaleness that is seen as the key influence, not their technical competence. The discussion below will support this assertion arguing that the impact of female sexuality within construction is multifaceted, with women being seen as potentially useful in closing a deal with a client but acting as an irritating distraction on a building site.

The vulnerability of women in minority professional roles is inscribed by normative stereotypical assumptions about male leadership qualities and technical prowess that position women as secondary players. Wider cultural perceptions of women as the weaker sex are difficult to dislodge, even within sophisticated business environments where women are represented at all organizational levels. This wider cultural orientation has subtle effects with men disowning a propensity for vulnerability and women all too ready to absorb it as a function of the splitting and projection response pattern (Kram and Hampton, 2003). Minority professional women, particularly those in leadership or management roles, are more likely than their male peers to be the target of projected vulnerability and this can undermine their personal authority in the role and limit their effectiveness. As this occurs they are watched ever more closely to produce a spiralling dynamic that is experienced as highly stressful.

Dryburgh (1999), in an important Canadian study of female engineers, draws together these threads to present a Goffmanesque interpretation of the ways in which women professionalize their engineering identity. Her critique centres on adaptive behaviour of female engineers in relation to rites of passage that specifically engage women in managing others' impressions of them to inspire confidence and respect. This entails developing technological self-confidence and portraying themselves as competent to their employer organizations, clients and male colleagues. Dryburgh identifies three features of the professionalizing process: adapting to the professional workplace culture, internalizing professional identity and demonstrating solidarity with others in the profession (mainly men). The difficulties women encounter in becoming incorporated within the professional, industry and company cultures that comprise UK construction are discussed below in three later sections that debate the research findings. The first of these considers the particular visibility issues of the construction site, the second highlights the token status of women in the complex processes involved in 'winning' work and the third draws out the ambiguous position of women within the ritualized 'machinery' that drives the work of the Institution of Civil Engineers (ICE). The operating framework that underpins UK construction is the focus of the next section that introduces the context of the research.

Context

The context for this chapter is the UK civil engineering profession that is historically, normatively and numerically male-dominated with women currently comprising just over 5% of the total (Watts, 2007b). Much of the UK profession is embedded within corporate enterprises, many of which are now foreign owned. Civil engineers work in all sectors of the profession which operates alongside town planning, structural engineering, architecture, surveying and building engineering as part of a huge UK construction industry employing around 1.3 million people (Greed, 2001: 4). Civil engineering (along with architecture) is at the elite end of the building cycle with its key function characterized as applied design. This contrasts with the image of creative flair that attaches to architecture (Cohen *et al*, 2005). The profession is socially constructed as technical, male and often dirty work and, despite attempts by the industry to mediate these stereotypes, this powerful cultural imagery continues. More progressive characterizations of the profession have been hampered by formal engineering education programmes that remain allied to the 'old economy' that focuses predominantly on technical competence and presents the discipline out of context, without reference to local, social or political issues. The abstraction of the curriculum, with its lack of relevance to the outside world, coupled with its gender-exclusivity (Moxham and Roberts, 1995) that fosters an impersonal learning environment, does not welcome women.

Civil engineers design and construct the infrastructure of the built environment including transportation, building and utility construction and energy plants. These functions are delivered by a complex mix of technical and managerial tasks that includes: design, computer modelling, testing, bid preparation, report writing, client liaison, project and people management and high levels of team working. This variety is seen to offer diverse career opportunities and, with more than 50% of UK consultants' work now being undertaken overseas (Watts, 2009), the possibility of living and working abroad is increasingly likely in the wake of a move towards a globalized marketplace for construction services. Construction is big business and increasingly engineers are being forced to confront the tensions between business and professional interests (with meeting the deadline often the dominant factor) in a climate in which ethical decision-making has begun to be seen as part of the construction industry's wider social responsibility.

The dominant cultural values of the profession operate in a strongly defined macho environment moulded by conflict and crisis management (Langford *et al*, 1995) with its organizational processes ordered through rites and rituals that are embedded in patterns of behaviour differentiated by role and hierarchy. Women are under represented at senior levels within the industry and discussion about 'how equal is engineering' (NCE, 17 July 2003, p. 46) is a topic of continuing debate, with the current concern about differential salaries now publicly positioned as a gender issue (NCE, 22 May 2008; NCE, 3 July 2008). As with other professions civil engineering is tightly regulated and has strict accreditation procedures that are overseen by the Institution of Civil Engineers (ICE). The ICE sees itself as having three main functions, that of a learned society, as a qualifying body and as a voice for the civil engineering profession with a remit to guard against the uncritical application of construction technology (Druker and White, 1996). Its registration processes that lead to the chartering of civil engineers (that acts as a licence to practice) have in recent years come under scrutiny in relation to their rigid, lengthy and inconsistent nature (NCE, 23/30 August 2001). Whilst the ICE has historically been a bastion of male influence, a few women have found themselves elected to the ICE council (its governing body) while the first female president took office in 2008.

Methods

This chapter's analysis draws on qualitative research in which 31 women civil engineers were interviewed about their career experiences. Access for the research was straight forward as I had been an independent training consultant within the industry for some years and was almost 'one of them' adopting the role of insider researcher (Watts, 2006). I was, therefore, not dependent on gatekeepers which some researchers (Miller and Bell, 2002, for example) document as problematic. However, though not reliant on the gatekeeper interface I chose to involve some senior industry figures in identifying potential interviewees as a way of validating the research with respondents. The interview schedule ran smoothly due, at least in part I believe, to participants feeling that they were contributing to a legitimate study with their involvement inscribed by a form of professional etiquette (Christians, 2005). Participants ranged in age from 23 to 56 years and were employed in both the consulting (design side) and contracting (building side) of the business almost exclusively in the private sector. The group included women in director posts and others in junior/middle management roles. Of the 31 participants, 16 were married, five were living with a partner, eight were single, one was separated and one divorced; 13 had school age children.

The aim of the research was to explore women's experience and views of the profession; semi-structured interviews addressed topics such as career choice and advancement, professional registration processes, equal opportunities, workplace culture in the settings of the office and the construction site, business expectations and support structures. My insider researcher role facilitated a broadly functional ethnographic approach (Holmes and Marcus, 2005) enabling a good rapport with research subjects that fostered a rich sharing of information with humour as a feature of both the interviews and of the accounts (Watts, 2007a). The interviews lasted from one to two hours and were audio taped, transcribed and then thematically analysed according to the grounded theory tradition (Glaser and Strauss, 1967).

Three overarching themes emerged: professional and business subcultures that shape workplace presence; work/life balance that is moulded by the industry's 'presenteeism' ethic related to its long hours culture and, lastly, the issue of change within the sector. The 'presenteeism' culture fosters a climate of not leaving before the boss with associated visibility a requirement of the professional workforce. The theme of this chapter, however, is the issue of construction culture with a particular focus on the elements of building site fraternity, standard business practices of commercial contracting and the industry's systems of professional accreditation. What is reported highlights women's place on the visibility continuum (Cohn, 2000) that informs their professional contribution to the live building process, to contract negotiation and their involvement with ICE activities, both as candidates for the award of chartered status and as reviewers of that process.

Leading the building team

The particular power relations that operate in the setting of the construction site have been the focus of critical debate (see Watts, 2007b, 2009 and Greed, 2000), with this setting continuing to provide the arena for macho gender display that has a significant impact on women. A building site operates as a function of several occupations shaping both its culture and its product (Gherardi, 2006). Working on site thus appeared to require regimented visibility criteria with all grades of worker knowing their place and having discrete but clear levels of incorporation.

This functions as a 'banding together' of men most usually in relation to 'craft loyalty': steel fixers with steel fixers, joiners with joiners and so on (Watts, 2007a: 260). Periods of site work are obligatory for candidates preparing to become chartered engineers and, as a majority of participants were either already chartered or working towards this, there was much discussion of their site experience. Roles on site for civil engineers revolve mainly around the position of resident engineer who has the responsibility for directing the actual building process (laying out of site plans, checking measurements and overseeing the delivery and installation of materials) that always retains an element of experimentation (Schinzinger and Martin, 2000). This role is one of leadership and carries significant responsibility connected to monitoring health and safety on site, identifying risks and providing clients (and sometimes the public) with appropriate information on the progress of projects.

Nearly all the participants spoke with enthusiasm about the satisfaction they derived from this aspect of their job and their desire to design structures, build them and make them work. Their accounts, however, were set against the backdrop of cultural constraint, threats to their safety and varying forms of sexual harassment though the naming of the practice of sexual harassment was absent from their stories. Some participants used the language of battle to describe their periods of site work as 'trench warfare', involving men who want women out and women who are determined to stay. Despite the sexist and antagonistic work setting of construction sites, being part of the live building process was experienced as very rewarding and, for several participants, was the main reason for joining the profession. The satisfaction gained from building structures appeared to compensate for the generally negative attitudes of male colleagues that appeared inextricably linked to the performative requirements of masculinity (Quinn, 2002) involving girl watching, rough humour, profanity and crude behaviour.

The concerns expressed by participants were interwoven with their high visibility on site as physical spectacle contrasting with their invisibility in relation to their authority that went unrecognized and was subject to resistance by male colleagues. The following accounts illustrate the duality of the problem:

When I showed him (the site foreman) the plans and how the base-laying was a bit skewed he just turned round and walked off. He didn't want to have to tell the men to re-do it. I caught up with him later in the cabin and he started having a go at me but he got the message we were out of tolerance so he knew it would have to be done (a senior project engineer, aged 49).

One site foreman on a job in Wales gave me hell all the way through the project. He just refused to take any notice of my instructions, especially when I had to condemn some concreting. In the end I had to report him to his boss and then he never spoke to me again. He spoke about me, though, all the time to the lads and the mickey-taking, it was merciless. It got me down after a while and ruined what was a very interesting project (a graduate engineer well over half way through the chartering process, aged 26).

These accounts demonstrate the potential vulnerability of women acting in authority roles on construction sites and illustrate how site officials, such as the foreman, openly disputing decisions can seriously undermine the credibility of any resident engineer, particularly a young female engineer who may feel very conspicuous. These visibility tensions can also create overwhelming pressure to perform successfully, particularly in an industry where jobs are priced very competitively with increasingly narrow profit margins that do not allow for mistakes. The accounts also reflect the added labour of negotiating a legitimate presence to enable them to carry out their supervisory function. For some this appeared to be connected to ensuring congruence between image presentation and role expectations (Cohn, 2000). The youngest participant in the study (age, 23) recounted how, on just her second time on site, during a particularly hot spell of weather, she had worn a skirt and in her words 'not a short one or anything like that' and had been humiliated by the site workforce. Her words provide some insight into the disempowering effects of this behaviour that contribute to a culture of fear for some women working in the industry:

When I got out of the car there was a whole lot of them walking through the site gate and they all started whistling at me and making suggestive remarks. I was so embarrassed but it got worse and the ganger started to proposition me and said he would be waiting for me when I went to use the toilet. I was really frightened and sat in the site office and was terrified to go outside.

Concerns about managing self-image on site featured throughout the women's narratives with a clear emphasis on the cultural requirement to 'tone down' the use of make-up and wear only the plainest of clothes all in pursuit of assimilation to reduce their visibility as spectacle or object. Most of the participants said that they paid more attention to their dress and appearance during their periods on site than they did for their office-based role, an approach that seemed to be connected to their perceived greater vulnerability as managers in the setting of the building site. This supports the view that 'without constant vigilance regarding self-presentation at work, women run the risk of not being treated seriously as managers' (Edwards and Wajcman, 2005: 84). Trying to ensure that their sexual attributes do not eclipse their technical ability becomes a daily project for women in this setting. This theme of personal appearance and image, particularly in relation to constructs of femininity, is now explored in the context of the supplier/client interface with particular focus on securing the deal.

Closing out the deal

All the research participants referred to their involvement with what one of them described as 'winning new business' that is a regular feature of project-dominated income generation for all civil engineering consultants. Whilst most of the comments related to the contribution this activity made to work overload and the long hours culture that pervades the sector, four of the women discussed ways in which they were, at times, expected to 'wine and dine' clients, join contract discussions to (as one of them called it) 'smooth over some of the politics' and, in one case, to initiate a 'charm offensive' with a particularly difficult client at a pivotal stage of a contract negotiation. This demonstrates the (in)visibility paradox for women within the sector revealing how a male-dominated culture that renders them invisible as engineers can be conveniently manipulated, as circumstances require, to make visible their 'femaleness' within organizational processes that serve both the business and male majority interest (Cockburn, 1991). Within the negotiation process taking advantage of feminine practices of expressiveness, mutual recognition and empathy (Putnam and Kolb, 2003: 148) is not an acknowledged strategy within construction but its informal and discrete application is uncovered by this research and has been found to be present in other areas of construction culture such as surveying (Greed, 1991). The empirical detail that follows about some of this feminine 'charm work' demonstrates how male sexuality underpins the patriarchal culture of professional and organizational life in the construction sector.

One participant working as a middle manager for a prominent consulting firm described how pressure was put on her to attend what she called an 'intimate dinner' with her boss and the director of a potential client company.

> *He said 'try and doll yourself up a bit, maybe a little black dress. We have got to pull all the stops out to win this job. You'll be working on the job and I want him to see how well it's all going to work'. I thought, right, at least I have got something to offer – half the time you have to shout to make yourself heard with this lot.* (Middle Manager, aged 35)

A similar story was recounted by another participant who, having graduated from Oxford University, had embarked on a management career only to find that her usefulness to the company was increasingly measured by what she could bring to help 'iron out difficulties with stroppy clients'. She recalled one incident in particular where she felt that it was not her technical skill that was called upon but her feminine charm to ensure that the right social environment was created for the detailed project negotiation:

> *They asked me to join this meeting with a client we had done a lot of work for before. My divisional director explained that the atmosphere had become strained when they had been discussing the modelling strategy and the testing schedule and he wanted me to come and flutter my eyes at them and sell it to them. Well, I ask you, what can you say to that? Part of me took it as a compliment but really you would think that we have moved beyond that sort of thing, wouldn't you?* (Middle Manager, aged 34)

Hochschild's (1983) analysis of the commodification of emotional labour as a tool of organizational capital can explain the appropriation of this form of visibility in the context of an unequal power relationship between the powerful customer and the less powerful service supplier but also between the powerful 'boss' and the relatively powerless subordinate. This analysis suggests that the skills required by engineers are social and personal and not just technical, as was once thought to be the case (Watts, 2007b). The degree of choice, however, that less powerful employees can exercise within capitalist relations in agreeing (or refusing) to undertake this kind of emotional labour is a function of organizational context but this research demonstrates that gender is one factor likely to shape individual agency in this area, particularly within a male-dominated profession.

Professional advancement

One of the subcultures operating within the civil engineering profession concerns the recognition and accreditation of professional expertise arising from achieving chartered status that is seen as the key to career progress (Watts, 2007b). One theme of participants' comments on the topic of career advancement was the need to become chartered to 'fully join the club'. The criteria for the chartering process laid down by the ICE are intended to ensure that engineers have sufficient knowledge and expertise in design, construction and project management so that schemes are built according to best practice principles, with safety of structures the highest priority. In short, becoming a chartered civil engineer is akin to a licence to practice and is awarded on successful completion of a structured training programme that culminates in what is known as the Corporate Professional Review (CPR). Usually these stages would not be accomplished in less than four years and two participants in the study took ten years to complete the process. In recent years some concern has been voiced about the consistency, transparency and fairness of the process, particularly in respect of the CPR (NCE, 23/30 August 2001). Some of these concerns were echoed by several women in this research whose experience of the CPR was less than professional on a number of levels. Every woman in the study who had taken their CPR had had the experience of facing an all-male panel and the accounts that follow offer a snapshot of the kinds of difficulties that minority status and its attendant high visibility can bring in this situation:

> *They didn't pay any attention to anything I said at the interview. They had decided before I walked in what they were going to do. They were shouting at me during the interview and one man just kept interrupting every time I tried to answer a question.* (Senior Manager, aged 39 who failed the first review but passed at the second attempt)

> *I felt really isolated in the waiting room as all the other candidates were men. When I got into the room the chair of the panel said 'isn't it nice to see a lady come to do her professional review?' That was the sort of thing I really didn't want to be hearing. I was there to demonstrate my professional experience, not to sort of talk about what gender I was. All the way*

> *through, though, one man was trying to look up my skirt. I got through OK but it was a horrible experience.* (Main Board Director, aged 37)

> *My experience of the review was very grim. When I walked in all the men looked me up and down and one of them continued to stare at me throughout the interview. At one point they asked me if I thought that women were team players. I felt that that was discriminatory but I couldn't say so, how could I?* (Principal Engineer, aged 49 who passed this review and who, because of this negative experience, subsequently offered her services as a CPR panel member)

Some women in the study were involved in the committee and council work of the ICE and voiced their determination to lobby for a fairer chartering system. These participants demonstrated a keen awareness that those who benefit from inequalities have an interest in defending them whereas those bearing the costs have an interest in ending them. In this context they saw their visibility arising from a minority position as a moderate advantage. One of the participants, who is a very prominent supporter of the construction industry's equal opportunities and diversity initiatives, offered the following rationale to explain this advantage:

> *As a woman if you are on any of the ICE committees and you get yourself nominated to go on the council ballot paper you are sure to get elected. It's the novelty value you see. Getting any further though such as in a position of succeeding vice-president (in this position one would be assured of eventually taking up the post of ICE President regarded as the pinnacle of professional success) is what's difficult. You see they don't mind including women at one level but they don't want a woman at the top.* (Self-employed Consultant in private practice, aged 49)

The above participant, commenting on the impossibility of a woman becoming ICE President, could not have foreseen the influence exerted by the woman who, in 2008, became the ICE's first female President. This points to the issue of exceptionality where women who succeed in high profile corporate and professional roles within construction are highly visible because they are so rare. This scarcity value, however, barely reaps positive results commensurate with the disappointingly small proportion of women in professional roles within the sector. Their success is closely watched and dissected (Watts, 2007b) and dependent on the co-operation of male colleagues.

Conclusion

Because women in construction form such a small minority of the total workforce, with their representation fragmented across a large number of small and medium sized firms, they do not share a collective interest. Their visibility within construction is experienced as highly individual and has to be negotiated on a micro-level within their particular employing organization, leaving most women in professional roles isolated without a network of social support. This isolation is especially acute within the setting of the construction site where women in positions of authority contradict stereotypical expectations, adding a further gender dimension to an already strongly hierarchical workplace culture (Greed, 2000). Women's management style in this setting is subject to close surveillance and variously perceived as too masculine, too consensual, not firm enough and certainly a legitimate topic for open criticism and discussion (Watts, 2007b, 2009) heightening their vulnerability with the potential to undermine their self-esteem and personal effectiveness (Kram and Hampton, 2003: 219). In the construction industry allowing oneself to be seen as vulnerable, particularly in any leadership or supervisory role, is an index of weakness likely to incur the condemnation of co-workers in the form of challenging behaviours. Self-doubt or 'lack of self-belief', as one participant termed the consequence of women's readiness to internalize criticism, acts to limit women's professional progress.

Workplace visibility has potential for both positive and negative effects but where heightened visibility operates for a minority they become subject to different kinds of exclusionary treatment that both arise from and reinforce unequal access to networks and resources. Where women are expected by male colleagues to step into a feminized role as part of a business strategy, the choice not to act in this way is an illusionary one, as marginalization and loss of career opportunity are likely to result if they decline to co-operate. This raises the question of whether women should use their female attributes and differences from men to advance their individual position or does this just reinforce the negative stereotype? Whittock (2000) argues that the use of 'womanly ways' by females in male majority workplaces can be positive for both the women (in according them status even if it is not the status they want) and the organization, but may hinder assimilation and generate role entrapment. Alongside this, Gherardi (1995) takes the view that many women do not want to banish sexuality from the workplace because having a sexualized status is preferable to having no status and being invisible.

Application of Kram and Hampton's (2003) conceptual model of the visibility/vulnerability spiral to the data on which this paper draws has highlighted the ways in which the workplace dynamics within construction mean that women will be seen as violating traditional role expectations, either of engineers (especially as managers) or of women or both. The minority/majority dynamics both drive and are driven by visibility that results in role overload, role confusion and damaged self-esteem, especially for women in construction management functions. For example, having on a daily basis to carefully attend to all aspects of self-image in order to be appropriately visible as a woman manger is one example of role overload whereas cultivating 'femaleness' to influence business negotiations contributes to role confusion, with negative and positive visibility integral to both activities. Dealing with the contradictory demands of suppressing and accentuating the 'feminine' both in pursuit of corporate goals is psychologically wearing and may lead to strained relationships with colleagues. Returning to the Kleinian 'splitting and projecting' thesis discussed above, female construction managers are more likely than their male peers to be the target of projected vulnerability and, given the social roles they carry, may be seen as either too (and by inference inappropriately) powerful or completely vulnerable. Thus the real vulnerability of women in role as construction professionals is greater than that for men in the sector with a consequent pressure on women to achieve assimilated status. This research demonstrates that this is almost impossible to achieve and sustain and, in the absence of what Kanter (1993) describes as 'solidarity behaviour' between women in construction, it is difficult to be optimistic about their future prospects in this most 'male' of male work settings.

In summary, the ideas and analysis in this chapter offer insight into the ways in which women negotiate their professional roles within the built environment sector, with both their scarcity and their gender central to Kanter's (1993) model of person-of-one kind and person-of-another-kind interaction. Added to this, Acker's (2003) summary of the patterns of advantage and disadvantage, exploitation and control and meaning and identity, that are central to gendered organizations, reminds us of the inescapable truth about the reality of workplace minority visibility/vulnerability. Those who succeed by virtue of, or in spite of, their heightened visibility can look forward to further success but those who fail will be rewarded by a shift into oblivion finding themselves marginalized and deprived of access to the arenas wherein organizational power resides.

References

Acker, J. (2003) 'Hierarchies, jobs, bodies: A theory of gendered organizations'. In Ely, R. J., Foldy, E. G., Scully, M. A. & The Center for Gender in Organizations Simmons School of Management (eds) *Reader in Gender, Work and Organization*, pp. 49–61. Malden, MA, USA: Blackwell Publishing Ltd.

Blair-Loy, M. (2001) 'Cultural constructions of family schemas: The case of women finance executives', *Gender & Society*, 15(5): 687–709.

Christians, C. G. (2005) 'Ethics and politics in qualitative research'. In Denzin, N. K. and Lincoln, Y. S. (eds) *Sage Handbook of Qualitative Research* (3rd ed.). London: Sage Publications.

Cockburn, C. (1991) *In the Way of Women*. Basingstoke: The Macmillan Press.

Cohen, L., Wilkinson, A., Arnold, J. and Finn, R. (2005) 'Remember I'm the bloody architect!' Architects, organizations and discourses of profession, *Work, Employment and Society*, 19(4): 775–796.

Cohn, S. (2000) *Race, Gender and Discrimination at Work*. Colorado, USA: Westview Press.

Davies, C. (2003) 'Workers, professions and identity'. In Henderson, J. & Atkinson, D. (eds) *Managing Care in Context*. London: Routledge.

Dellinger, K. (2004) 'Masculinities in "safe" and "embattled" organisations. Accounting for pornographic and feminist magazines', *Gender & Society*, 18(5): 545–566.

Druker, J. and White, G. (1996) *Managing People in Construction*. London: Institute of Personnel and Development.

Dryburgh, H. (1999) 'Work hard, play hard: Women and professionalization in engineering – Adapting to the culture', *Gender & Society*, 13(5): 664–682.

Edwards, P. and Wajcman, J. (2005) *The Politics of Working Life*. Oxford: Oxford University Press.

Gherardi, S. (1995) *Gender, Symbolism and Organisational Cultures*. London: Sage Publications.

Gherardi, S. (2006) *Organizational Knowledge: The Texture of Workplace Learning*. Malden, MA: Blackwell Publishing.

Glaser, B. G. and Strauss, A. L. (1967) *The Discovery of Grounded Theory. Strategies for Qualitative Research*. Chicago: Aldine.

Greed, C. (1991) *Surveying Sisters – Women in a Traditional Male Profession*. London: Routledge.

Greed, C. (2000) 'Women in the construction professions', *Gender, Work and Organization*, 7(3): 181–196.

Greed, C. (2001) *Social Exclusion or Inclusion: The Continuing Story of Women and Construction*. Paper presented to the Planning and Environment Research Centre Seminar, 7 March 2001, University of the West of England.

Hochschild, A. R. (1983) *The Managed Heart: The Commercialization of Human Feeling*. Berkeley, CA: University of California Press.

Holmes, D. R. and Marcus, G. E. (2005) 'Refunctioning ethnography: The challenge of an anthropology of the contemporary'. In Denzin, N. K. and Lincoln, Y. S. (eds) *Sage Handbook of Qualitative Research* (3rd ed.) London: Sage Publications.

Kanter, R. M. (1993) *Men and Women of the Corporation* (2nd ed.) New York: Basic Books.

Klein, M. (1959) 'Our adult world and its roots in infancy', *Human Relations*, 12: 291–303.
Kram, K. E. and Hampton, M. M. (2003) 'When women lead: The visibility-vulnerability spiral'. In Ely, R. J., Foldy, E. G., Scully, M. A. & The Center for Gender in Organizations Simmons School of Management (eds) *Reader in Gender, Work and Organization*, pp. 211–223. Malden, MA, USA: Blackwell Publishing Ltd.
Langford, D., Hancock, M. R., Fellows, R. and Gale, A. W. (1995) *Human Resources Management in Construction*. Ascot: Longman Group Ltd.
Lewis, S. (2002) 'Work and family issues: Old and new'. In Burke, R. J. and Nelson, D. L. (eds) *Advancing Women's Careers*. Oxford: Blackwell Publishers.
Lewis, S., Rapoport, R. and Gambles, R. (2003) 'Reflections on the integration of paid work with the rest of life', *Journal of Managerial Psychology*, 18(8): 824–841.
Lewis, G. (2004) '"Do not go gently...": Terrains of citizenship and landscapes of the personal'. In Lewis, G. (ed.) *Citizenship: Personal Lives and Social Policy*. Milton Keynes/Bristol: The Open University/The Policy Press.
McIlwee, J. and Robinson, G. (1992) *Women in Engineering: Gender, Power and Workplace Culture*. Albany, NY: SUNY Press.
Miller, T. and Bell, L. (2002) 'Consenting to what? Issues of access, gate-keeping and "informed" consent', in Mauthner, M., Birch, M., Jessop, J. and Miller, T. (eds) *Ethics in Qualitative Research*, pp. 53–69. London: Sage Publications.
Moxham, S. and Roberts, P. (1995) *Gender in the Engineering Curriculum*. Melbourne: University of Melbourne.
NCE, *New Civil Engineer*, 23/30 August 2001, 'Tales of mystery and imagination', pp. 14–17.
NCE, *New Civil Engineer*, 17 July 2003, 'A gender agenda – Working lives: Women in engineering', p. 46.
NCE, *New Civil Engineer*, 22 May 2008, 'Mind the gap', pp. 14–15.
NCE, *New Civil Engineer*, 3 July 2008, 'Civils careers: The woman's point of view', pp. 10–11.
Putnam, L. L. and Kolb, D. M. (2003) 'Rethinking negotiation: Feminist views of communication and exchange'. In Ely, R. J., Foldy, E. G., Scully, M. A. & The Center for Gender in Organizations Simmons School of Management (eds) *Reader in Gender, Work and Organization*, pp. 135–150. Malden, MA, USA: Blackwell Publishing Ltd.
Quinn, B. A. (2002) 'Sexual harassment and masculinity: The power and meaning of "girl watching"', *Gender & Society*, 16(3): 386–402.
Schinzinger, R. and Martin, M. W. (2000) *Introduction to Engineering Ethics*. Boston: McGraw Hill.
Wajcman, J. (1998) *Managing like a Man*. Cambridge: Polity Press.
Watts, J. H. (2006) '"The outsider within": Dilemmas of qualitative feminist research within a culture of resistance', *Qualitative Research*, 6(3): 385–402.
Watts, J. H. (2007a) 'Can't take a joke? Humour as resistance, refuge and exclusion in a highly gendered workplace', *Feminism and Psychology*, 17(2): 259–266.
Watts, J. H. (2007b) 'Porn, pride and pessimism: Experiences of women working in professional construction roles', *Work, Employment and Society*, 21(2): 297–314.

Watts, J. H. (2008) 'Impression management: A form of emotion work for women in a male-dominated profession', *International Journal of Work Organization and Emotion*, 2(3): 221–235.

Watts, J. H. (2009) 'Leaders of men: Women managing in construction', *Work Employment and Society,* forthcoming.

Whittock, M. (2000) *Feminising the Masculine*. Aldershot: Ashgate Publishing Ltd.

10
The Critical (and Subversive) Act of (In)visibility: A Strategic Reframing of 'Disappeared and Devalued' Women in a Densely Masculinist[1] Workplace

Susan Harwood

Introduction

This chapter offers an exploration of some important research findings about how 'disappeared women' in a highly masculinist organization were able to bring about positive changes to their workplace by engaging with each other in some collaborative and subversive 'critical acts' (Dahlerup, 1988). Drawing on a three-year PhD research project[2] in a policing organization, I describe how women working on this project were able to use their invisibility to engineer positive change, to reframe their deferential behaviour to subvert male authority, to mask their collective activity, and to advance their radical cause. Whereas I have discussed elsewhere (Harwood, 2006) how the engagement of men in the research practice was crucial to our positive research outcomes, my focus here is on reframing the invisibility of women in densely masculinist organizations as a positive force for change.

The impetus for this participatory action research project was created when a (then) incoming police commissioner expressed disquiet about the culture of his new organization; he focused on a number of reform issues, including the need to redress the gender imbalance. He was presented with a complete absence of women at senior levels and, a worrying number of harassment complaints. My PhD research project was specifically and carefully designed to provide new insights and possible solutions to a pervasive question: how can gendered workplace cultures be successfully redressed? The answer to this question has eluded a raft of well-intended equal opportunity and affirmative action initiatives for more than 20 years, both within Australia and overseas, and has been a subject of interest to a broad range and extensive body of researchers.

My methodological framework comprised a complex interplay between four qualitative models: participatory action research, quality management, a gender lens interventionist approach and feminist ethnography. That combination of feminist goals and action research techniques drew men and women into insider teams for the purpose of conducting a thorough, forensic examination of the gendered organization of their workplace. The goal was to develop recommendations for change, linked to a framework for successful implementation.

Once the formal collaboration between my university and the policing organization was completed, we established a commissioner-endorsed reference group, comprising a mix of senior and middle-ranking men and women. The intent of the teams-based research methodology was to bring together men and women in small research teams, training them in strong group process skills and tools and, in how to apply a 'gender lens'[3] approach to their workplace. After establishing a shared understanding of the research problem, each of the reference group members selected a topic and established and led a project team. Reference group members reported back at regular meetings on the process and findings of their project teams and over time, these internal forums provided an ongoing and safe space for both men and women to engage in robust dialogue about the contentious issues that they were identifying in their workplace. The major test was how to apply the gender lens to each of their nominated projects. These projects were entitled 'Barriers to women's advancement in policing'; 'Why do women resign?'; 'Improving access and availability of training and development for female public service officers'; 'Women in a goldfish bowl'; 'Diversity'; and 'Mentoring'.

The data collected by these insider project teams began to bring into sharper focus some of the practices that were enacted to suppress and silence women in their organization. In her discussion of gender, power and practice, De Francisco reminds us of why we need the power of a gender lens tool to illuminate the full range of gendered practices:

> Gender is constructed in a complex array of social practices within communities, practices that in many cases connect to personal attributes and to power relations but that do so in varied, subtle and changing ways.
>
> (De Francisco, 1997: 38)

As a team of collaborative researchers, the reference group became more skilled in its examination of what De Francisco (1997) refers to as layers of cultural and interpersonal context and privilege within their workplace. The application of the gender lens not only provided a clearer view of the links between these layers, but also illuminated some of the subtleties and complexities of gender relations within this policing organization. The particular pressures that form part of women's experiences were highlighted as the data gathering process yielded women's previously untapped stories of their lived experiences.

My focus here however is on presenting and discussing case studies that focus on some of the women involved in these research projects. I do so to surface and discuss the subterfuge and other subversive activities that the women in the research teams had to employ to protect their participation, their research practice and their findings. Referring to Clare Burton's (1991) research on the price women pay for the promise of change, I refocus the 'gender lens' approach we adopted throughout the life of the research project, turning their lens inwards to concentrate on the experiences of the women in four of my six project teams. I do this to demonstrate that, despite our best efforts to ensure equality among project team participants, the discriminatory practices we were researching in the wider workplace had a differential impact on the experiences of men and women while they conducted their research. In describing how the women shouldered most of the burden of the project team work, I argue that they not only had more to lose than their male counterparts on these teams but were apparently more than prepared to pay a higher price for their participation. I also suggest that a highly visible, interventionist, feminist research project of this kind will impose a particular set of new challenges to women working in densely masculinist, gendered workplaces. I conclude the case studies with a personal account of what happened to the feminist researcher when her role continued and broadened beyond the anticipated life of the initial research project to both embrace and drive a cultural reform agenda.

A brief overview of the research methodology

As outlined earlier, the feminist framework underpinning my research methodology comprised participatory action research, the gender lens approach developed by researchers at the Centre for Gender in Organizations and, the tools and techniques of quality management. This integrated approach was designed to create an inclusive, participatory working environment for all research participants. In collaboration with key stakeholders I had developed a structured research plan to ensure close engagement with a carefully selected advisory group[4] (the reference group) and operational groups (the project teams). The idea was to ensure that men and women with a firm commitment to gender equity shared their experiences in order to identify and analyse problems of the gendered workplace culture. Integral to the engagement of this group was the building of a sense of team endeavour. After the establishment of the reference group, members collaboratively decided on specific initiatives designed to change the masculinized culture of policing. They then led and guided those initiatives. As both the project team leader and the facilitator, I provided each of the six project teams with training in how to conduct their research; this model ensured a transfer of learning from the reference group to the teams that would gather and analyse the data. The methodological approach also enhanced the insiders' capacity to maintain their focus on the application of the gender lens, while engendering their development of a sound group process. The role of the reference group throughout the life of the project was to offer support, guidance and encouragement to each of the project teams and to act as a repository for the dissemination and analysis of information presented at each meeting. The role of each of the project teams was to explore their research topic by developing a research plan, gathering and analysing their data and preparing and presenting a final report to the reference group on their findings and recommendations. Each of these elements proved to be significant in laying the groundwork for a robust methodology that directly engaged over 1000 personnel over the two-year life of the research project.

Information was passed between and shared amongst all stakeholders by means of the regular reference group meetings, at which project team leaders would report on their group's findings. Through their application of this research methodology, the women and men within the reference group and project teams became adept at identifying some of the long established, gendered workplace practices around them. However, the women had to do more than recognize these practices – they also had to manage a number of testing oppositions. For example, most of the women on these teams were caught between their desire to lead and drive change and their low status and profile. Whereas the women carried most of the weight of the project workloads, they were still expected to defer to the demands of their predominantly male supervisors and colleagues. Moreover, despite making a major contribution to a project endorsed by the head of their organization, these women were not protected from discriminatory practices being visited upon them as they conducted their research. Indeed, I argue that in various cases the potential for this research to uncover and report adverse findings against men in this workplace ensured that some women were targeted for further discriminatory treatment.

The following four case studies from the research project show how these particular women (with some receiving support from their male colleagues) separately and collectively engaged in critical acts at crucial points in their research journey to avoid and resist detection. That is (and as I will show) some of these women had to actively 'hide' their project participation from their colleagues, their supervisors and their work units; they variously reported that they deemed such subterfuge necessary if they were to survive in an environment in which their visible participation would render them as 'feminazis', 'stirrers' or worse, 'lesbians' to those men (and some women) who would be challenged by their change in status. In so doing, these women chose to render 'invisible' their ongoing engagement in our research project while simultaneously performing circumscribed and highly deferential roles within their gendered workplace. I note here that rendering these women invisible was just one element of our *modus operandi*, and that at other times (and for a variety of purposes) these same players joined their various cohorts for some highly visible, strategic acts that were played out on centre stage.[5] In short, their capacity to move between the visible and the invisible was crucial to their continuing project participation.

The case studies focus on 'Naomi', who led an all-women team of public service officers working in policing; 'Melinda', a police officer who was the leader of a small mixed team; 'Andrea', a participant in an all-women team comprising public service as well as police women; and 'Gail', a police officer whose participation as the subject of an ethnographic study was sponsored and supported by her male boss. In presenting each of these studies I will outline how these women, in different situations and in different ways chose to make invisible various aspects of their research work to protect the project findings, their career aspirations and their team. I conclude with a forensic examination of the feminist facilitator.

'Naomi'

Participatory action research (PAR) had the potential to be both liberating and dangerous for the teams of researchers at my research site. This 'double-edged sword' was no more apparent than for Naomi and her team members, all of whom occupied lower level public service positions. Over the extensive period of their research work on this project, there was evidence that these women became increasingly liberated as they shared their knowledge and personal experiences of the gendered practices of their workplace; further, they became more confident about naming and discussing the behaviours and attitudes of the men with who they worked. Despite their low pay and low status, these women were the keepers of corporate knowledge for their particular work units; they were expected to identify, retrieve and prepare crucial, high-risk data that allowed their (male) managers and directors to respond swiftly to their superiors' requests for information.

At the same time, exclusionary practices ensured that most of these women were kept out of the official communication loop. Their lack of profile and status seemingly precluded them from being formally notified about changes to the structures, functions and staffing of their organization. This selective communication model constrained them as individuals from fully engaging in the higher-status work of their organization. In the face of these hierarchical impediments to information sharing, the women in this group created their own pathways and means of access. In their ascribed roles in their separate workplaces, they prepared reports, drafted documents for their supervisors and gathered data from departmental files. They discovered that when they came together as a collective for their team meetings, they could pool the capital gleaned from their disparate support roles, combining their fragments of information into some cohesive knowledge. For these reasons the regular project team meetings became an information clearing house. My researcher status gave me access to various forums around the organization and as a result I was able to elicit and share information not normally available to women at this level. One of the team members commented favourably on this aspect of her project team participation in her final evaluation:

> We received a lot of information from Susan regarding the 'goings-on' and 'happenings' in the agency. This is because she attended a lot of meetings we never had the opportunity to attend (or be invited to) ourselves and she was willing to share the information with us.

The women on this team were very keen to share their knowledge with each other, their work colleagues on this project. Their commitment to openness and transparency was somewhat challenged by their associated need to 'hide' their activities. They often had to employ a range of tactics to maintain their links with their research. Most managed to at least preserve their place on the project through some subterfuge and skilful manoeuvring.

Naomi began to play a more visible and active role when the original leader had to leave and encouraged Naomi to take on her role, which also meant representing the public service officers' team on the reference group. While initially wary of these roles and what they might entail, Naomi very quickly discovered that her access to reference group meetings afforded new insights and knowledge about her organization. Seemingly poised for some kind of action, this strategic opportunity was something that she capitalized on as her involvement increased.

Over time, the reference group and project teams had to come to terms with some of the inherent contradictions in the choices that women like Naomi make in this workplace. Judy Wajcman's (1999) discussion of this issue is based on her research on men and women managers. However, her comments about the choices that some women make could also be referring to coping strategies that women employ within highly masculinist organizations like policing:

> *Various constructions of femininity which women deploy in relating to men in power involve being flirtatious, admiring and generally supportive. In this way, women are actively reconstituting heterosexualized forms of dominance and subordination.* (Wajcman, 1999: 165)

The issue of dominance and subordination was raised when Naomi prepared to take on a role that appeared to her project team colleagues to be contradictory. Naomi reported excitedly to her project team that she would be attending senior management forums for a period of time. However, several group members, attuned by now to see their organization through the gender lens recoiled in horror when she reported that her role would be to work the power point (that is, 'press the buttons' on the computer) for the senior males when these men talked to their data show presentations. Effectively, she was to reduce herself to the role of a handmaiden.

What we discovered was that Naomi was prepared to 'do' subservience as a means of collecting 'insider' knowledge about the organization. She suggested that playing the deferential and anonymous role in the meeting process suited her intent very well. In fact, she would be appropriating the submissive identity of an acolyte to empower herself with privileged information. Thus, Naomi planned from the outset to subvert the button-pushing role. She knew that through her attendance at these regular senior management forums she would be able to hear everything that was going on and would have access to privileged information that, in normal circumstances, could take months to filter down into the ranks. This unfettered access would transform her, for this space and time, into a privileged knower about future directions and about who the key players were on the management platform. In short, she would come back to her group and share this knowledge, informed about who is in, who is out, and to whom we should be directing our recommendations. During the ensuing months, Naomi demonstrated her skilful capacity to juggle several mental models of femininity to her advantage, moving between her public service officer day job, her leadership role for her project team and her performance as an acolyte at the senior managers' forums.

Naomi's ability to engage with others in the wider organization was premised on her acknowledgement and maintenance of certain class and gender distinctions. Acker (1990: 146–147) refers to these demarcation lines in her discussion of how gendering occurs in organizations. She suggests 'interactions between women and men, women and women, men and men' include 'all those patterns that enact dominance and submission'. The gendered nature of an administrative support role often means that women's performance is unrecognized, undervalued and not seen as contributing to the more important, strategic agendas that belong to the domain of men's work in gendered workplaces. For Naomi, however, there were further strategic advantages in playing the subservient, and invisible, role. After performing in the role of handmaiden for several senior management meetings, she reported that she had gained more information for the project than she had originally anticipated. Assuring her colleagues that her gender lens was still working, she told us that she had not quite recognized the full dimensions of the gendered nature of the 'button-pushers' role until there was a change in who performed the role. She reported that when she had not been able to attend the senior management meetings, it had been arranged that a relatively junior, male police officer would take her place. This male officer's enactment of what was obviously the 'woman's role' of button-pushing was not only visible but was also reported to be offensive to those present. There were complaints from the senior managers present about the misuse of this male police officer's skills, time and training. He was told that he would not be performing this role again. Naomi commented that while it was apparently acceptable to senior men for her to be seen (or not seen) in her subservient performance, it was unacceptable for them to see a male, uniformed officer of equal status performing the same role.

Naomi was challenged when she first began to perceive these forms of everyday discrimination around her. Later, when asked to evaluate her participation on the reference group and project team, she provided the following comment:

> *After being in this agency for many years, I know at times I begin to regard as 'normal' practices and behaviours that would be regarded as 'abnormal' through the eyes of equity. I felt validated whilst participating in project meetings.*

Naomi's account became an important piece in the truth telling about the subordination of women's knowledge and experience in this organization. As Joyce Fletcher's (1999: 22) account of 'disappearing acts' suggests:

> *Subversive stories usually take the form of personal accounts of members of a marginalized group whose voice has been silenced and whose experience has not been counted as knowledge....The goal is to offer the dominant group an opportunity to question these truths, or at least to consider that they are not universal.*

Naomi's subversive story helped flesh out the overall narrative of the research project, creating some small, incremental changes to the ways in which women's and men's roles are described within this workplace. To use Meyerson and Scully's (1995: 596) terms, Naomi had engaged in two change-oriented strategies: a 'small win' and a 'local, spontaneous, authentic action'. Playing the role of a power-point operator gave her access to a high level, senior management forum that was otherwise off limits to low-level public service women. This small win for women enabled her to gain further knowledge about strategic directions and the gendered nature of decision-making in her workplace. At the same time, by taking advantage of an unexpected opportunity, Naomi had been able to 'push change while maintaining her identity' (Meyerson and Scully, 1995: 596).

Over the next 12 months, Naomi was presented with a range of new opportunities, some of which involved her in very public, very visible demonstrations of her newly-honed skills as an advocate for women public service officers. On one of these more public occasions, Naomi used her presentation to a group of senior managers to reflect on her experiences and to share her learning. Subverting the respectful 'feminine' tone normally adopted by women public service officers in such a setting, Naomi appropriated language more commonly identified with her male audience to describe her new identity:

I have learned how to stand up for myself, to stand up for what I believe in. I've become more 'ballsy'. I'm not going to put up with things the way I have in the past.

Yet, the status of this emerging, assertive identity was fragile. This much was evident as soon as Naomi stepped back into the confines of her everyday work. There, she experienced regular threats to her newly won sense of achievement. The prevailing norms of this organization served to constantly remind public service women like Naomi of their prescribed roles. Once outside the safety net environment of the reference group and project teams, there were inherent difficulties of being involved in a change process that could backfire on individual careers within the organization. Naomi described this as one of the difficulties associated with occupying such disparate spaces:

At times it's hard to personally reconcile pressures to retain the status quo with the desire for change. It feels like being involved in a group that's pressing for change is a CLM (career limiting move).

Naomi's fears about backlash and possible retribution were very real, and were expressed by other group members at various times during the research journey. However, this research project was specifically designed to engender strong team building among all participants. The teams-based approach to problem-solving meant that all project participants, including Naomi, could turn to their own project teams for support, as well as to a larger cohort of 'tempered radicals'[6] among the reference group and other project teams.

'Melinda' was a relatively young police officer who led a project to determine whether the barriers to women's advancement were perceived or real. She made her own challenging discoveries about what can happen to women police officers when they have to juggle their expected, deferential and relatively invisible roles with the 'pushback' that comes with being seen and recognized as an emerging contender for a leadership role in the hierarchy.

'Melinda'

Melinda's project team comprised herself as leader and two male officers. Despite their being a higher rank than Melinda, both her male colleagues on this project were assiduous in their efforts to support and advance her in her leadership of this team, as well as in her career prospects. Melinda discovered that outside this supportive environment she could not always count on other males for the same level of respect and collegiality. Indeed, her leadership of this team could offer no safeguard against the expectations of a new male supervisor at her workplace. Like the women on Naomi's team, Melinda knew and understood the importance of deference in her workplace. Moreover, as a uniformed officer, she was attuned to the particular kinds of power plays that were associated with gender and rank in this organization.

Arriving late for an early morning meeting, Melinda explained that she had been tasked with an unexpected role that had disrupted her plans to travel into head office in a timely fashion. Our project team meeting, arranged some time before, had been scheduled to start very early in the day. Melinda's new boss only recently promoted to Inspector rank, made it clear that his arrangements took precedence over hers: he required her services as a driver. Moreover, it was apparent from his instructions to Melinda that he believed that his new status demanded a chauffeur. Accordingly, Melinda was expected to drive her supervisor to a meeting that was at the opposite end of town to her own. He was aware that this would make Melinda late. He also expected her to leave her meeting early so that she would be in time to collect him again. In this male officer's terms, his 'requirement' for a driver entitled him to a display of deference and duty from his subordinate; the importance of her role as a team leader was invisible to him.

Fletcher (1999) suggests that there were particular feminine and masculine practices that act to keep prevailing power systems in place. Describing some of these masculinity practices from a poststructuralist framework, Fletcher argues that there are 'aspects of work that are congruent with idealized masculinity'. These are the aspects defined within the organization as 'real work'. Therefore, those practices 'associated with idealized femininity' (Fletcher, 1999: 30) cannot be so defined. Given the research topic it is unlikely that Melinda's supervisor would regard her project team meeting as 'real work'. Later, when Melinda recounted the same story to the reference group, the more experienced members provided some of their observations about the links between such an arrogant waste of a valued worker's time and the masculinity practices enacted with the acquisition of commissioned rank. While remarking that this kind of behaviour was not all that unusual for this workplace, they were in agreement that these practices tend to emerge at inspector level, and were seen by the newly anointed as entitlement of office, and therefore part of their 'real work'. This cynical disregard for Melinda's team leader role on this project, and the blatant misuse of her time and the department's resources, was not an unusual practice. Reference group members agreed that upwardly mobile males seem keen to find ways to visibly demonstrate the accoutrements of their new office when they reach this rank (only two women had to this point).

As Melinda's profile began to take on more prominence in the organization, her experiences of new forms of discrimination began to inform her understanding of her gendered workplace. Increasingly, she used her own project team, as well as the reference group to report and discuss these changes. One of the unwelcome experiences she reported occurred when she was performing in an acting role in her workplace. Melinda recounted that as she walked into a meeting room, she observed a male officer of lower rank checking her badge. This officer then turned to another male officer next to him, and speaking loudly enough for Melinda to hear, said *'how come a token woman who has got [only this] _____ [number],[7] has got an acting inspector?'* In sharing these and other stories with us, Melinda demonstrated that her newly honed skills in applying the gender lens had begun to clarify her perceptions about such behaviour. However, as an upwardly mobile woman officer, she needed to remain vigilant to the threat of diminished credibility. As a young woman on an upward trajectory, her increasing visibility meant that she found herself being confronted with the reality that some males would invariably denigrate her efforts and abilities. While not wanting to abandon her hard won credibility and beliefs (Meyerson and Scully, 1995), Melinda's reporting of such incidents (within the safety of our research teams) demonstrated her awareness that her identity was changing; that as she became more visible within the organization, some of her male colleagues were targeting her with the same hostile and discriminatory practices she was researching. Melinda continued to mediate her performance within the organization, carefully walking a very fine line to ensure that she could continue to conceal the extent of her participation in and contribution to a highly visible project: she learned to play down her role to men in the wider organization while also enjoying the benefits from revealing her skills and knowledge to senior men on the reference group and project teams, each of whom supported and sponsored her work on this project.

I now turn to 'Andrea', to report on how some different, yet related masculinity protection practices were drawn into play as the women in her team began to write up their final report on why women police officers had left their organization.

'Andrea'

This policing organization had neither current data on the numbers of women who had left the organization, nor their reasons for leaving. Women police officers with a wealth of knowledge and experience had simply disappeared from the organizational radar. Through her position on the union, the reference group member who selected this topic had gathered some anecdotal data about the numbers of women who had left policing and she wanted to locate them and ask them why they had left. No-one could have anticipated that the response from some of these former police women would be so explosive; so much so that the particular challenges for the women on this project team were to remain in control of their research data and retain their autonomy as researchers, while ensuring that some significant findings were not 'disappeared' (Fletcher, 1999).

With their telephone surveys of former women police officers completed, this group had some explicit data from their interviewees in hand. Team members now needed to collate this material. They had invested a considerable amount of time determining how to best categorize the multiple and diverse responses to survey questions. Recognizing the amount of work still to be completed, 'Andrea', one of the younger members of this group offered to take on the twofold task of organizing and analysing the collated data, and then writing up an initial draft of the report.

When the project team leader reviewed Andrea's first draft, she was surprised to discover that most of the more contentious material was missing. The missing data included verbatim accounts from interviewees recording their individual experiences of the corruption, sexual harassment and discrimination they said they had witnessed and experienced while they were serving police officers. The language used, and some of the incidents described, were colourful, explicit and in many cases, quite confronting. Andrea had cut many of these accounts from her version of the report. On discovering this, we learned that this project presented Andrea with a problem that not only threatened to sabotage the integrity of the final report, but also had the potential to impact on her future career aspirations.

According to Andrea, her manager had instructed her to ensure her team's report was not 'too controversial'. As an organizational appointee on the reference group, Andrea's manager had become aware, through discussions on this particular project that the findings were likely to reflect badly on his area of influence. His intervention in the collaborative and democratic process of the project was designed to censor the proposed contents, to erase evidence that perhaps he considered could be 'too explicit' or 'too critical' of the organization. On hearing what had happened, several of the other team members stepped in and re-inserted the material that had been excluded. While recognizing that what they had was almost 'too hot' to handle, this group was nonetheless determined to give voice to those women whose departure from their organization had left their experiences of policing unremarked and unacknowledged. Andrea's manager placed her in an invidious position, and yet, she was also part of a team whose groundbreaking research would make visible for the first time the lived experiences of women who felt that they had no other choice than to leave their chosen profession.

In Fletcher's (1999) terms, Anderea was still learning to cope with the fear factor, unsure of the price she would personally pay for her team engaging in 'the politics of speaking out' (Fletcher, 1999: 158). Later, this young woman demonstrated her personal commitment to the project through her continuing participation. With her team's support and the weight of the collective project findings behind her, Andrea appeared to overcome her fear of displeasing her manager and became a more visible, quietly assertive advocate for the project and its outcomes.

The subject of my next case study, 'Gail', discovered that her new officer-in-charge role in a small town created more than the anticipated ripple across the organization; the impact of this placement, when combined with her participation on my research project generated such a level of (unwelcome) interest that she seemed to be living her life in a goldfish bowl.

'Gail'

Gail made history as the first female officer with children to be placed in charge of a country police station in this policing jurisdiction. Whereas my role was to interact with Gail in my capacity as a feminist ethnographer, she played the unusual, dual roles of being both subject and narrator of her own case study. A range of pressures were brought to bear on this particular officer because of her groundbreaking role. To begin with, she was provided with better accommodation than the small dwelling previously occupied by a series of male officers who were either single or married with grown children. Whereas the purchase of a new and better home was highly visible within the town, more controversial was the considerable investment of departmental funds on Gail's behalf, rendering her own placement highly visible to other officers within her organization.

These 'firsts' created some unwanted attention for Gail and it would be fair to say that being part of our project undoubtedly added to the scrutiny. Accordingly, she and I worked very hard at hiding the extent of her project participation by ensuring that all of our communication was outside of normal communication times and channels.

Very soon into her new role Gail clearly understood that her entry into this male-dominated community would be contentious, and that men in particular would not only have difficulty with the concept of a woman officer in charge of their local police station – they would also be watching her every move. She reported to me that she had not expected the same level of scrutiny from her male supervisors. Gail soon found that she was overburdened by inadequate staffing, a hostile community and the pedantic demands of her new male supervisor. She described this supervisor's demands and his scrutiny of her paperwork as excessive and his feedback to her as largely negative. It appeared that some members of the community were in agreement with her inspector's assessment of her unsuitability for the role, complaining bitterly that a woman was not adequate for this town. Gail told me that some of this animosity was undoubtedly related to her tough stand on domestic violence among indigenous community members, and her vigilance for maintaining the law on drinking hours at the local hotels. As one of the women police officers in Gerber's (2001: xii) study comments, community members see women police officers differently:

When you're in uniform, and you're a man, people see a cop. If you're a woman and you're in uniform, people don't see a cop, they see a woman.

During this time, Gail commented that while she did not attempt to hide the fact that she had two young children, it annoyed her greatly that her role as a mother had become the focus for a lot of the additional scrutiny of her performance in the workplace. Whereas she and I often discussed her children's state of health and her difficulties with suitable childcare arrangements, these elements of our ongoing dialogue were peripheral to the issues that she raised about the challenges of her daily working environment. However, these issues were of little concern to Gail's many detractors. From accounts she received, and those passed through to the reference group, officers looking into the goldfish bowl seemed more interested in devaluing Gail's professional expertise; these internal reports focused on relatively minor issues, such as Gail breastfeeding on the job, breaking down in tears and employing the wife of one of her officers to babysit. She complained to me that no one seemed interested in applying the same level of scrutiny to examine the operational policing issues confronting officers in this isolated town. If they did, she suggested, they would find she and her team of officers were confronted by a complex array of entrenched social problems that required additional policing support as well as some innovative and well-resourced remedies. Her high-level visibility as a woman 'doing a man's job' got in the way of her delivering the services required by this isolated community.

Despite having to deal with this intense and ongoing speculation about her suitability and performance in her management role, Gail's persistence, capacity and sheer determination ensured that her experiences were recorded and made visible for this project. She remained committed to the completion of the case study, delaying her report for a short while as she began a new job in a challenging work environment and juggled a different workload.

A new round of changes – including relocation to a much larger town – resulted in Gail needing to engage in a range of subversive practices to hide her ongoing participation on the project. For example, I used her private email address to make contact and we did not ever speak with each other on her work phone or during work hours. Instead, we continued our practice of working on this research behind the scenes, speaking to each other out of hours, on weekends and late at night, and often while she was attending to one or other of her children. Finally, when her draft was finished, we engaged in a lengthy but vital final act of consolidation when we each read, edited and revised the three versions of the same case study: those prepared by her superintendent, Gail and me. It was only when we had the composite version that each of us, finally, had a complete picture of the high costs Gail had paid for maintaining her commitment to telling her story.

Double duty, double bind, double the rise

These case studies provide a representative sample of the experiences cited by many of the women in my research teams. All of these women expended considerable energy in their project work. Much of this energy involved them in managing a range of professional identities. While they were effectively going out on a limb for other women in their organization, the women on these teams were potentially placing themselves at considerable risk by participating in their projects. In contrast, the men working on the reference group and/or project teams assessed their level of risk as minimal. One of the senior men, for example, reported that from time to time his male colleagues commented that they thought he was a little 'crazy' for participating on the reference group but he retained and improved his status and recognition.

The women used different criteria to assess their degree of risk. Their research was throwing the spotlight on to multiple examples of gendered practice within this workplace. Moreover, they were drawing these anomalies to the attention of various stakeholder groups within their organization, the majority of which were presided over by men. For women such as 'Naomi', this could only be construed as a 'career limiting move' in an organization where there was barely any upward movement for women police or public service officers. Women like 'Gail' were required to lead dual lives while they worked on their projects. As I have discussed, some reported in confidence to their team members that they were living some of the same harassment and discrimination scenarios that other women were revealing to them through their researcher roles. Others, such as 'Melinda' were beginning to frame recommendations that should improve the working lives of all women; however, they knew that the success of some of these recommendations would depend upon the punishment and/or removal of perpetrators, some of whom were currently subjecting individual researchers to a range of discriminatory, demeaning and sexist behaviours. These women therefore had to balance their own, personal experiences with the altruistic goal of making things better for all women. Some said that they felt a personal responsibility to name and shame known perpetrators; others, such as 'Andrea' reported that they were living in fear throughout this period, aware of the risks involved for anyone to have, or to share this knowledge. One of the women on the project teams provided the following comment, in which she was responding to a male supervisor who had complained about the length of time that the research was taking, and questioned the necessity for further meetings:

> *I am sure that you will agree that the experience of women in [our organisation] are largely viewed through the eyes of our male colleagues. And although they may be keen to ensure parity in the workplace I do not*

believe that they should dictate the conditions under which women can tell their stories.

The women within the project teams expressed their sense of collective empowerment from working with each other over an extended period of time. It is not surprising, therefore, that men in their workplaces noticed these changes and had to face the possibility that some women appeared to have new and unusual access to power. Yet, as they came together to participate in the collaborative, democratic and supportive environment of their project team meetings, the women project team members continued to separately pay the accustomed deference to their male supervisors and colleagues in their individual workplaces. Therefore, they were operating in two worlds, with two sets of accepted norms and practices. Burton (1991: 11) cautions that women's unequal position in the workplace is sustained by paying deference because such subservience helps to legitimize male authority. I argue that in particularly gendered workplaces, such as policing, women make strategic use of deferential behaviour to mask their activities and to advance their radical cause.

Many of the women on the project teams had to hide their ongoing participation by engaging in subterfuge and other subversive activities. According to the women, they were prepared to do this so that they could comply with their supervisors' requests to be available to support their work on other, competing priorities. This lack of support for their project work meant that, by the time we were compiling the final reports for each of the projects, these women were performing 'double duty'. Not surprisingly, these were the people in this organization who were in the least powerful position to negotiate with their supervisors.

Fletcher's (1999: 117) analysis of the 'masculine logic' underpinning organizational practices provides some means for understanding the nature of the double burden for the women in these teams. She suggest that 'what is seen as important work in organizations' is largely shaped by that 'masculine logic', so argues that issues that 'fail to fit the masculine ideal' are the ones that 'get disappeared and devalued' (Fletcher, 1999: 117). The capacity for their work to meet this fate underpinned some of the ambivalence women expressed about the sustainability of their project team findings. Through their new understanding of the practices that gendered the organization, they were able to see and articulate some of the inherent contradictions confronting them as they tried to manage their own and others' expectations. The last stage of their research work was the most difficult and time-consuming and required even more concentrated time and effort. However, these women were expected to perform the same or greater workloads, juggling the demands of their supervisors and colleagues with the final, very busy stages of their project team involvement.

From my discussions with various team members it was apparent that they were aware of the inherent inequities in this organization's expectations that the women would and could carry these double workloads. At the same time, there seemed to be general consensus among the women themselves that this price would be worthwhile if they could deliver on their promise of bringing about change for all women. Fletcher (1999: 113) describes this kind of altruism as indicative of 'empowered workers'. She suggest that people who engage in such practices are those 'who not only take responsibility for their work and their own learning but accept a more general responsibility for the whole' (Fletcher, 1999: 113–134). In the recent past, the usual experiences for women at my research site were more closely aligned with Burton's (1991: 36) assertion that women in their position had 'little power to define the new situation and to make claims on the more interesting work that is created'. With this new shared sense of optimism then, the women on the project teams were juggling their double burdens with their eye on the prize. Just like Bruni and Gherardi's (2002: 193) case study of 'Omega' each of the women on the project teams were taking the opportunity to construct 'a professional self' while acting on their new awareness of 'a gendered self'. By Bruni and Gherardi's (2002) account of Omega's journey, we learn that women have to continually switch between feminine and masculine behaviours to accommodate men's differential responses to women's biological and professional entities. Further, they suggest that women have to participate in the kind of self-management in which their male colleagues never have to engage. Such self-management is also subject to intense scrutiny, as was evident in Gail's story.

As a result of the experiences of their women members, the project teams understood much more about some of the pitfalls that lay ahead with the implementation process for their draft recommendations. What we had not understood however was the extent of the hostility towards me as a result of my continuing and increasingly visible presence in this organization.

A forensic examination of the feminist facilitator

Gatenby and Humphries (2000: 103) offer some cautions about the researcher's need to balance explicitly feminist agendas with the research objective. Importantly for my research, these authors canvas some of the difficulties that may result from researchers playing multiple roles in the process of engaging with their subjects:

> *We sense the tension in the possibilities for various roles we may undertake, as observers, supporters, listeners, advisors and so forth. Decisions about what issues to raise with participants and how to raise them or lead discussions are often difficult...Our own participation and disclosures vary, not only according to the practical realities of our lives, but also according to the emotional realities of living with feminist ideals in a patriarchal world.*
>
> Gatenby and Humphries (2000: 98)

There is no doubt that the participatory intent of my methodological approach was realized through the high level of interaction we were able to achieve within and between the reference group, the project teams, the wide range of research subjects and then later, the implementation group. However, this was not without cost and required far greater facilitation than had been originally anticipated. When the project recommendations were accepted and we entered the implementation process, I negotiated the role of paid facilitator and became deeply involved in driving a number of the key initiatives. This meant that my profile within the organization became more complex, more visible and accordingly, more open to conjecture and speculation. Not surprisingly I was subjected to some increasingly forensic examination by a variety of observers, some of whom could neither understand nor condone the continuing presence of a non-police officer in their jurisdiction, with the authority to call on resources and high-level contacts.

The complexity of my roles increased over time, requiring me to mediate a fine line between my formal insider/outsider status, and my informal roles as colleague, coach and group leader. There were undoubted benefits to this level of facilitation, and many internal supporters argued that without it, the research project would not have been completed or realized and the ensuing recommendations might not have been implemented to the degree that they were. This level of interaction made it difficult at times to maintain some objective distance from the subjects and the results of the research, and, from the internal politics of this policing organization.

Earlier, during the research project, a high level of trust developed between most project team members and myself. This fact, when combined with the focus of our research topic, meant that I was often asked to provide support, advice, and at time, to take action, on harassment and discrimination issues that were impacting directly on some of the researchers, and/or on their work colleagues during the life of the project. In performing these roles I was clearly caught between the gaps that defined my insider/outsider status. According to Ellis and Bochner's (1996: 19) definition, I was also performing my ethnographer role, not standing 'above or outside' what I was studying.

Some of the simmering, internal frustrations about my continued role boiled over during the implementation stage when a series of changes occurring under the sponsorship of a new commissioner prompted backlash that for the first time was aimed directly at me. The commissioner had understood the importance of the implementation of the project recommendations; indeed he had addressed the implementation group at the commencement of his term suggesting that he considered the work of this team to be driving the cultural reform agenda within his organization. However, my relative visibility and associated longevity as a privileged outsider was now subjecting him to some tensions with his new senior management team. My privileged insider/outsider status had become somewhat blurred around the edges and I learned that I needed to reposition myself from what Sandra Acker (2000: 198) refers to as the researcher's 'insiderness' to 'outsiderness'. This was a dramatic shift from my original positioning within this organization when the unassailable support from the top for redressing the gendered workplace culture had provided a protected and very privileged position. This protection had created a false perception about the responsiveness to truth telling in this organization.

Conclusion

The data gathered through this PhD research project illustrates and informs our understanding of how women can strategically move between visibility and invisibility when responding to the gender dynamics at play in their workplace. Mediating such movement, however, was not without cost. My study showed that women did the bulk of the project work, were less visible within the wider organization, and were less likely than men to be rewarded appropriately for their efforts. Just like the four women I highlighted through the case studies – Naomi, Melinda, Andrea and Gail – the majority of women on my research teams had to manage the additional burden of conducting research into a contentious, feminist topic within an environment that was hostile to their presence, their performance and their project topics. In contrast, rank and gender enabled the men on my project to make choices about how, where and when they placed their efforts. Moreover, in keeping with the masculinist, hierarchical culture of this workplace, the men on these teams were less likely than the women to be held accountable and/or admonished for the choices they made about where they placed their priorities. Importantly, they were also more likely than any of the women to be able to enlist administrative support for the increased workloads created through their involvement in the project teams.

However, despite the lack of future prospects, or perhaps because of this bleak scenario, these women were still prepared to 'rock the boat'. They had neither the accompanying status nor the rank to countermand the gendered practices of their workplace. For this reason, their project teams afforded some degree of protective invisibility; their teams became a safe haven where they quickly developed a level of camaraderie, mutual respect and sense of purpose that was not always available to them in their daily work. This achievement was due not only to the calibre of those chosen to participate but also to the sound group process and robust methodology, which gave participants access to a new, and apparently welcome forum for their discussion and reflection. Many of their robust discussions were reflective of the desire to lead the organization forward, to nullify the impact of past discriminatory practices and to engage with men and women in practices that were fair, equitable and collegial.

Cockburn's (1991: 46) research provides some good reasons for why the women on the project teams faced such a difficult task in their research practice. She argues that equal opportunity is not an easy policy to implement because it means 'confronting head-on men's sense of owning the organisation'. The women on the project teams actively engaged in such confrontation, but did so by quite deliberatively and effectively engaging in a range of subversive tactics, in keeping with some of the cultural practices they learned within their policing environment. To varying degrees, these manoeuvres enabled them to maintain a sense of ownership, efficacy and control over their research practice. They embraced and enacted leadership practices that to a large degree were invisible to others outside the project; nonetheless they engaged these alternative practices in the hope of moving their organization forward. As Sinclair (1998: 119–120) suggests, there are some positives for women in being able to hide their competencies behind some cultural perceptions about women's limited roles: 'Women are accustomed to being sex-stereotyped and are adept at using the complacency of others' comfortable categorisations to achieve particular ends'.

Such contradictions formed the basis for the dialectic I have outlined: the women on the project teams quickly understood that to lead change, they would need to embrace some strategies, learning and behaviours that were a radical departure from their confined, constrained and stereotyped professional selves. They could only do so if they kept themselves and these activities below the organizational radar. To ensure the success of their mission, they would need to remain visible in their usual roles, continuing to make overt displays of submission, deference and appeasement in their normal operating environments. For these reasons, the equal opportunity environment engendered within the teams, supported by the ground rules and the strong team-working ethos, were significantly at odds with the same women's experiences outside these forums.

Many of the women police and public service officers involved in the research project have now achieved greater visibility in their organization through their attainment of higher ranks and levels. One of the women public service officers, speaking from her more senior and highly visible role, reflected on the double-edge sword of having a new perspective, along with her new status:

You've ruined it for us now you know. We will never be able to look at this organisation the same way again. Now we see everything, know what is going on – nothing is hidden. We can see it all.
(Team member to research student at the end of the project)

While offering some support for Fletcher's argument that 'certain [relational practices] get disappeared', I assert that this is not always a negative outcome. For some of the players in my research teams, such disappearing was both a critical and subversive act. At various, crucial stages, these women were able to reverse the disappearing act to cross their own personal and professional boundaries, bringing new knowledge and fresh insights to the gendered practices of their workplace.

Notes

1 Dr Sue Lewis, formerly Swinburne University, Victoria, coined the term 'dense masculinity' to describe the gendered work practices at her research site, a fire and emergency services organization. As with similar paramilitary organizations such as policing, the excess of men, comparative to women, results in practices, policies and behaviours that are imbued with masculinist characteristics. Personal communication, September 2005.

2 This chapter draws on research conducted by the author for her PhD thesis 'Gendering Change: An Immodest Manifesto for Intervening in Masculinist Organisations', University of Western Australia, 2006.
3 This term was coined by researchers associated with the Center for Gender in Organisations [the CGO]; it describes an approach that offers a tool for fleshing out 'masculine definitions' and the 'gendering' of job descriptions that work against women (Kolb and Meyerson, 1999: 141).
4 The advisory group and the operational groups are referred to in this chapter as the 'reference group' and the 'project teams' respectively.
5 See Harwood (2006: 266–271) 'Presenting the Evidence: the Power of Numbers'.
6 Meyerson and Scully (1995: 586) describe 'tempered radicals' as 'individuals who identify with and are committed to their organizations, and...to a cause...that is fundamentally different from, and possibly at odds with the dominant culture of their organization...[they are] called 'radicals' because they challenge the 'status quo'. The applicability of this concept to individuals and teams at my research site is examined in greater detail in Harwood (2006).
7 In this policing jurisdiction [and many others], officers are assigned a number when they join the police service; the lower the number, the greater the longevity as a police officer. It is still common practice within policing to read an officer's number [displayed on their uniform] to determine their seniority. It is then possible to compare their years of service with their current designation [as signalled by a name badge and/or the number of stripes and 'pips' they are wearing on their sleeves]. Melinda's observers in this example were clearly of the opinion that someone with such a relatively 'high' [more recent] number should not have been acting in such a senior position. Melinda had been an officer for 17 years at this stage of her career.

References

Acker, J. (1990) 'Hierarchy, jobs, bodies: A theory of gendered organizations', *Gender and Society*, 4(2): 139–158.
Acker, S. (2000) 'In/out/side: Positioning the researcher in feminist qualitative research', *Resources for Feminist Research*, 28: 189–208.
Bruni, A. and Gherardi, S. (2002) '"Omega's Story": The heterogeneous engineering of a gendered professional self'. In Dent, M. and Whitehead, S. (eds) *Managing Professional Identities: Knowledge, Performativity and the 'New' Professional*. London: Routledge.
Burton, C. (1991) *The Promise and the Price: The Struggle for Equal Opportunity in Women's Employment*. Sydney: Allen and Unwin.
Cockburn, C. (1991) *In the Way of Women: Men's Resistance to Sex Equality in Organizations*. London: Macmillan.
Dahlerup, D. (1988) 'From a small to a large minority: Women in Scandinavian politics', *Scandinavian Political Studies*, 11: 275–298.
De Francisco, V. (1997) 'Gender, power and practice: Or, putting your money (and your research) where your mouth is', in Wodak, R. (ed.) *Gender and Discourse*. London: Sage.
Ellis, C. and Bochner, A. P. (eds) (1996) *Composing Ethnography: Alternative Forms of Qualitative Writing*. Walnut Creek: Alta Mira Press, a division of Sage.

Fletcher, J. K. (1999) *Disappearing Acts. Gender, Power and Relational Practice at Work*. Cambridge, MA: The MIT Press.

Gatenby, B. and Humphries, M. (2000) 'Feminist participatory action research: Methodological and ethical issues', *Women's Studies International Forum*, 23(1): 89–105.

Gerber, G. L. (2001) *Women and Men Police Officers: Status, Gender and Personality*. Westport, Connecticut: Praeger.

Harwood, S. (2006) *Gendering Change: An Immodest Manifesto for Intervening in Masculinist Organisations*. Perth, PhD Thesis: University of Western Australia.

Kolb, D. M. and Meyerson, D. (1999) 'Keeping gender in the plot: A case study of the Body Shop', in Rao, A., Stuart, R. and Kelleher, D. (eds) *Gender at Work: Organizational Change for Equality*. West Hartford, Connecticut: Kumarian Press.

Meyerson, D. E. and Scully, M. (1995) 'Tempered radicalism and the politics of ambivalence and change', *Organization Science*, 6(5): 585–600.

Sinclair, A. (1998) *Doing Leadership Differently: Gender, Power and Sexuality in a Changing Business Culture*. Melbourne: Melbourne University Press.

Wajcman, J. (1999) *Managing Like a Man: Women and Men in Corporate Management*. Sydney: Allen and Unwin.

11
A Reversal of the Gaze: Men's Experiences of Visibility in Non-traditional Occupations
Ruth Simpson

Introduction

This chapter explores how men experience visibility. In particular, it considers the challenges men face in the 'eye of the gaze' (Townley, 1992). The gaze captures some of the power dynamics of visibility and the disciplinary and controlling effects of surveillance as individuals are subject to normalizing scrutiny and judgements. Power is implicated in the relationship between gazers and those captured in their view in that, through systems of classification and categorization, a form of reality or knowledge is created and maintained. Drawing on a research project which focussed on the challenges men face in four non-traditional careers (nursing, primary school teaching, cabin crew and librarianship), I explore the different ways visibility 'plays out' for men in these roles. These occupations are defined as non-traditional on the grounds that they are numerically dominated by women and because they draw on skills and attributes, such as nurturance, service and care, which are culturally associated with femininity. Here, men 'stand out' as gendered subjects and are visible as 'exceptions to the rule'. Masculinity is 'on the line' (Morgan, 1992) and available for scrutiny in contexts where women's dispositions and women's experiences represent the unmarked case. In these respects, while in general terms gender can be seen to be a problem that attaches to women, in non-traditional work contexts it becomes an issue that is visibly associated with men. Moreover, while activities of service and care are assumed to be the domain of women, tied essentially to skills and attributes of femininity, such work is often perceived as incongruent with the embodied dispositions of men. Men can thus face a double bind. If they perform femininity they bring their masculinity as well as their sexuality to question; if they perform masculinity they are seen to be unsuitable for the job. This raises questions about how men negotiate the tensions between gender and occupational identity and how men manage the visibility that is heightened in their occupational role. This chapter draws on the concept of the 'gendered gaze', a power dynamic that is commonly applied to examine the subjection of women by men, to explore the visibility of men. In other words, it considers the implications of a 'reversal of gaze' when it is men, outside the norm, that are under view.

The power of the gaze

Inherent in much of the current work on women's experiences in non-traditional occupations, where much of the work on these contexts is located, is the notion of surveillance. For Kanter (1977) for example, token women are subject to scrutiny which serves to constrain women into defining 'role traps' (pet, seductress, mother, iron maiden) that limit available repertoires of power and influence. Women may respond to constant scrutiny by avoiding conflict, by being over cautious or by exhibiting a fear of failure in order to avert possible retribution. Keeping a low profile (seeking invisibility) is thus a common strategy for women. This appraisal or 'gaze' can therefore be seen to have a disciplining and normalizing effect in that it helps to structure thought and action into pre-existing norms, categories and behaviours – so that knowledge about individual women and about women as a gendered group is created.

The concept of the gaze, and its power, is captured in Foucault's (1977) Panoptican. Originally conceived by the utilitarian philosopher Jeremy Bentham in the context of the need to control the behaviour of convicts, the Panoptican comprised a 12 sided polygon with a central tower through which surveillance could take place. Inmates may or may not be actually under view – but there was always the possibility that they were so. It was through the constant possibility of surveillance that conformity and discipline would eventually take place. In this way, for Foucault, the gaze is a source of power and discipline. In fact, it need not be incorporated into an external edifice but can be institutionalized and projected through internal systems and procedures. A managerial gaze for example can be exercised through targets, accountability and control or through performance appraisals. As Townley (1992) argues, the gaze is thus a form of government achieved through the practice of total visibility. Moreover, if individuals can be encouraged to 'want' what these systems deliver, then the 'inspecting gaze' can become internalized and discipline, regulation through self surveillance can be achieved. Being constantly seen or able to be seen produces the disciplined individual – influencing individual experiences as well as organizational structures.

The concept of the gaze therefore captures the disciplinary power of surveillance. Through systems of classification, codification and measurement, it constitutes for Foucault (1977) both power and knowledge. In terms of the latter, a partial reality or form of invention (Townley, 1992) is created through the gaze. The knowledge is partial because it leaves those aspects which it does not highlight or classify 'in the dark'. In other words, it visibly highlights that 'on which it alights, leaving in darkness that which lies outside its sphere' (Townley, 1992: 189). Those aspects that are rendered invisible constitute the gaze because the invisible, what lies outside, serves to define what we see.

Through examination and surveillance, knowledge of the individual accordingly emerges but this is both defining and incomplete in that the individual is visible only in relation to a 'hypothesised essence' (ibid) – a norm from which it is characterized and derived. The individual is accordingly known through a series of normative judgements. Thus, in being assigned to stereotypical 'role traps', women managers from Kanter's work are known according to gender conforming norms of behaviour and, as she found, strong sanctions are mobilized in the form of marginalization and ridicule, if women step outside of these roles. This is the reality created around women irrespective of individual and personal dispositions. In this way, the gaze allows knowledge to develop and control (through correction, classification, exclusion) to be exercised over those in view – leaving similarly defining and non-conforming or oppositional features in the dark.

The practices and relations embodied in the gaze have strong gender associations. In this respect, a gendered vision is often bestowed on women by the 'gazer' (Perriton, 1999), capturing the power asymmetry that exists between the viewer and the viewed. As Snow (1989) points out, the 'male gaze' is founded on voyeurism, objectification and patriarchy – as well as phallocentrism. Tyler and Abbott (1998) for example refer to how female flight attendants are subject to instrumentally imposed aesthetic codes and manage themselves as 'ornamental objects'. Through the gaze of airlines in particular and patriarchally determined aesthetic codes of femininity more generally, women are expected to manage and maintain their bodies to reach an aesthetic ideal. As Tyler and Abbott argue, the production and maintenance of 'gendered bodies' is part of the control of women's behaviour through appearance (see also Adkins, 1995; Hall, 1993). Similarly, Alvesson (1998) has examined how men working in the 'feminized' context of an advertising agency, where a focus on team-working and the need for creativity and sensitivity in relationships afforded few opportunities for displays of traditional masculinity, activated a sexually appraising 'gaze' on women in the firm and so consigned to women a subordinated and objectified position of being 'viewed'. The emphasis on the sexual attractiveness of female employees, a 'hyper-feminization' of women, therefore placed women in a subordinate position and allowed men to recapture a masculinity undermined by the symbolically feminine. In general terms, the gaze thus has a constitutive role (of subjectivity, of knowledge) which results in and emanates from the operation of power, so helping to define organizational reality.

While work has suggested that women are often subject to the controlling gaze of others, the gendered nature of the gaze may also be significant and subordinating for men in contexts where masculinity is subject to challenge. In the context of non-traditional occupations, where women's experiences and women's embodied dispositions are the norm, men stand out as different. They become visibly gendered and doubly Othered in the sense that they lie outside dominant notions of work-based masculinity (hierarchical, detached, disembodied) as well as outside the norm of service and care that are tied to essentialized notions of femininity. This raises questions about the implications of heightened visibility for men and how they respond to being 'under view'.

Method

Against this background, this chapter sets out to explore how men experience visibility and the gaze in their non-traditional roles. In so doing, it draws on data from a larger project which sought to investigate the challenges and experiences of men in four occupational categories: nurses, primary school teachers, cabin crew and librarians. The project was based on interviews with 74 men working in these occupations in the UK and Australia. The UK study comprised 49 in-depth interviews, conducted in London and the South-East, with male workers from across the range of levels and roles within each group. Sixteen male nurses and nine primary school teachers took part in the smaller Australia based study. All were located in and around Sydney, New South Wales. In each context, the sample was established by advertising the project on intranet sites and through professional journals and associations.

The research adopted a social constructivist approach in that it explored how men give meaning to their experiences at work and how they make sense of their reality. The goal of constructivism is to understand the world of lived experience from the point of view of those who live it (Schwandt, 1998) and how seemingly 'objective' features are constituted by subjective meanings of individuals and inter-subjective processes (Eriksson and Kovalainen, 2008: 19). This approach challenges the hegemonic status of taken for granted knowledge on the grounds that the world is known through human experience, mediated through language and sustained by 'conventions of communication'. The aim is therefore to challenge previously taken for granted understandings and to reveal alternative meanings. On this basis, interviews became an active resource for exploring men's experiences in that the stories and interpretations offered were seen as part of an identity management process that highlighted tension and challenge. The question was not therefore whether interviews reflected 'true' attitudes, feelings or experiences but how interviewees constituted themselves with reference to their work contexts.

Interviews were semi-structured, following a set of themes that concerned career issues (career background, motivation, aspirations, attitudes of friends and family to career choice); issues relating to minority status (potential advantages/disadvantages; experiences of marginalization and inclusion); perceptions of 'caring' (e.g. significance and perceptions of personal attributes, of gender difference in performing emotional labour, of challenges faced in this work) and issues concerning implications of career choice for identity and self image (image of the job, its fit with self identity and self perception, possible challenges to masculinity and associated response). Interviews mainly took place in the place of work and lasted between one and one and a half hours. All interviews were recorded and subsequently transcribed.

In recognition of the researchers' implication in the production of accounts (Pullen, 2006), interviews took the form of a dialogue. Reflexivity was sought through a shared process of exploration. Here, interviewer and interviewee discussed the meanings of recounted experiences and respondents were encouraged to consider, in the manner of reflexivity put forward by Martin (2006), their attitudes, emotions and behaviours. As Whitehead (2004) has pointed out, located in the 'mainstream', men often fail to reflect on themselves as gendered subjects or to understand experiences in the margin. Men in this study were unusual in the sense that they had to some extent 'broken the mould' in their occupational choice and had thought carefully about their decision. As one nurse pointed out, he came into nursing 'against all the odds' in terms of giving up a previous career and coping with the disapproval of family and friends. Reflexivity had been involved in their journey and was in some ways built into everyday practice as men coped with challenges to their masculinity and as they performed, in many cases, care and emotional labour. Therefore, while conversations in interviews often took a turn which was new, in the sense that respondents had not thought about or reflected on certain issues before, many reflected ably on their attitudes and experiences.

The analysis comprised a critical reading of the text, paying attention to, from Essers and Benschop (2007), what was said, how it was said and the context in which the statements, descriptions or interpretations were made. In these accounts issues of visibility emerged as a key theme, provoking narratives and emotions relating to the often unwelcome experience of being conspicuous and under view. Within this broad category, sub themes emerged. These related to the gaze as pleasurable, enabling; the gaze as uncomfortable and constraining; and the desire for invisibility.

The gaze as pleasurable, enabling

As tokens in their occupational roles, men were highly visible – a situation which was often unusual for them in that, in other (e.g. non-work) contexts, they were often invisibly gendered. For many men, standing out in the crowd and being highly visible was a source of pleasure and allowed the uptake of a 'special identity'. Others experienced the 'gaze' and the knowledge created about men within this vision as enabling and potentially developmental. Visibility was thus welcomed:

> *God yes for me being in a minority is fantastic! Especially if you're liked as that minority, people know who you are, people come to you for things. I guess I'm relatively popular.*

While visible and Othered in a feminine role, the cultural privileges of masculinity ("liked as that minority") can translate into a privileged ontology and a source of value. Men are accordingly sought after and included:

> *I actually like being one of the few men or even the only man in a school full of women, because they treat me like one of the girls to be perfectly*

honest and that's absolutely fine, I love it, I don't have a problem at all.

Visibility thus conferred symbolic value on men who could draw on the cultural resources of masculinity to give them a privileged and special status that might be less marked in an all male group. Visibility could be pleasurable in other ways as men conformed to organizationally prescribed aesthetic ideals and 'paraded' an exclusive identity in the 'eye of the gaze'. This was particularly pertinent in the case of cabin crew. Here, men often enjoyed the presentation of their bodies to fit a corporate image as well as the high levels of visibility on the job.

> That's partly why I chose the job. I love being clean (laughs) I love looking smart, the uniform and that. It's expected that you be like that, to look professional and I don't mind at all, I enjoy looking good and parading if you like up and down the aisle!

> I always wanted to strut through the terminal with my uniform on after flying or like going to the plane and it's like the passengers go oh it's the crew.

As with female crew (Williams, 2003; Tyler and Abbott, 1998), men were expected to embody the organization in that physical appearance was symbolic of the organization 'brand'. All men spoke of the need for a smart and clean image. Like women in Tyler and Abbott's (1998) study, men routinely exercised a form of self surveillance, undertaking body work to comply with managerial prescriptions of presentation. However, rather than experiencing the 'panoptical gaze' as oppressive, male crew appeared to celebrate their bodies as the bearers of an aesthetic ideal, relishing and enjoying the visibility their work afforded them in the terminal and the aisle.

The knowledge created and maintained through the gaze was advantageous to men in other ways. In many cases, men were assigned to stereotypical roles that exposed them to developmental and learning opportunities. Assumptions that men were careerist and, through their gender, the possessor of special expertise and authority often translated into a 'father' role where men were expected to take the lead, to take on challenging situations (e.g. giving advice, chairing meetings, dealing with difficult children or patients). One nurse recalled how as a student his female supervisor routinely asked his advice as if she did not know herself what to do – deferring to his judgement even though he was not yet trained. A teacher recounted how he was often expected to be the 'spokesman' at staff meetings and raise controversial issues on behalf of female colleagues. In other words, men were exposed to situations which were challenging and demanded resourcefulness. Rather than leading to cautious behaviour, as in Kanter's study of women who sought to evade belittling role traps, these situations and expectations could be developmental for men, exposing them to situations that demanded initiative and resourcefulness.

The gaze as oppressive, constraining

Visibility was not always, however, a welcome and comfortable experience for men. In this respect, men were often subject to performance pressure under the gaze of female managers and colleagues. It was anticipated that men would not be able to 'care' appropriately and men felt the pressure of being 'under view':

> *You can't display bad nursing skills because they're watching you all the time. You've got to keep your skills you know spot on. You've got to do all those things, be a caring person, be empathetic towards the patients, don't shirk your responsibilities, take responsibility for what you're doing, be the technical expert...it's not always easy.*

> *She thought I was a smart alec – she told me so – and that I wouldn't last five minutes. It was like she was watching and waiting for me to fail.*

Men routinely reported perceptions that they were not suited to the demands of a caring role. One Australian teacher referred to assumptions that, because he was a man, parents would automatically believe he was incapable of dealing adequately with problems a child might be experiencing:

> *I know that if any of the children have an issue like maybe they're being taunted or something, a parent will immediately assume that I'm not sensitive to the situation...that frustrates me because I'm actually very sensitive and caring...I find I get a lot if OK, you're a man, you're not really in touch, you don't really care, you don't really understand about my daughter's feelings.*

The idea that men were seen by women as 'unsuited' for the job was a common theme. Bolton (2005) found similar attitudes among women in her study of gynaecology nursing where male colleagues were presented as lacking the necessary emotional labour skills and hence unable to sufficiently 'care' (as one female nurse pointed out, men were only good for 'horse doctors'). In the present study, these pressures often spurred men on to work harder and succeed. One man recalled how he broke the rules and took a ventilator home from intensive care to dismantle – so that if it went wrong he was 'technically ready for it'. Another confessed that he studied his medical texts into the night to prove to a particularly exacting ward manager that he could excel at the job.

Being marked as different could be an uncomfortable and painful experience and could provoke feelings of resistance towards an identity imposed through a traditionally gendered (and Othering) gaze.

> *I remember walking down the corridor one day in the hospital and there were visitors waiting to go onto a ward for visiting time and I heard them say look there's a male nurse, I've never seen one of them before and actually feeling them staring at me as I walked down the corridor and I found that so odd because I thought why are they saying it, I'm not a male nurse, I'm a nurse, a student nurse...*

In these contexts, the gaze could be oppressive, containing critical appraisal of men in their non-traditional roles. Unlike the appraisal of women, embodied in the gaze of men is a suspicion of their motives and of their sexuality. The gaze is thus traditionally gendered and fundamentally heterosexual – felt particularly keenly in the company of male peers and supporting Kimmel's (1994) contention that it is men rather than women who 'police' the gender boundaries in terms of the appraisal of male behaviour.

> *I can see it in their eyes – I can see them* (male acquaintances) *wondering why has he chosen that job? Library work is for women – that's an odd job for a man to go into.*

> *Men in particular – they laugh and say oh you're a man for goodness sake, why have you chosen to do nursing? Why can't you be a doctor?*

Intimations of homosexuality were encountered by men across the four occupational groups in the present study. For cabin crew these intimations were particularly prevalent and men spoke with feeling of the abuse they often had to endure in the course of their work. Men's accounts of the gaze – from male and female passengers, from pilots – were infused with negative imagery:

> *They* (the pilots) *look at you in disgust sometimes like they assume you're gay and you're going to jump on them.*
>
> *I was leaving the plane and these guys started shouting at me, like where's your boyfriend then you dirty bugger.*

Assumptions of sexual deviance permeated male teachers' accounts in particular and had strong discursive (i.e. for management of subjectivity) and material (i.e. for work practices) implications. Here, men's motives for entering the profession was often scrutinized and in the process men came under suspicion, their bodies marked as potentially dangerous in their work with children. As one teacher commented:

> *There are certain things I can't do with the children, I can't hug children as much as a woman teacher would be able to do, because again it would be seen as too close and too intimate with them, which is nonsense, but it would still be seen…(as inappropriate). I should be able to hug somebody as much as a woman should be able to hug someone…*

As Sargent (2001) argues, the social construction of homophobia acts as a ritualized mechanism of social control especially when it is conflated erroneously with paedophilia. For men to nurture children is to judge them as also being dangerously close to molesting them. In this respect, from men's accounts, the gaze is a construct that is a hybrid of two 'symbolic statuses': homosexual male and child molester – the person that parents fear most to have in charge of their children. In an evocative quote, one teacher from Sargent's study described his feelings:

> *I've been teaching second grade now since I started teaching. I guess I wanted to teach little kids all along. Actually I'm kind of offended by this constant reminder from other teachers and from the principal that, as a man, I have to be particularly careful how I behave with children. I know what has happened. I know, um, how do I say this. I understand I guess that there have been some horrible incidents and most of them have involved men, but you know there have been some pretty terrible incidents that have involved women too. They're just not all over the headlines. Molestation is one issue but you know slapping kids around, yelling, calling them names, demeaning them – that's pretty awful too. And that happens more in the women's classrooms than in the men's classrooms, I've noticed. There isn't this big push*

on to make women understand they're being you know watched more closely. I think that just because people assume that just because a child is in a class with a women a child is safe. Hey that's just not true look at the evidence. (Sargent, 2001: 69)

While women evade the gaze in the context of teaching, it has strong and unwelcome implications for men. The gaze accordingly reveals and conceals, supporting partial truths and obscuring what remains outside its view. Women are assumed to be safe, despite some evidence to the contrary. All men are a source of danger, despite the countless teachers who are not. From the quote above, male teachers are marked as potentially dangerous while female teachers lie outside the line of vision.

The desire for invisibility

From the above, we can see that men can be visible in their difference and positioned uncomfortably as Other. This is in contrast to more traditional contexts where, as Butler (1990) has argued, men and masculinity are concealed within the norm. As 'the absolute One', they are in other contexts gender neutral and, unlike the men in this study, their bodies unmarked within a 'disembodied normativity'. However, this invisibility is challenged when men enter non-traditional work contexts where, like women, they are visibly defined by their gender, visibly categorized and essentialized by their masculinity. Men as a gendered subject are thus visible in these contexts.

In the context of nursing in particular, as I have argued elsewhere (Simpson, 2007, 2009), men engage in practices that can be interpreted as a desire for invisibility. Here, male nurses have been shown to draw on ties of fraternity and expert knowledge to seek entry into the centre of male medical practice and to have exhibited conflict and resentment when they felt outside of that sphere (Simpson, 2007, 2009). They accordingly present themselves as having special ties with male doctors, based on shared 'masculine' interests such as sport and on an expertise associated with their often specialist status.

I do have a close relationship with the (male) *doctors – I find that I can be pally with them and sit down and chat with them and we can talk about men things.*

Associations with femininity and men's marginal occupational status mean, however, that entry into the dominant centre is never fully secure and there can consequently be tension around male nurses' uncertain position in relation to this 'norm'. Tension is evidenced in stories of encounters with (always male) doctors where practices of deference and of hierarchy were challenged by male nurses and overturned.

> *I've sent doctors out of my unit before – I've sent them off because I felt they were behaving inappropriately in front of my patients and I've said don't come back to my unit until you either apologise or you can conduct yourself appropriately.*

> *I was at a meeting yesterday and there was three consultants just chit chatting away while I was trying to discuss something and I asked them if they could keep quiet and they just carried on chatting so I said if you don't **** shut up I'm going to walk out of here...*

The need to enter and the subsequent antagonism towards the (masculine) dominant centre can be interpreted as resistance to a visible Other status and to its hierarchical implications – in other words as a desire to evade the gaze. As pointed out in the Introduction, in other contexts men may well have experienced the privileges of invisibility, their gender and cultural advantage hidden within the norm. They may have had few occasions to reflect on or problematize the privileges of men. These privileges may become more visible from their position as Other. The struggles around this centre – of resistance and overtly aggressive displays – may be interpreted as firstly, a recognition of the material and cultural rewards associated with that location and secondly as a desire to enter that domain. The 'quest for invisibility' (Lewis, 2006) i.e. for an invisible gendered subjectivity unmarked by alterity and for access to the cultural rewards of the norm, may partly explain the levels of antagonism when those privileges are effectively denied.

Conclusion

In this chapter we have explored some of the implications of visibility and of the reversal of gaze, for men's experiences in a non-traditional role. We have found that some men claim to enjoy the visibility their token status brings, both as the basis of a 'special' identity and, in some contexts, the means of displaying an aesthetic ideal as well as how they are exposed through assumptions of careerism and special expertise, to opportunities for development and challenge. At the same time, visibility and marking can be an uncomfortable experience when that is associated with Other (different, devalued) identities. Identity work can also be seen in the struggles that take place around the dominant centre as men resist Otherhood and seek the invisibility and privileges of the norm.

The gaze can thus be experienced as pleasure and as a source of discomfort and pain. We have also seen how it both highlights and conceals – supporting partial truths and obscuring what remains outside of its view. Men may seek to escape its sights and strain against its ideological framing – but its disciplinary power remains. As Sargent argues, many of the behaviours that men adopt (moving into management and away from classroom teaching; minimizing physical contact with children) are intended to distance themselves from this symbolic status – symptomatic of the disciplinary and normalizing power of the gaze. Across the occupational groups, men encounter an appraisal that is based on traditional notions of gender and of sexuality – often incorporating homophobia and with painful implications for those under view.

Overall, while the gendered nature of the gaze has been based in the main on a masculine source of vision with women as its object of appraisal, we can see that men can also be part of the 'viewed'. Men in 'feminine' occupations challenge traditional notions of masculinity and in so doing become subject to a conventional, disciplinary appraisal in these contexts from peers, acquaintances, parents, patients and passengers. The gaze has discursive and material consequences as men resist subordinated identities and as they conform to (or evade) its normalizing tendencies in specific work practices. In the reversal of the gaze, men become aware of and resent their marking as gendered subjects – and resist an Other status. As the nurse complained in an earlier quote, painfully experiencing a reversal of gaze, *I'm not a male nurse, I'm a nurse, a student nurse...*

References

Adkins, L. (1995) *Gendered Work*. Buckingham: Open University Press
Alvesson, M. (1998) 'Gender relations and identity at work: A case study of masculinities and femininities in an advertising agency', *Human Relations*, 51(8): 969–1005.
Bolton, S. (2005) 'Women's work, dirty work: The gynaecology nurse as other', *Gender, Work and Organization*, 12(2): 169–186.
Butler, J. (1990) *Gender Trouble: Feminism and the Subversion of Identity*. London: Routledge.

Eriksson, P. and Kovalainen, A. (2008) *Qualitative Methods in Business Research*. London: Sage.
Essers, E. and Benschop, Y. (2007) 'Enterprising identities: Female entrepreneurs of Moroccan or Turkish origin', *Organization Studies*, 28(1): 49–69.
Foucault, M. (1977) *Discipline and Punish: The Birth of the Prison*. Harmondsworth: Penguin.
Hall, E. (1993) 'Smiling, deferring and flirting: Doing gender by giving good service', *Work and Occupations*, 20(4): 452–471.
Kanter, R. (1977) *Men and Women of the Corporation*. New York: Basic Books.
Kimmel, M. (1994) 'Masculinity as homophobia: Fear, shame and silence in the construction of gender identity'. In Brod, H. and Kaufman, M. (eds) *Theorising Masculinities*, pp. 119–141. London: Sage.
Lewis, P. (2006) 'The quest for invisibility: Female entrepreneurs and the masculine norm of entrepreneurship', *Gender, Work and Organization*, 13(5): 453–469.
Martin, P. Y. (2006) 'Practising gender at work: Further thoughts on reflexivity', *Gender Work and Organization*, 13(3): 254–276.
Morgan, D. (1992) *Discovering Men*. London: Routledge.
Perriton, L. (1999) 'The provocative and evocative gaze upon women in management development', *Gender and Education*, 11(3): 295–307.
Pullen, A. (2006) *Managing Identity*. London: Palgrave.
Sargent, P. (2001) *Real Men or Real Teachers: Contradictions in the Lives of Men Elementary School Teachers*. Harriman TN: Men's Studies Press.
Schwandt, T. (1998) 'Constructivist, interpretivism: Approaches to human enquiry'. In Denzin, N. and Lincoln, Y. (eds) *The Landscape of Qualitative Research: Theories and Issues*. Thousand Oaks, CA: Sage.
Simpson, R. (2007) 'Emotional labour and identity work of men in caring roles'. In Lewis, P. and Simpson, R. (eds) *Gendering Emotion in Organizations*. London: Palgrave.
Simpson, R. (2009) *Men in Caring Occupations: Doing Gender Differently*. Basingstoke: Palgrave Macmillan.
Snow, E. (1989) 'Theorizing the male gaze: Some problems', *Representations*, 25: 30–41.
Townley, B. (1992) 'In the eye of the gaze: The constitutive role of performance appraisal'. In Townley, B., Barrar, P. and Cooper, C. (eds) *Managing Organizations*. London: Routledge.
Tyler, M. and Abbott, P. (1998) 'Chocs away: Weight watching in the contemporary airline industry', *Sociology*, 32(3): 433–450.
Whitehead, S. (2004) 'Man: The Invisible Gendered Subject'. In Whitehead, S. and Barrett, F. (eds) *The Masculinities Reader*. Cambridge: Polity Press.
Williams, C. (2003) 'Sky service: The demands of emotional labour in the airline industry', *Gender, Work and Organization*, 10(5): 513–550.

12
Gender, Mask and the Face: Towards a Corporeal Ethics

Alison Pullen and Carl Rhodes

> It is like us, but it responds with strangeness because it is not like us [...] The mask stands in an intermediary position between different worlds. Its embodiment of the fragile, dividing line between *concealment and revelation*, truth and artifice, natural and supernatural, life and death is a potent source of the mask's metaphysical power (Tseëlon, 2001: 20, italics added).

The processes of revealing and concealing gender are easily taken for granted as a simple matter of considering something as being either exposed or covered up such that it might at times be more visible and at other times less visible. Here, revelation is associated with the uncovering of something that exists beneath that which is over it. The very idea of the revealing and concealing of gender already implies the donning or removal of a mask. To reveal – quite literally to lower or remove the veil that masks the face – is to show the face so that its bearer can be seen without obscurity or adornment. Such a consideration of gender as something subject to potential revelation suggests a performance where gender can be surfaced and hidden, highlighted and suppressed, overt and covert, processual and fixed. Countering such a view, this chapter argues that rather being something that might be concealed or revealed (i.e. through the donning or removal of a mask) gender is itself a mask. Here gender is not something that can be revealed so as to be known, but is that which does the concealing. On this basis we ask our central question: *what lies beneath when the gendered mask is removed?*

To address this we turn to the ethical philosophy of Emmanuel Levinas, and in so doing argue the face revealed beneath the mask of gender is the originary site of ethical relations with the other. Levinas casts ethics as being located in the primary ontological relation with the face of the other. But the ethical relationship with the face Levinas proposed is not one where revelation yields knowledge as if once the wearer's mask is removed her true identity can be known – nothing could be further from the ethical relation. It is in the face of the other that one is rendered destitute in the abyss of *unknowability* that separates self from other and renders the other absolutely particular. One does not know the face of the other but, ethically, is hostage to its mystery. To unmask, ethically speaking, would not reveal knowledge, but unknowability. It is on these grounds that we see the gendering of human bodies as being an ethically questionable practice that over-writes people with masks that violate their status as unique and particular.

What is revealed when all of the masks are removed cannot be understood in relation to categories of knowledge such as gender; the face of the other is entirely unique, irreplaceable and incomparable to any other others. By this account the categorization of persons in terms of gendered identity is best regarded as a violation of their ethical character as infinitely other – as one of a kind. As Diprose (2002) would have it this relation to unknowability is pre-reflective, affective and corporeal such that ethics comes to bear in the intercorporeal generosity between people and prior to their categorization. This thinking suggests that the politics of knowledge about gender is to be preceded and overcome by a corporeal ethics that would arise *before* gender, and where *gender as mask* is to be regarded as a violation of ethics. We thus consider how the gendered inscription of persons and their identities is a violation of ethics such that any politics of gender is one that must work towards undoing and unmasking gender itself. Such a gendered politics, we conclude, rests on an ongoing resistance to gender as means of controlling and defining the other. This politics of resistance relies on an ethical position which puts corporeal difference and affectivity at the heart of any self other relationship. This we propose is a politics of affectivity which as its ethical horizon displaces gender and the violence it entails.

Revelation and gender

The relation between unmasking and revelation speaks from the bedrocks of phallogocentric knowledge – that is, as if emerging from Plato's cave, is that which should be pursued with sufficient effort and earnestness is the one truth that lies behind the shadowy artifice of the masks of language and culture. The goal is to reveal the face in its nudity, its bare truth free from adornment and artifice. The male knower, he who pursues such knowledge, is a truth adventurer, boldly going where no man has gone before... and later coming back with the treasure of the truth as if it were he, by virtue of his strength, intelligence and courage, who is the only one who can reveal that truth. Knowledge here is the stuff of the gods, it is primary and originary; it is that which existed in the beginning and that which human intellect is demanded to pursue through processes of revelation. And he who can lay the claim to the power to unmask naked knowledge gets just that one step closer to the throne...a hero's journey embarked upon through the rustling of the mouth, the sweeping of the pen and the click-clacking of the keyboard.

Conventionally a mask is understood as a device that shrouds identity with artifice. From its etymological trace in the Italian *maschera*, a mask involves a disguise achieved through covering, and through covering the face in particular. Back further to the medieval Latin *masca*, masking is about blackening the face – obscuring its features with darkness so that the identity of its bearer cannot be known. But to suggest that masks simply hide the true identity of their wearers elides the historical meaning of the mask. As Tseëlon's (2001) explains the relation between masks and identity in Western culture can be traced back to ancient Greece in terms of the relation between culture and the theatre. In this sense a mask is analogous to a social role where mask and role are associated with particular moral obligations as well as particular rights and privileges. In that context:

> [The] mask did not hide the true identity of its wearers. It declared who and what they were, and so made public discourse possible It provided a role and bestowed the right to speak (Donald, 1996: 177).

Masks connect the individual person with the social and cultural in that they express the 'duality of private agency and social control' (Tseëlon, 2001: 5) while at the same time resolving 'the apparent contradiction between social identity and individual political agency' (Moruzzi, 2000: 1). With the mask 'the distinction between self and role is not between a deeper truth and a surface appearance but between two masks, two ways of speaking, two modalities'. Such a view disrupts the commonplace modern idea that a mask is something that covers and conceals and suggests instead that it is something that enables or inhibits the identity of its wearer. When self and role are no longer so firmly distinguished a mask does not hide the true identity of its wearer such that a false or *different* identity assumed; rather, the mask is identity.

From such a starting point we can question the idea that in masking gender we purposely hide that which is masculine and/or feminine such that our performance of self is one of concealment, containment, and protection. We can also question masking as a blackening of gender as it would involve the performance of gender in a less pronounced way – again so as to hide it away from view, to block it out from the gaze, or to pretend it is not there. Clearly such practices of covering gendered visibility can be identified – think for example of the woman manager who masks her femininity in response to the demands for 'managing like a man' (Wajcman, 1998), or the woman under pressure to perform a feminine self when this is alien territory. But although such practices hide gender, they do so with gendered masks, transforming what it means to have a gendered identity. This does not mean that to unmask is to perform an act of revelation and enlightenment – to lay bear the truth obscured by the artifice of its covering or the shadow of its darkness, in this case such that gen0der can be brought to the light of day and rendered visible. Instead we find a set of layered practices of masking through which gender is performed.

When we start thinking about living our gendered existences, issues of sameness and difference are central to the formation of gendered selves. We consider with whom we regard our selves as being of the same type, and from whom we think of ourselves as different. Our identity is not our own, it always rests on how we see ourselves, as well as how we develop ourselves, in relation to others. Identity emerges in relation to the matrix of ways we mark the divisions between us and them; those with whom we identify, and those with whom we do not. These relationships of identification between self and other inform gendered masks as we consider, adopt and fuse our self to the characteristics, habits and behaviours of those we seek to identify with. These make us look and act the self that we wish to be identified by. For one person to be a woman is for that person to have become in some way like other women who came before her, just as 'being a man' is to adopt the characteristics that one associates with one sort of masculinity or other. These identities do not originate with the person who claims them, they are taken on from culture through the adoption of masks that that culture provides us with. Mask upon mask our identity mutates and develops with each additional adornment, and with each additional scar, making and changing who we are and how others see us for who we are. In the same way, difference is rendered mobile through masks, setting us apart from the others as well as from our former selves through dynamic and multiple identifications. And it is not just about ourselves; with the reading of masks we come to know the other person, inquiring, caring, judging and analysing exactly who they are by locating them in relation to the categories of identity that we have learned through culture. To know another person is know the masks that s/he wears, especially those that no longer appear like masks. Masks become; they become us.

What is a mask?

As Tseëlon (2001) explains, masks perform an act of representation – their symbolism is that of repeating particular cultural meanings as they relate to the identity of persons. The mask is thus intimately related to the face for which it offers a partial cover; protecting and hiding the face from view. But a mask is not the same as a disguise. Disguise involves hiding or concealing but, unlike a mask, its aim is to misrepresent. A disguise is a full covering which erases the wearer from view such that he or she might be mistaken for someone else. Mask is also different to masquerade with the latter being an intentional, a deliberate covering that can be pleasurable, excessive or subversive. Like disguise, masquerade involves assuming a false appearance, and further it is deliberate and overstated – it is a performative caricature. A mask however holds a more ambiguous relation between the character of the mask and the identity of its wearer (Tseëlon, 2001). With the mask, identity is enabled as well as disguised, with its wearer becoming themselves through their masked performances.

Reflecting on masks provides a means through which we can interrogate the revelation and concealment of identity from a non-essentialist standpoint – one that starts from the position that meaning and identity are 'situated not within the self, but in a series of representations mediated by semiotic systems such as language' where the self is 'no longer an essence but a description' (Benwell and Stokoe, 2006: 31). Unlike the performance of masquerade or the deceit of disguise, the mask is a cultural metaphor that can understand identity without recourse to the idea that there is an essential or authentic identity somehow lurking behind the mask as if awaiting to be uncovered so as to reveal one's originary identity. Wearing a mask transforms rather than just conceal identity, and removing a mask can diminish as well as reveal identity.

Considering identity in relation to masks asserts a relation between self/other since masks enable self to become other, and to incorporate other; relating as they do to paradoxes of sameness and difference. Masks enable one self to become the same as others, while at the same time differentiating self from other; they question the very idea that one has some essentially authentic identity that can somehow be recovered as if the artifice of culture might be removed to reveal a natural self in all its nudity. With the mask, fundamental issues such as the nature of identity, the truth of identity, the stability of identity categories and the relationship between the supposed identity and its outward manifestations (essence or appearance) are brought into question. As Kaiser puts it:

> masking enables the interrogation of identities, partial identities, potential identities and non-identities [...] it provides a means for both delineating self from other and interrogating the other within the self (xv, in Tseëlon, 2001: 2).

More radically, following a long line of gender theorists (see Lloyd, 2005) reading the wearing of masks as a non-essentialist identity performance allows the possibility of transgression of gender boundaries. Masks enable us to become someone that we could not otherwise be; constrained by the cultural existence of masks, perhaps, but unconstrained by the idea that men and women must be locked within the confines of some pre-existing and immobile identity to which they are enslaved. As Napier (1986) says, masks:

> testify to an awareness of the ambiguities of appearance and to a tendency toward paradox characteristic of transitional states. They provide a medium for exploring formal boundaries and a means of investigating the problems that appearances pose in the experience of change (Napier, 1986: xxiii cited in Tseëlon, 2001).

As we have discussed so far, the notion of a mask disturbs the idea of concealing and revealing identity, because it is the mask itself that enables identity to be formed. As Tseëlon (1992: 125) puts it "appearances do not mask reality but are reality" – in this case the reality of identity. Furthermore, masks might be thought of as artifice, pretence and disingenuity, they are identity. It is not the case that there is *an authentic self* where real or metaphoric masks cover and deceive by pretending to be the real self. Instead masks are *authentic manifestations* that mark the multiplicity of identity (a distinction offered by Tseëlon, 2001). Building on this idea that masks bring into question the idea of an authentic self filled with essence and therefore culture, this chapter suggests that *gender is a mask*, entailing multiplicity and fluidity and that which questions the apparent naturalness of dominant categories of gender identity and the 'oppressive effects of institutionalized binarity' (Garber, 1992: 161). A mask represents both self and other, but also allows the possibility of the self to become other through processes of inversion and transcendence that defies order and introduces ambiguity (Tseëlon, 1992).

What is *under* the masks?

If, as we have suggested so far, there is no solid, essential and originary identity that can be located beneath the masks, what then might be located there? The simple answer of course is that before the mask is the *face*, and it is a reflection on the meaning of the face that can begin to consider what is revealed once the concealing mask is removed. It is with the ethical theory of Emmanuel Levinas that we make this consideration, and in so doing move our discussion of identity and masks into the realm of ethics.

Perhaps the most lasting and profound contribution of Levinas to ethical theory is his locating of ethics in the primary encounter with the face of the other. With this move Levinas strips ethics back to its more rudimentary and profound meaning in the relations between human beings. For Levinas, being face to face with the other is the 'original ethical relation' (Levinas, 1987/2008: 32) and one where the self becomes exposed to the other in its vulnerability and sacrifice. Levinas' ethical self is hostage to the other in an ethics that is radically antithetical to selfishness and where 'the only absolute value is the human possibility of giving the other priority over oneself' (Levinas, 1991/2006: 93). It is responding to the demand of this possibility that marks the ethical life – a response where in place of the self what comes first is a responsibility to the other, a care for the other and a love for the other.

The face of the ethical encounter is not one apprehended as a matter of knowing other people, of subsuming them within the categories of knowledge with which they can be identified in relations of sameness and difference with others. Instead, the encounter with the face of the other attests to the other's very unknowability; it is a spiritual encounter with the 'idea of infinity' (Levinas, 1969/1991: 48). The other is a radical alterity that is not an other of me, but is absolutely particular – a one of a kind that cannot be replaced and resists comparison with the other others. From this irreplaceability 'the Other lies absolutely beyond my comprehension and should be preserved in all its irreducible strangeness' (Davis, 1996: 3). The other, encountered in its face, is not to be reduced to the self as if s/he were merely a mirror for the self's reflection or a canvas for its projection but is sacred and unfathomable.

It is with this conception of the primary and radical alterity of the face that Levinas extends ethical responsibility to its full possibilities. This is an 'infinite responsibility' to the other – a responsibility that exceeds reciprocity and self interest such that I am responsible to others 'without concerning myself about their responsibility for me' (Levinas, 1972/2006: 57). The face of the other demands my responsibility, not in the equality of exchange and politics, but as a form of non-reciprocal giving. Ethics register in 'response, help, solicitude [and] compassion' (Hansel, 1999: 122).

The idea of an ethics of the face, is an ethics before social identity, and ethics before masks. As Levinas explains: 'The sensible presence of this chaste bit of skin with brow, nose, eyes, and mouth, is neither a sign allowing us to approach a signified nor a *mask* hiding it' (1991/2006: 29, italics added). The face of the other that is ethics is one without any mask, stark in its nudity and expression:

> The nudity of the face is a stripping with no cultural ornament [...] The face enters our world from an absolutely foreign sphere [...] The signification of the face in its abstraction is, in the literal sense of the term, extraordinary, exterior to all order, to all world (Levinas, 1972/2006: 32).

Levinas's challenge to ethical thought surpasses the idea that ethics emerges from the thinking and acting subject, however constituted. This is an ethics that challenges the egoism of the knowing *I* as the locus and foundation of responsibility; that challenges self obsession. It does so by insisting on the primacy of the other before the self. There is no self without other first, and that other is that to which the self owes its being; the self is hostage to the other in the ethical relation. Ethics begins 'before the face of the other which engages my responsibility by its human expression' (Levinas, 1987/2008: 26). This ethics is an awakening where the self is disturbed and put into question by the radical alterity of the other; an awakening that is 'outside of knowledge' (Levinas, 1991/2006: 76) and expresses itself in 'terms other than those of knowledge' (p. 75).

The mask of knowledge

The mask is something that comes after the face that covers it over or obscures it so as to reveal something other than the face. This is not to say that masks are somehow meaningless or false; on the contrary masks overflow with significance – as we argued earlier the mask is identity. However, whereas the face is the unknowability of the other constituted in the ethical encounter, masks are quite amenable to knowledge – both self knowledge and the knowing of the other. It is here that ethics/face become contrasted with knowledge/mask. Ethics can be seen in the face of a baby – unperturbed by knowledge in its expression of being alive, crying out for care, demanding responsibility, yet without subjectivity and without knowledge of how to perform gender. The baby's face is unmarked by the violence of gender – it is entirely unmasked. 'Is it a boy or is it a girl?' asks the stranger in the street looking for clues in the colour of the mask of clothing. Knowledge, gender, is added to the baby through the discourse that covers the face that renders the child knowable before it is even close to acquiring consciousness of its own subjectivity. The child is operated on by 'seizure and comprehension' (Levinas, 1987/2008: 30) that pushes aside the wonder of its purity and particularity, and replaces them with no indefinite terms. These are the terms of the mask, the terms of knowledge that covers the infinitude of otherness and gives them the identity of belonging to a category.

What we know as knowledge (of other people) is a 'way of approaching the known being such that its alterity with regard to the knowing being vanishes' (Levinas, 1969/1991: 42) – it is a 'suppression of the other' (p. 302) in a mundane yet violent exercise of power. The mask covers and erases the ethical relation, and moreover, it is this mask, this knowledge, that marks the entry of the subject after ethics. The donning of a mask enacts a metamorphosis that objectifies the face and transforms its bearer into a subject (Levinas, 1987/2008). Here, life is 'betrayed by knowledge' (Levinas, 1991/2006: 71) because with knowledge 'the other finally finds itself stripped of its alterity [...] it becomes interior to my knowledge' (Levinas, 1991/2006: 155). And the idea of a gendered identity categorizing all against the master tropes of the feminine and the masculine are perhaps the most brutal categories of such knowledge. With gender the entire totality of humanity in all the vastness of its difference becomes reduced to comparison against these two tropes. Gender is a category of knowledge that, par excellence, violates the alterity of the other by masking that alterity with knowledge.

And this masking is not something that is done to us just by others – it is something that all of us allow as we graft knowledge onto our faces in the form of masks for others to see and for ourselves to imagine in the reflection in the mirror.

> The human being clearly allows himself to be treated as an object, and delivers himself over to knowledge in the *truth* of perception and the light of the human sciences (Levinas, 1987/2008: xxii, italics in original).

This delivery is the delivery of the mask – the visible and symbolic artifice that makes it possible to pretend that we can generate knowledge of the other despite the infinite abyss that separates 'me' from 'you'. To be sure, we cannot do without masks in the function of pretending that the unknowable alterity of the other can be comprehended and possessed. But ethics puts the meaning of the mask, in its 'synthetic plasticity', into question such that responsibility can be 'described as a breaking of the plastic forms of the phenomenality of appearance' (Levinas, 1987/2008: 33). The ethical significance of the other signifies 'from beyond the plastic forms which do not cease covering [the face] like a *mask* with their presence in perception' (Levinas, 1991/2006: 125, italics added). What is demanded is not the naivety that would hope for the abandonment of the mask in the name of ethics, but a recognition that masks and faces are not alternative forms of representation. This means not confusing the 'significance of the face with the plastic forms of representation which already *mask* it' (Levinas, 1991/2006: 130, italics added). It is in this sense that whilst the mask denotes subjectivity, the ethical self is 'outside the subject' – a 'self without reflection' (Levinas, 1987/2008: 122).

Corporeal ethics

Although Levinas does not, to any great extent, consider the idea of the mask in his philosophy, it follows from his thinking that while masks are identity and knowledge of the self and other, ethics operates before the mask. Ethics is 'outside the subject' as well as prior to it. Moreover, despite our human will to work the power of knowledge and to valorize knowing and thinking, with ethics there is 'the wonder of a mode of thought better than knowledge' (Levinas, 1987/2008: xiii). The other is only known through its masks as it is rendered as an object to be apprehended. But in that appearance it holds too that the other 'cannot be reduced to the presence of an object that my gaze determines and upon which it makes predictive judgements' (Levinas, 1987/2008: 9). Despite all efforts and all violation, the other remains unknowable even as knowledge claws and fights in its indefatigable desire to capture the other once and for all in concrete terms. Additionally, it is such terms which constitute

> identity, and recuperate the irreversible, coagulate the flow of time into a 'something', thematize, ascribe a meaning. It would take up a position with regard to this 'something', fixed in a present, repres*ent it t*o itself, and thus extract it from the pliable character of time' (Lévinas, 1978/1991: 37).

At the birth, it is the gleeful declarations of 'it's a boy', or 'it's a girl'.

How then might we approach alterity ethically without seeking to mask it with knowledge by locating it in this or that category of identity? What might be the practice of an ethical relation with the other if that relation is made from a pre-reflective self, a 'self without reflection' and 'prior to knowledge' (Levinas, 1987/2008: 122, 123); prior to masks. It is in approaching and responding to the unmasked face of the other that we can consider, taking the lead from Rosalyn Diprose (2002), a corporeal ethics grounded in generosity – a generosity that 'involves a dispossession of self [that] is born of an affective, corporeal relation to alterity that generates rather than closes off sexual, cultural and stylistic differences' (p. 127). Such generosity manifests in a breaking free from the privileging of reason and knowledge as the ultimate pursuit of masculine forms of knowing in favour of a feminine 'welcoming of the alterity of the ethical relation' (p. 140). This knowledge and the masks that it gives us to wear come to be understood as 'imperialism and violence' that impose limits on alterity through the 'imposition of familiar ideas' (p. 137) that marks a closure to the other through rigid perceptions that render the other as 'finished' (p. 177). It is prior to and against such things that ethics operates. An ethics before knowledge, an ethics before the masked inscription of gender. If gendered practices seek freedom from, then they become free of the containment that repress and oppress.

Corporeal ethics is not about passing judgements as it is about *disrupting* the taken for granted means through which judgement is violently imposed. Its corporeality rests with the fact that it is primarily informed by a bodily practice that precedes rationality and intellect in an affective dimension where bodies move and respond to bodies as unassimilable. With this ethics the 'man of reason' (Lloyd, 1993) recedes from his privileged place and is replaced by the affective body. As Gatens (1996) explains, the separation of mind over body, and the privileging of the former over the latter that privileges reason and knowledge, is a central foundation of Western thinking. This foundation can be traced through a series of dominant dualisms that inform our understanding of the social, political and ethical dimensions of life. The divisions Gatens highlights are those between the bodily, natural and feminine on the one hand, and the rational, cultural and masculine on the other. Moreover, these divisions marks the foundation of the dominant Western 'politico-ethical structuring of the "universal" human subject' (p. 57) that at its core eliminates difference by appropriating it. With the knowing mind in control '[r]ational knowledge has been constructed as a transcending, transformation or control of natural forces; and the feminine has been associated with what rational knowledge transcends, dominates or simply leaves behind' (Lloyd, 1993: 1). Moreover, with corporeal ethics this privileging of the masculine over the feminine is reversed on its own terms such that the ethical self is feminine in that it precedes and is other to rational knowledge.

Corporeal ethics enacts a generosity that is an overflowing 'life force' which 'defies the culturally informed habits of perception and judgement that would perpetuate injustice by shoring up body integrity, singular identity, and their distinction between inside and outside, culture and nature, self and other' (Diprose, 2002: 190). Remembering our introductory arguments of the dangers of representing masks as essentialist, this generosity dislodges the masks that we have come to confuse with our faces and renders our knowledge of our selves and other insecure – it is a 'prereflective activity mediated by the cultural-historical that haunts my perception, but an activity that surpasses that perception and the modes of being that it supports' (Diprose, 2002: 193). It is this position as prereflective that marks generosity's corporeality – its affective operation through the body before reflection. On account of this it is a generosity that 'eschews the calculation characteristic of an economy of exchange' (p. 5) in favour of relations of giving. This ethical generosity works through the body in connection with other bodies, but in doing so takes one outside of one's self – outside of the subject that is defined by the masks we wear. Through these corporeal interfaces gendered relations are emancipated in and through alterity.

Ethics against gender

Masks understood as knowledge of the subject are indispensable to social life, they allow us to become who we are as we identify with and differentiate ourselves from other people. They allow us to know other people, to compare them to each other and ourselves. And as we have argued in this chapter, gender, as a central part of identity, itself is such a mask – a culturally dominant means through which we become who we are by locating ourselves in relation to what we understand to be masculinity and femininity. We have also argued that when such masks of gender are removed what is revealed is a face that precedes gendered description. It is this unmasked face that, following Levinas, is the originary site of ethics, founded as it is in the ethical relation of the face-to-face. Whereas identifying others in relation to gender categories renders those others knowable, in so doing it conceals the very ethical uniqueness of each and every one of them – it masks the ethical mystery of the other. Accounting for gender, even more troubling when the knowledge that is embedded in gendered difference 'embodies traces of the interests of men and so exhibits the world in a way that conflicts with ideas I live from and that contribute to my existence as a woman, then the path of thinking that this disturbance provokes is likely to be feminist' (Diprose, 2002: 142). Here in our terms a feminist removal of the gendered masks that seek to define masculinity and femininity in the hard and fast terms of masculine knowledge.

At the heart of ethics is a 'relationship with the other as such and not a relationship with the other already reduced to the same, to "one of mine"' (Levinas, 1991/2006: 160). Such reduction is achieved not in awe of the face of the other, but on reflection of the masks that cover that face so as to make its bearer appear knowable and comparable to others. It is in this way that a Levinasian ethics of radical alterity that privileges the face of the other as the originary site of ethics sees gender as a form of masking that violates ethics. Having come to that point, however, we are not keen to be read as dismissing gender as somehow un-ethical. Instead gender as mask is a mask that divides people into categories that violates each one's absolute uniqueness. We argue for a politics that seeks to disrupt gendered distinctions between persons. This is a 'politics of generosity [that] begins with all of us, it begins and remains in trouble, and it begins with the act' (Diprose,

2002: 188), a 'passionate politics that would work through generosity for a justice that is yet to arrive' (p. 194).

A politics of affectivity authorized by the ethics of the face takes as its target the masking of people through restrictive and oppressive gendered performance and expectations that are understood as a violation of the ethical unknowability of the other. The task of such a politics, therefore, is that of 'diminishing the violence to which [human persons] are exposed in the order, or disorder, of the determinism of the real' (Levinas, 1987/2008: 95) – in this case the reality of gender. The means through which such a task can be achieved is in the realm of knowledge; not through the acquisition of knowledge, but through its disruption. The knowledge to be disrupted is that through which gendered masks are created, performed and worn. This suggests that we do not need to generate better knowledge of gender and its practices, but rather to usurp the very privileging of knowledge ahead of ethics. In place of knowledge, ethics favours thinking; thinking that is 'productive in its political task of transforming both the self and the social realm' (Diprose, 2002: 126) through the 'production of ideas against convention' (p. 127). Positioning this thinking as not being a matter of knowledge is itself an example of the corporeal ethics that we discussed earlier – this is an affective openness and response to difference that questions the 'maleness of reason' (ibid., cf. Lloyd, 1993) and its desire to fix the world and house identities into oppressive cage-like categories.

Conclusion

By way of bringing this chapter to a close we need to remind ourselves that the ethical relations that Levinas attests to, while pointing a way to an ethical basis for a politics of affectivity, are no guarantor of ethics, and nor should they be. Indeed, if such guarantees were put in place in advance then ethics itself would become reduced to the calculations of knowledge that would close down the openness to alterity that inspired it in the first place. As Diprose puts it, there is no 'particular program of political practice that could better regulate unconditional generosity, ethical openness to the other [...] unconditional generosity, of the kind Levinas envisages is at the basis of sociality, is never present in any pure form' (p. 186). Generosity does not achieve justice (p. 193) and this is precisely what demands an eternal vigilance to its pursuit.

There will always be masks, gendered or otherwise, that are generated in the presence of such a multitude of others; comparisons will be made, categories will be established and, in the process, the ethical sanctity of the absolute other will be violated. But this is not cause for despair. Ethics could never be a closed project whose pursuit pre-empted its capture – indeed it is in pursing itself that ethics is practiced. As we have argued elsewhere:

> responsibility can be considered as a horizon of possibility that, while demanding vigilant attention, is not something that can be achieved once and for all in the administrative arrangements of the here and now. This means that ethics and responsibility are not things that can ever be governed by organizational programs, rules or codes and, moreover, might be diminished by such arrangements (Rhodes and Pullen, 2009: 353–354).

What we have been testifying to in this chapter is that although gender might be something that can be revealed and concealed in various social processes, gender is a form of knowledge and practice that performs an act of concealment – it is a mask. That which is concealed by gender is ethics – ethics understood as the openness and generosity to the uniqueness of the other and revealed as unknowable. The social practice of gender enacts a structuring of power and privilege that is achieved through the ways that, through gendered categorization and discrimination, people are rendered knowable. It is this knowledge that manifests in a mask that covers over the alterity of the other so as to make that other subject to the exercise of power. What this calls for is an ethics of 'undoing gender' (Pullen and Knights, 2007) that begins prior to knowledge in the intercorporeal and pre-reflective realm of the face-to-face relation – a relation prior to the imposition of the mask of subjectivity.

References

Benwell, B. and Stokoe, S. (2006) *Discourse and Identity*. Edinburgh: Edinburgh University Press.

Davis, C. (1996) *Levinas: An Introduction*. Notre Dame, France: University of Notre Dame Press.

Diprose, R. (2002) *Corporeal Generosity: On Giving with Nietzsche, Merleau-Ponty and Levinas*. Albany: Stage University of New York Press.

Donald, J. (1996) 'The citizen and the man About town'. In Hall, S. and du Gay, P. (eds) *Questions of Cultural Identity*, pp. 170–190. London: Sage.

Garber, M. (1992) *Vested Interests: Cross-Dressing and Cultural Anxiety*. London: Routledge.

Gatens, M. (1996) *Imaginary Bodies: Ethics, Power and Corporeality*. London: Routledge.
Hansel, G. (1999) 'Emmanuel Levinas (1906–1995)', *Philosophy Today*, 43(2): 121–125.
Kaiser, S. (2001) 'Foreword', in Tseëlon, E. (ed.) *Masquerade and Identities: Essays on gender, Sexuality and Marginality*, pp. xiii–xv. London: Routledge.
Levinas, E. (1969/1991) *Totality and Infinity*, trans. Alphonso Lingis, Pittsburgh: Duquesne University Press.
Levinas, E. (1972/2006) *Humanism of the Other*, trans. N. Poller, Urbana: University of Chicago Press.
Levinas, E. (1978/1991) *Otherwise Than Being or Beyond Essence*, trans. A. Lingis, Dortrecht: Kluwer.
Levinas, E. (1987/2008) *Outside the Subject*, trans. M. B. Smith, London: Continuum.
Levinas, E. (1991/2006) *Entre Nous: Thinking-of-the-other*, trans M. B. Smith and B. Harshav, London: Continuum.
Lloyd, G. (1993) *The Man of Reason: 'Male' and 'Female' in Western Philosophy* (2nd ed.) London: Routledge.
Lloyd, M. (2005) *Beyond Identity Politics: Feminism, Power and Politics*. London: Sage.
Moruzzi, N. M. (2000) *Speaking Through the Mask; Hannah Arendt and the Politics of Social Identity*. New York: Cornell University Press.
Napier, D. (1986) *Masks, Transformation and Paradox*. Berkeley: University of California Press.
Pullen, A. and Knights, D. (2007) 'Undoing gender: Organizing and disorganizing performance', *Gender, Work and Organization*, 14(6): 505–511.
Rhodes, C. and Pullen, A. (2009) 'Organizational moral responsibility'. In Clegg, S. R. and Cooper, C. (eds) *The Sage Handbook of Organizational Behaviour: Macro Approaches*, pp. 340–355. London: Sage.
Tseëlon, E. (1992) 'Is the presented self sincere? Goffman, impression management and the postmodern self', *Theory, Culture and Society*, 9: 115–128.
Tseëlon, E. (2001) 'Introduction: Masquerade and identities', in Tseëlon, E. (ed.) *Masquerade and Identities: Essays on Gender, Sexuality and Marginality*, pp. 1–17. London: Routledge.
Wajcman, J. (1998) *Managing like a Man: Women and Men in Corporate Management*. PA: Pennsylvania State University Press.

Index

Abbott, P. 221–2, 225
accessibility 30
Acker, J. 116, 144, 153, 190, 201
adaptive behaviour 179
aesthetics 25
affectivity 246
Africa, pregnancy in 65
alpha males 40–1
Alvesson, M. 222
Anthonissen, A. 140
assertiveness 61
attractiveness 222
Australia 172
Austria, self-employment 101
author, (in)visibility 159–60, 214
authority 43–4
autonomy 126
availability 15, 30

baby bar, the 90, 96
Baszanger, I. 106
Baudrillard, J 50
Beck, U. 124
Beck-Gernsheim, E. 124
benchmarking 48
Benschop, Y. 224
Bentham, Jeremy 220
Binns, Jennifer 8, 10, 12, 13, 18, 158–72
biology, and gender differences 97n6
black power 7
Bochner, A. P. 214
body work 225
Bolton, S. 81, 226–7
boundaries 26, 30–1, 33, 177, 227
Bourdieu, Pierre 55
Bruni, A. 36, 105
bullying 65
Burton, Clare 196, 211, 212
Butler, J. 229

care responsibility 49, 76–87, 131, 133, 208–9, 226 *see also* childcare
Carter, S. 101, 102
castration, fear of 43–4
Centre for Gender in Organizations 196
change, promise of 196
charm work 185–7, 189
childcare 102, 115–16, 119, 127, 128, 131, 208–9
civil engineering 19, 175–200
  adaptive behaviour 179
  client relations 185–7
  context 180–1
  cultural values 181
  gendered visibility 176–8
  isolation 189
  leadership 182–5
  male domination 180
  methodology 181–2
  power relations 182
  presenteeism 182
  professional advancement 187–8
  roles 180, 183
  under representation of women 181
  visibility tensions 183–5, 190
  visibility/vulnerability spiral 178–9, 189, 190
Cockburn, C. 215
Cohen, Laurie 7, 8, 9, 12, 13
Cohn, S. 176, 177
concealment, of privilege and advantage 11
conformity 50
control, loss of 34, 35
conversations, safe 86
coping mechanisms 8–9, 33, 34, 35–6, 200
corporate knowledge 199
corporeal ethics 242–5, 246
Cromie, S. 127

249

cultural marginalization   9
cultural values, densely
    masculinist   194–216
culture change project   19

Davies, C.   80
De Beauvoir, S.   36
De Certeau, M.   42–3
De Francisco, V.   195
defensive strategies   5–6
deference   203–6, 211, 216, 225–6
Dellinger, K.   176
de-mothering strategies   16, 85–7
demotivation   87
densely masculinist workplaces
    194–216 *see also* civil engineering
  case studies   198–209, 214–15
  coping strategies   200
  deference   203–6, 211, 216
  disappearance   194
  empowerment   211, 212
  exclusionary practices   199
  female leadership   198–203
  female status   198–203
  the feminist facilitator   212–14
  invisibility   198
  knowledge sharing   199–200
  masculine logic   211–12
  masculinity protection practices
    206–7
  methodology   195–8
  power relations   203–6, 212
  risk   210
  visibility tensions   207–9
Department of Trade and Industry
    (DTI)   100
detraditionalization   125, 126–9
difference   236
Diprose, Rosalyn   243, 246
disappearance   12–13, 19, 45–6,
    194, 202
disembodied normativity   229–30
disguise   237
Dodier, N.   106
domestic cleaning   9
dominance   200–3
Dryburgh, H.   179
du Gay, P.   125
dualisms   244

Eagleton, T.   50
Eckenrode, J.   102
Ellis, C.   214
embodied femininity   163
emotion work   8, 15, 25, 32, 186–7,
    226–7
emotional support   114
empowerment   211, 212
enterprise: and detraditionalization
    126–9
  discourse   125
  and retraditionalization   129–35
  retraditionalization   136
entitled agents   141
entrepreneurship   17, 100–20 *see
    also* female entrepreneurs
    Mumpreneurs; self-employment
  feminized   130–1
  and gender   101, 103–6, 116–20
  as masculine domain   105, 117,
    120, 128–9
  methodology   106–7
  personal characteristics   101
  support programmes   102–3
equal opportunities legislation   1, 51
equality   18, 82, 140–1, 147, 148,
    151–2, 153
erasure   11, 30, 56–8
eroticism   2
Essers, E.   224
ethical responsibility   240
ethics and ethical relations   234,
    239–41, 245–6, 246–7
ethnography   106–7
ethno-mimesis   29
exclusion   3, 92
exile   45
expectations   30
exposure   12

face   234, 241
  and ethical relations   245–6
  ethical significance   242
  and masks   239–41
  revelation   235
failure   43
fascinum, the   44
fathers   88–90, 90–1, 96
fear   184

female advantage 14
female body 167 *see also* pregnant bodies
  display of 2
  in management theory 56–8
  as other 55
female entrepreneurs 6, 12, 17, 100–20, 136n1, 168 *see also* entrepreneurship; Mumpreneurs; self-employment
  barriers to entry 102–3
  methodology 106–7
  types 103–4, 126–7
female managers 49
feminine, constructions of the 50
feminine skills 1
femininity 18, 245
  compensating for 176
  and corporeal ethics 244
  idealized 130, 163–4
  juggling 201
  and leadership 163–4, 168
  masking 236
feminism 7, 50
feminist facilitator, the 212–14
Fenwick, T. 118, 130
field hockey *see* sport leadership
financial risk 133–4
Firth-Cozens, Jenny 39–40
Fletcher, J. K. 202, 204–5, 207, 211, 212, 216
foreigners 40–1, 45, 46–7, 47
Foucault, M. 104, 220–1
fracture 31–3
fragmentation 31–3
freedom 126

Gatenby, B. 212–13
Gatens, M. 244
Gatrell, Caroline 8, 12, 15–16, 54–74
gaze, the 219, 231
  enabling 224–6
  and the gender 221–2
  power of 220–2
  visibility tensions 226–9
gender
  cultural performance 104–5
  denial of 6

and entrepreneurship 101, 103–6, 116–20
  ethics against 245–6
  and the gaze 221–2
  and greyness 28
  identity 23, 168–9, 245
  and knowledge 241–2, 247
  and leadership 159
  as a mask 239
  material actuality 105–6
  normative position 5
  and revelation 234–7
  unmasking 234
gender differences 97n6
gender discrimination 58
gender identification 36
gender justice 1
gender lens 195–6, 197, 205
gender management 2
gender relations 129–30
gender research 1
gender switching 36, 169–70
gendered Other, the 2
gendered visibility 176–8
gendered work 104–6
gendering 168
generosity 242–5, 244, 245–6, 246
Gerber, G. L. 208
Gherardi, S. 189
Gore, S. 102
Gregson, N. 25, 36
'Grey Area' (video installation) 15, 23–5, 24, 27–8, 29, 31, 34
Grise, J. 130
Grosz, E. 58
guilt 114–15
gynaecology nursing 227

Hampton, M. M. 176, 178–9, 190
Harwood, Susan 9, 11, 13, 19, 194–216
Hayes, J. 127
Haynes, K. 55, 70–4
health 55
Hearn, J. 5, 167
hiding 27, 34, 198, 209, 211, 215–16, 236
Hillary Commission for Sport, Fitness and Leisure 146

Index

Hochschild, A. R.   186
Hokowhitu, B.   140
Holliday, A.   107
homologation   51–2
homophobia, social construction of   228–9
homosociability   3
Höpfl, Heather   6, 7, 11, 15, 39–52
Hulten, Sofia   15, 23–5
humour   11, 72, 177
Humphries, M.   212–13
hyper-feminization   222
hyper-sexualization   11
hypothesised essence   220–1

identity   5, 125, 130, 135, 243
  assertive   202–3
  authentic manifestations   239
  gender   23, 168–9, 245
  impact of masculine symbolism   113
  imposed   227
  and knowledge   241
  and masks   235–6, 236–7, 237–9
  and revelation   238
  stripping of   34, 35
  trailblazing   9
  victim   4
identity work   32, 159, 167–72
individualization   124–5, 126, 129–30, 131
infantilization   41, 42
inferior men   57
infinite responsibility   240
insider/outsider status   214
Institution of Civil Engineers (ICE)   181, 187–8
International Federation of Women's Hockey Associations (IFWHA)   145
interpersonal skills   49
(in)visibility   1, 18
  author   159–60, 214
  conceptualizations of   3–5
  corporeal   18, 159, 162–7
  discursive   18, 158, 160–2
  embodied   167
  as identity work   159, 167–72
  in leadership   158–72

  vortex   9–10, **10**, 13–14
invisibility   25, 33
  densely masculinist workplaces   198
  making visible   93–4
  within the margins   8–9
  normative position   4, 5–8
  protective   215
  seeking   12–13
  strategic use of   13
invisible privileges   4
Ireland, self-employment   101
isolation   189
Italy, self-employment   101

Jackson, S. J.   43–4
Jennings, J. E.   128

Kaiser, S.   238
Kanter, R. M.   35, 176, 176–7, 190, 220, 226
Kerfoot, Deborah   17, 100–20, 172
Kimmel, M.   227
Knoppers, A.   140
Know Your Place Campaign   103
knowledge   235, 241–2, 242–3, 246, 247
Kram, K. E.   176, 178–9, 190
Kristeva, J.   40–1, 45, 46–7, 51

Lagan, B.   58
law firms, Norwegian   76–87
  career track   77–82, 86–7, 90–3
  de-mothering strategies   85–7
  exclusion of women   81
  farewell interviews   94
  gender invisibility   81
  male domination   76
  masculine norms   80–2, 96–7
  and parenthood   82–5, 88–90, 94–6
  pregnant bodies in   84
  visibilization of motherhood   88
leadership   17–18
  camouflage   165–6, 167
  civil engineering   182–5
  corporeal (in)visibility   158, 162–7
  discursive (in)visibility   158, 160–2

female in densely masculinist
  workplaces 198–203
female managers 49
female presence and ethos 145–7
female visibility 162, 163, 166–7
feminine conceptualizations 161
and femininity 163–4, 168
and gender 159, 169–72
gender (in)visibility in 158–72
gender switching strategy 169–70
gendered images 164–5
heroic models 140, 161–2, 164
identity work 159, 167–72
male invisibility 164
masculine ideals 158, 160–2, 162, 168, 169, 179
methodology 159–60
research 141–2
skills 49
styles 170–2
women trespassers 165–6
Lee-Gosselin, H. 130
Levinas, Emmanuel 20–1, 233–4, 239–41, 242–3, 245, 246
Lewis, Patricia 6, 12, 17, 25, 36, 93, 124–36, 165, 168
Longhurst, R. 57, 58, 60, 71
Lyng, Selma Theresa 7, 12, 16, 76–87

McDougald, M. S. 128
McIlwee, J. 176
McNay, L. 128, 129
McRobbie, A. 124–5, 125
male body: as the norm 15–16
  as universal 54, 55, 56–7
male competition 39–40, 40, 45–6
male domination 1, 76, 139–42, 147, 153, 180
male fear, of failure 43
male privilege 7
management identity 2
management theory
  female body in 56–8
  and maternal bodies 56–8
  and the pregnant body 56–8, 73
management tools 48–9
marginalization 3, 8–9, 25, 26, 116, 141

Marshall, J. 165
Martin, E. 55, 57, 60
Martin, Patricia Yancey 172
Martin, Y. M. 141
masculine discourses 1
masculine subjectivity 172
masculinity 1 2, 11–12, 14, 167–8, 245
  hegemony 18, 104, 168
  idealized 130
  invisible privileges of 4
  in leadership research 141–2
  and membership 15
  in Non-traditional Occupations 219–20, 224–6, 227–9, 229, 231
  privileges 18
  protection practices 206–7
  and rank 204–5
  and sport 140
  stereotypes 168
  symbolism 15
masks 20–1, 233–47
  and corporeal ethics 242–3
  definition 235–6, 237–9
  disruption of knowledge 246
  and ethical relations 245–6
  ethical significance 242
  and face 239–41
  gender as 239
  and identity 236–7, 237–9
  of knowledge 241 2
  and revelation 233–4, 234–7
maternal bodies see also pregnant bodies
  definition 54
  erasure of 56–8
  invisibility of 54
  and management theory 56–8
  in medicine 55
media portrayals of women 132–3
membership 15, 39–52
  conformity 47–8
  definition 40–1
  entry into 41–2, 46–8
  and failure 42–3
  pecking order 39–40
  token 44
  women as foreigners 40–1
  women's lack of 43–4

men
  advantages of visibility to 2
  emotion work 226–7
  experience of visibility 219–31
  gender blindness 1–2
  invisibility 164
  in Non-traditional Occupations 19–20, 219–31
  normative position 5
  self-employment 100–1
  stereotypes 225–6
  visibility 158
menstruation 55
meritocracy 1, 148
Messner, M. A. 146
Meyerson, D. E. 202, 217n6
Miller, Caroline 17, 100–20
minority corporate actors, gendered visibility 176–8
minority status 176–7, 178–9
Mone, Michelle 129, 131, 135
Morgan, D. H. J. 167
motherhood 16, 17, 82–90, 94, 125–6, 132, 136
mothering 82–5, 87, 88, 95
Mumpreneur Directory, the 124, *134*, 134–5
Mumpreneurs 12, 17, 124–36
  see also female entrepreneurs
  business profiles *134*, 134–5
  detraditionalization 126–9
  financial risk 133–4
  media portrayals of 132–3
  retraditionalization 129–35, 136
Muzio, D. 81

Napier, D. 238
National Governance Board of Field Hockey 147
National Hockey League (NHL) 149
netnography 58–9
Nettleton, S. 55
New Zealand Olympic Committee (NZOC) 139, 141
New Zealand, sport leadership in 139–54
New Zealand Women's Hockey Association (NZWHA) 145–6

Non-traditional Occupations, men in 19–20, 219–31
  desire for invisibility 229–30
  masculinity 219–20, 224–6, 227–9, 229, 231
  methodology 222–4
  negative imagery 227–9
  visibility 224–6
  visibility tensions 226–9, 231
Norway 16, 76–87

object relations theory 178
O'Neill, M. 29
order 48
organization studies 1–2
organizational performances 44
organizational space 14–15, 23–36, 24
  claustrophobia 34
  fracture and fragmentation in 31–3
  gendering 25
  literature 24–5
  methodology 26–9
  over-exposure 30–1, 35–6
organizations
  constructions of the feminine 50
  directedness 42–3
  entry into 46–8
  female managers 49
  logic of 50–2
  management tools 48–9
  relationships 40–1
  representations 44
  trajectory 41–2
ornamental objects 221
Other, the 6–7, 24, 240, 245–6
  ethical significance 242
  gendered 2
  men as 229–30
Othering 16, 82–5, 88, 92, 93–4, 95
Otherness 177
over-exposure 30–1, 35–6
overperformance 178–9

Panoptican, the 220
parental leave 85, 86, 88–90, 97n2

parenthood 94–6
　and career track 92
　gendered meanings of 88–90
　and othering 82–5
participatory action research
　(PAR) 198–9
passions, control of 48
patriarchal discourse 48
patronage 50
pay gap 26
pecking order 40
performance pressures 3
perpetual immanence 36
phallogocentric knowledge 234
Phoenix Fund 103
physicality 48
playthings, women as 41
police, the 9, 19, 194–216
　case studies 214–15
　coping strategies 200
　deference 203–6, 211
　female leadership 198–203
　invisibility 198
　masculinity protection
　　practices 206–7
　methodology 195–8
　reasons for leaving 206–7
　risk 210
　seniority 217n7
　visibility tensions 207–9
power relations 2, 7, 11, 219
　civil engineering 182
　densely masculinist
　　workplaces 203–6, 212
　gendered 11
pregnancy 8, 12, 15–16, 54
　in Africa 65
　health issues 64–7, 68–70, 86
　ignored 62–3, 64–5
　morning sickness 69–70
　negative responses to 57
　revealing 60–1
　and workplace routines 63–7
pregnant bodies 15–16, 54–74, 84
　abjuration of the 70–4
　and changes to workplace
　　routines 63–7
　disruption of workplace
　　practices 61, 62, 70
　exclusion from literature 54–5
　fears of revealing pregnancy 60–1
　health issues 64–7, 68–70
　ignored 62–3, 64–5
　invisibility 59–60
　and management theory 56–8, 73
　methodology 58–9
　ridiculing of 71, 72
　size 71–2
　supra-performance 67–8
　unreliability of 57–8, 68–9, 70–1
　visibility 67, 68–74
preservation, of order 11
Pringle, R. 55–6
privileges 5
Probyn, E. 136
professionalism 11
professionalizing process 179
professions, female proportion 76
projection 178, 190
'Proposed Effects of Gender
　Differences in Entrepreneurs WFI
　Experience and Coping Strategies
　on Business Performance'
　(Jennings and McDougald) 128
Pullen, Alison 8, 14, 20–1, 233–47
Puwar, N. 55

quasi-men 41, 47–8, 51–2

rationality 48, 49, 50
recognition 87
reflexivity 223–4
responsibility 240, 241, 247
retraditionalization 125–6, 129–35,
　136
revelation 11–12, 233–47
　and gender 234–7
　and identity 238
　and masks 233–4
Rhodes, Carl 8, 14, 20–1, 233–47
Richardson, L. 144
Robinson, G. 176
Robinson, S. 3–4, 5, 7, 11
role models 102
role traps 220
Rollins, J. 9
Rose, G. 25, 36
Ryan, Irene 8, 17–18, 139–54

Index

Sam, M. P.   143
sameness   236
Sargent, P.   228–9, 231
SBS Incubation   103
Scully, M.   202, 217n6
segmentation   26
Self-Employment Access and Learning Programme   105–6, 107–13, 116–20
self-confidence   87
self-employment   17, 100–20, 106–7 *see also* entrepreneurship; female entrepreneurs; Mumpreneurs
  case study   107–13
  figures   100–1
  freedom   118–19
  gender differentiation   116–20
  gender disadvantage   119
  interview data   113–16
  masculine symbolism   108, 109, 113, 118, 120
  motivations   118
  stereotypes   113
  work/life balance   113–16
Self-Employment Agency   107–8, 118
self-image   184–5
self-perception   167
sex discrimination legislation   177–8
sexual harassment   177, 183
sexuality   1, 7
sexualized status   189
Shell Livewire   102–3
Simpson, Ruth   13, 19–20, 25, 36, 93, 219–31
Sinclair, A.   141–2, 172, 215–16
Smith, Dorothy   160
Snow, E.   221
social compromise   131
social constructivism   223
socialization   97n6, 103
Spain   101
Spender, Dale   158
splitting   178, 190
sport
  administration   143
  gender regimes   139
  and masculinity   140
  values   142
  visibility in   147–9
Sport and Recreation New Zealand (SPARC)   143, 146, 148, 153
sport leadership   17–18, 139–54
  absence of women   139, 143
  barriers   150–3
  equal opportunities   140–1, 151–2, 153
  female presence and ethos   145–7
  government intervention   143
  male domination   139–42, 147, 153
  male/female differentiation   151
  masculine values   150
  methodology   144–5
  national governing body   144
  occupational closure   153
  organizational context   142–5
  organizational structures   149–53
  visibility of women   147–9
stereotypes   113, 164, 168, 175, 179, 215–16, 225–6
sterile perfection   48
strangers, women as   45
Strangers to Ourselves (Kristeva)   40–1, 45
subjectivity   104, 159–60, 172
subordination   200–3
support work   19
supra-performance   67–8
Sweden   101
symbolic negation   9, 25
symbolism, masculine discourses   15
synchronicity, lack of   128–9

Taylorism   54
tempered radicals   217n6
thinking   246
Thorp, H.   141
To Have and to Hold: Men, Sex and Marriage (Firth-Cozens)   39–40
token men   3–5, 19–20, 219–31
  desire for invisibility   229–30
  masculinity   219–20, 227–9, 229, 231
  symbolic value   225

visibility 224-6
visibility tensions 226-9, 231
token women 1, 3-5, 8, 175, 205, 220
totalizing discourse 48
Townley, B. 220
Train2000 103
Tseëlon, E. 235, 237, 238-9
Tyler, I. 55
Tyler, Melissa 7, 8, 9, 12, 13, 14-15, 221-2, 225

United States of America, female entrepreneurs 100
unknowability 234, 240, 243
unreasonable demands 12

visibility 25
  advantages to men 2
  conceptualizations of 3-5
  and exposure 12
  gendered 176-8
  within the margins 8-9
  men 158
  men's experience of 219-31
  negative 19
  in sport 147-9
  tensions 183-5, 190, 207-9, 226-9, 231

tokens 175
total 220-1
visibility/vulnerability spiral 176, 178-9, 189, 190
Vizard, Steve 164
vulnerability *see* visibility/vulnerability spiral

Wajcman, Judy 200
Watts, Jacqueline 8, 10, 11, 19, 175-200
Whitehead, S. 5, 167
Whitmont, E. C. 48
Whittock, M. 189
Willis, P. 107
Women In Enterprise Programme 103
work 175
work dedication 82
work-family interface 128
work/life balance 32-3, 87, 94, 103, 113-16, 119, 127-9, 129-35, 135-6, 176
workplace routines, and pregnancy 63-7
worthlessness 34, 35

Žižek, S. 43-4